Introduction to Educational Leadership and Organizational Behavior

Theory into Practice
Second Edition

Patti L. Chance

Routledge
Taylor & Francis Group
New York London

First published 2009 by Eye On Education

Published 2013 by Routledge
711 Third Avenue, New York, NY, 10017, USA
2 Park Square, Milton Park, Abingdon, Oxon OX14 4RN

Routledge is an imprint of the Taylor & Francis Group, an informa business

Library of Congress Cataloging-in-Publication Data

Chance, Patti L., 1955-
Introduction to educational leadership and organizational behavior: theory
into practice / Patti L. Chance. — 2nd ed.
      p. cm.
    ISBN 978-1-59667-101-0
1. School management and organization—United States. 2. Educational leadership—United States. 3. Organizational behavior—United States. I. Title.

LB2805.C445 2009
3 71.200973—dc22

2008041807

ISBN: 978-1-59667-101-0 (pbk)

Printed and bound in the United States of America by
Edwards Brothers Malloy on sustainably sourced paper

Also Available from EYE ON EDUCATION

**School Leader Internship: Developing, Monitoring,
and Evaluating Your Leadership Experience, Second Edition**
Martin, Wright, Danzig, Flanary, and Brown

**Introduction to Educational Administration:
Standards, Theories and Practice, Second Edition**
Douglas J. Fiore

Money and Schools, Fourth Edition
David C. Thompson, R. Craig Wood, and Faith E. Crampton

**Human Resources Administration:
A School-Based Perspective, Fourth Edition**
Richard E. Smith

Applying Servant Leadership in Today's Schools
Mary K. Culver

Transforming School Leadership with ISLLC and ELCC
Neil J. Shipman, J. Allen Queen, and Henry A. Peel

School-Community Relations, Second Edition
Douglas J. Fiore

**Instructional Supervision:
Applying Tools and Concepts, Second Edition**
Sally J. Zepeda

**The Principal as Instructional Leader:
A Handbook for Supervisors, Second Edition**
Sally J. Zepeda

**The Administrator's Guide
to School Community Relations, Second Edition**
George E. Pawlas

**Countdown to the Principalship:
A Resource Guide for Beginning Principals**
O'Rourke, Provenzano, Bellamy and Ballek

**What Great Principals Do *Differently*:
15 Things That Matter Most**
Todd Whitaker

About the Author

Patti L. Chance, Ph.D., is professor and chair of the Department of Educational Leadership at San Diego State University. She has experience in both rural and urban schools and has taught at the elementary, middle school, and high school levels. She has worked in various administrative capacities in K-12 schools, including elementary principal, assistant principal, and district coordinator for gifted education. She has served as a journal editor of a national, refereed education journal and currently sits on editorial boards for several national journals devoted to educational leadership. Her published research is related to instructional supervision, educational administration preparation programs, and leading for systemic change.

Table of Contents

About the Author v

Preface xiii

1 **Applying Organizational Theory to Educational Leadership:
   An Overview of Theoretical Foundations** 1
   Three Periods of Organizational Theory 3
       Classical Organizational Theory 3
       Behaviorist Period 5
       Systems Theory 7
   Application of Theory to Practice 8
   References 9

2 **Organizational Structure: Fundamental Constructs that Define
   Schools** 11
   Synopsis of Organizational Structures 11
   Organizational Typologies 12
   Formal Organizational Structure: Bureaucracy 17
       Division of Labor and Specialization 18
       Rules and Regulations 19
       Technical Competence and Career Orientation 20
       Impersonal Orientation 21
       Hierarchy of Authority 22
       Separation of Ownership and Administration 22
   The Informal Organization: Human Elements 23
   Structural Constructs of Organizations 25
   Persistent Dilemmas that Define School Organizations 29
   Summary 31
   Theory into Practice 33
       The Case of the Missing Microscopes 33
       Sample Analysis 34
   Reader's Application 36
       Rehab or Restructure? 36
   Student Exercise: Case Analysis 38
   References 38

3 **Systems Theory: Understanding the Dynamics of Schools
   as Open Systems** 41
   Synopsis of Systems Theory 41
   Social System Theory 42
   Fundamental Constructs of Social System Theory 43
   Nomothetic and Idiographic Components 47

Role Conflict 49
Leadership-Followership Style 49
Feedback Loops 52
Leadership Style. 53
Institutional Theory. 54
Summary. 56
The Case of No Band Marching. 57
Sample Analysis 57
A New Discipline Approach for Old Ways 59
Student Exercise: Case Analysis. 60
References 60

4 **Organizational Culture: Schools as Learning Organisms** 63
Synopsis of Organizational Culture. 63
Culture as a Defining Element of School Climate 64
Interrelationship of Structure, Climate, and Culture 66
Social Structure and Culture. 68
Schools as Learning Organizations 71
Culture and Community. 72
Considerations for Diversity and Social Justice 73
Summary. 76
Theory into Practice. 76
Big Horn and Deep Creek Come Together: A Case of School District
Consolidation 76
Sample Analysis 78
Reader's Application 79
Everyone's Kids 79
Student Exercise: Case Analysis. 80
References 80

5 **Leadership: Influencing Behavior, Relationships, and
School Effectiveness** 83
Synopsis of Leadership Theories 83
Trait Theories of Leadership. 85
Power Approaches to Leadership. 87
Behaviors of Leaders 88
Transformational Leadership 93
Critical Theory Perspectives on Leadership 97
Toward an Integrated Approach to Leadership Theory 98
Summary 100
Theory into Practice 102
Establishing Order at Jackson High. 102
Sample Analysis. 103
Reader's Application 104
What's Happening at Eastbrook? 104
Student Exercise: Case Analysis 106
References 106

6 **Contingency Theory: Variables Affecting Organizations and Leadership** **109**
  Synopsis of Contingency Theory 109
  The Uncertainty Factor: Contingency Theory Applied To Organizations . 110
    Open Systems 110
    Loose versus Tight 112
  Contingency Theory Applied to Leadership 113
    Fiedler's Leadership Contingency Theory 113
    Path-Goal Theory 116
    Situational Leadership 118
  Application to School Leadership 120
  Summary 121
  Theory into Practice 122
    A New Principal for Washington Middle School 122
    Sample Analysis 123
  Reader's Application 124
    Changing of the Guard 124
  Student Exercise: Case Analysis 125
  References 125

7 **Motivation: The Human Dynamics of Leadership** **127**
  Synopsis of Motivation Theories 127
  Individual and Group Perspectives: A Framework for Understanding
    Motivation Theories 128
    Motivation Defined 128
    Individual Motivation 128
      External Motivation Theories 129
      Internal Motivation Theories 130
    Motivation in Organizations 134
      Motivation-Hygiene Theory 134
      Expectancy Theory 136
      Goal Theory 138
  Group Dynamics 140
  Summary 144
  Theory into Practice 144
    Low Morale at Lincoln 144
    Sample Analysis 146
  Reader's Application 148
    Tensions in the Second-Grade Team 148
  Student Exercise: Case Analysis 151
  References 151

8 **Communication: The Impact of Organizational Structure on Information Flow and Perceptions** **153**
  Synopsis of Communication Theory 153
  Organizational Structure: A Framework for Understanding
    Communication Theory 154

Basic Elements of Communication 154
Organizational Structure. 157
Information Overload 159
Networks 159
Nonverbal Communication 162
Communication and Information Technology 163
Application to School Leadership 164
Summary 165
Theory into Practice 166
Who's on First? What's on Third? 166
Sample Analysis. 169
Reader's Application 170
I Heard It through the Grapevine 170
Student Exercise: Case Analysis 171
References 172

9 Decision Making: An Essential Function of Leadership 173
Synopsis of Decision-Making Theories 173
Rational Decision-Making Models 174
Descriptive Theories of Decision Making 178
Participatory and Group Theories of Decision Making 182
Limitations of Group Decision Making: Groupthink 187
Data-Driven Decision Making 189
Decision Making Filters 191
Summary 192
Theory into Practice 192
It's a Dirty Job, and Someone's Got to Do It 192
Sample Analysis. 194
Reader's Application 195
Controversy Haunts Spirit Day at Meadows Middle School. . . . 195
Student Exercise: Case Analysis 197
References 197

10 Organizational Change: Reforming and Restructuring 199
Synopsis of Organizational Change Theories. 199
Conceptualizing the Change Process 200
Second-Wave Change Theories: Rational, Linear Approaches to
Organizational Change. 201
Change as Innovation 201
Organizational Development 205
Total Quality Management 209
Third-Wave Organizational Change: Transforming Organizational
Structure 211
Application to School Leadership 217
Summary 218
Theory into Practice 219
Curriculum Change Not Flying at Eagle Elementary School. 219

Sample Analysis. 220

Reader's Application 221

    No Raise in Taxes If the Old School Is Razed 221

Student Exercise: Case Analysis 222

References 223

11 Applying Theory to School Leadership: Concluding Comments **225**

    References 228

Name Index **229**

Subject Index **231**

Preface

This book is written for the student-practitioner. Its intent is to raise theories of leadership and organizational behavior from the catacombs of library bookshelves and bring them to life in the everyday world of school leadership. This text introduces organizational and leadership theories that are especially relevant to educational administration programs that prepare students for school and district leadership roles. Moreover, theories are explained in terms of their application to educational settings.

In an attempt to focus on theoretical foundations useful to the school leader, two major themes are addressed: (a) organizational theories relevant to schools and (b) leadership processes essential to school effectiveness. Organizational theories relevant to schools are examined through fundamental components and structures of organizations to understand the systemic operations of educational organizations. Concepts and theories related to bureaucracy, social systems, power, and organizational climate are introduced as a framework for becoming acquainted with schools' organizational structure. Leadership theories, drawn from both the body of general leadership theory and the body of research associated with organizational theory, are addressed as the processes essential to effective school leadership, including decision making, communication, understanding human motivation, and guiding change.

Throughout the book, organizational theories are presented within the context of their usefulness in informing practice. Direct relationships and applications are made to the real world of school principals and superintendents. In addition, theories and concepts are explained through their historical perspectives, for it is important to recognize that larger social, cultural, and economic forces influence all organizations, especially schools.

The book begins with an historical overview of organizational theory in Chapter 1, to provide a framework for understanding the structure and operation of modern school organizations. In subsequent chapters, specific organizational theories, which have application to educational organization and leadership, are presented within the context of their historical development and their applicability to school leadership today. Basic concepts of organizational structure are presented in Chapter 2. Chapters 3 and 4 more fully explain systems theories and organizational culture. In Chapter 5, theories of leadership are presented in terms of traits and behaviors of leaders. In addition, bases of power, authority, and effectiveness of leadership are explored. Chapter 6 relates the concepts of leadership to organizational structures through the presentation of contingency theories. Chapter 7 focuses on the concept of motivation and explores human behavior and its impact on the organization. Chapters 8 and 9 discuss two primary functions of leadership—communication and decision making. The complexities of communication and decision-making processes are presented as dynamic functions related to the values, norms, motivations, and goals of the organization. Finally, Chapter 10 pulls together the concepts of organizational structure and leadership through the presentation of organizational change theories.

Each chapter concludes with two case scenarios relevant to the theories and concepts presented in the chapter. The first case is accompanied by a sample analysis illustrating the application of theory to practice. The author's sample analysis in each chapter represents only one of several ways to interpret and solve the situation. The second case is presented for the reader's application and is followed by questions intended to guide the reader's analysis. A variety of case situations are presented throughout the book and include problems of practice associated with the superintendency, the principalship, and the assistant principalship in elementary, middle, and high schools in rural, suburban, and urban settings. Diverse issues are presented in the case studies and include problems related to instructional supervision, finance, hiring, school improvement, curriculum development, district consolidation, and school reform.

In an introductory text, it is necessary to present a certain breadth of content. At the same time, however, it is important to provide the reader sufficient explanation and detail as to make the content understandable and useful. Thus, in outlining the chapters of this book, I chose a breadth of content that represents essential bases of knowledge for the educational leader; that is, fundamental organizational constructs and structures applicable to schools and generic principles and processes essential to all school leadership positions. In this second edition, I have included current themes of concern in educational leadership theory, such as leading for social justice, data-driven decision making, and organizational change in terms of global culture, diversity, and the impact of information technology. Within each chapter, however, I do not attempt to provide a panorama of theories related to that particular concept. Rather, I chose to focus on a few selected theories in enough detail to illustrate their applicability and usefulness to the practice of school leadership.

The primary purpose in writing this book is to bring together theory and practice. This is done by illustrating what theoretical concepts of organizations and leadership look like in real-world school settings and then showing how the educational leader can use the knowledge of theory to solve problems of practice.

1

Applying Organizational Theory to Educational Leadership: An Overview of Theoretical Foundations

It was Monday, August 1, and Sandra Jenkins' first day on the job as an elementary assistant principal. It was her first administrative appointment, and she was excited, nervous, and a little scared. She had completed her course work for administrative certification last May and had interviewed for this position shortly after that. The interview with the principal and assistant superintendent had gone well; they had seemed very pleased with her educational background and teaching experiences. She had immediately liked Mission School District and Summerset Elementary School. Today, she would be introduced to her new position, move into her office, and spend the day with the principal, Pat Larkin. Pat had many years of experience as a principal, and Sandra felt she could really learn a lot from someone like Pat.

When Sandra arrived at Summerset promptly at 8:00 am, Pat was already in his office. He greeted her enthusiastically, offered her a cup of coffee, and suggested they meet in the conference room. Pat was obviously prepared for their day-long orientation session, as Sandra noticed policy and procedure manuals, handbooks, and other files neatly stacked on the conference room table. After some brief chitchat, Pat began, "Well, Sandra, I'm really excited to have you on board the Mission District administrative team. Today is going to be like your first day of school. I know that you have been taking administrative classes at State University for your school administration credential. You've probably learned a lot of theories about leadership and school organization and reform, but now you'll learn about the real world of school administration. You can basically forget most of that stuff they taught you in your graduate classes, because it doesn't really apply in practice."

Sadly, too many school leaders agree with Pat's comments about the connection of educational leadership theory and practice. It is for that reason this book is written. This book is intended as an introduction to organizational and leadership theory for educational administration, and addresses fundamental processes inherent to school organizational behavior and leadership. Two major themes are developed. The first involves an examination of organizational structures and basic components of organizations to understand the systemic operations of educational organizations. Concepts and theories related to bureaucracy, social systems, power, and organizational climate are introduced as a framework for becoming acquainted with schools' organizational structure. A second theme involves leadership processes that are essential to school effectiveness. These include decision making, communication, understanding human motivation, and guiding change.

Throughout the book, organizational theories are presented within the context of their usefulness in informing practice. Direct relationships and applications are made to the real world of school principals and superintendents. In addition, theories and concepts are explained in terms of their historical perspectives, because it is important to recognize that all organizations, especially schools, are influenced by larger social, cultural, and economic forces. Thus, as work, lifestyles, and other aspects of modern culture change, so do the organizations that operate as part of the culture. However, history teaches us that change is not a re-creation, but rather an evolution of organizational systems. "Old" ways and methods may eventually give way to "new" means and structures, but not without retaining certain traditions and ways of operating, at least through periods of transition and reforming. Taking the historical development of culture and organizations into account, it follows that the study and conceptualizations of organizational theories offer views about school organization and leadership that reflect traditions, thoughts, and cultural perspectives relevant to a particular point in time. Schools today in many ways still resemble schools as they existed early in the twentieth century; in other ways, they are vastly different. An historical perspective on the development of organizational theory is essential to understanding the role of school leadership today.

Three Periods of Organizational Theory

The study of organizations and ensuing theory can be classified into three historical periods: (a) classical organizational thought; (b) behaviorist period; and (c) systems theory. Although each era distinguishes itself from the preceding period, organizational theory is continually evolving. Thus, more recent stages of theory development are built on previous understandings and conceptualizations of organizations.

Classical Organizational Theory

The classical organizational theory period is most aptly represented by the work of **Frederick Taylor**. Taylor, often referred to as the father of scientific management, viewed workers in much the same way as industrialists of the period thought of machinery and the assembly process. The following principles outline the basic concepts of Taylor's (1911) scientific management.

- A hierarchical chain of command with various levels of authority and an established division of labor is the most effective operational structure.
- Each person in the organization must be prescribed clearly defined tasks.
- Rules of behavior and a system of punishment are necessary to the efficient and effective management of an organization.
- Workers should be hired based on their abilities and expertise.
- Tasks and procedures should be standardized.

Taylor's notions about scientific management were obviously rooted in an industrial era characterized by mass production where factories produced manufactured goods with interchangeable parts. Mass production relied on an assembly-line approach to manufacturing, and efficiency was gained through specialization, with each factory worker performing a single task as a part of the total production process.

Efficiency was a primary concern of the industrial era, because the goal of mass production was the manufacturing of large quantities of goods at the cheapest cost. Taylor and his followers of "human engineers" concentrated on the efficient operation of factory production through time and motion studies and prescribed methods of work that required the least number of physical manipulations in the shortest time. Management studies in the classical period were characterized by a concern for planning, directing, and organizing the efficient operation of a mass production enterprise. Bureaucracy, discussed in more detail in Chapter 2, arose as an efficient organizational structure in the industrial era. Classical organizational thought was characterized by a concern for **specialization** and **division of labor**, where work was coordinated from the top-down through **formal structures** of communication and a well-defined **chain of command**.

Henri Fayol (1916/1949) expanded Taylor's view of management and administration to include that of the upper levels of the organization. Fayol indicated that organizational efficiency would result if issues related to planning, organizing, commanding, coordinating, and controlling were used by those in management positions. Fayol also espoused certain administrative precepts such as setting a good example, eliminating incompetents, being knowledgeable of personnel, and creating a shared organizational focus by periodically meeting with assistants.

Luther Gulick (1937) also contributed to the foundation of scientific management and the development of the modern bureaucracy. He is best known for his delineation of the functions of the chief executive, described as POSDCoRB. This acronym stood for planning, organizing, staffing, directing, coordinating, reporting, and budgeting. These ideals of management provided support for the departmentalization of businesses, the development of a defined span of control, and the delegation of authority to subordinates as it was deemed necessary.

Basic principles of management related to productivity, efficiency, the use of authority, and the coordination of institutional activities are rooted in research associated with the classical period of organizational theory. Fundamental principles of management science during the classical period called for a well-defined organization with a hierarchy of authority, established rules and regulations, and workers who were technically competent. These are the principles and assumptions on which bureaucratic theory is built. Ultimately, this approach to management migrated from the corporate world to that of education, resulting in an **industrial view of school.** This model equated schools to factories, where raw materials (students) were processed into finished products (productive citizens). Early scholars of educational administration, such as Ellwood Cubberly (1916), compared the management of schools to the management of business and industry. In his description of the role and function of the school principal, Cubberly (1923) outlined specific job descriptions for various school employee roles with rigid expectations and a defined hierarchy of authority. Concepts of specialization and measurement dominated his discussion of school organization, as evidenced by his references to classification of students and teachers and the measurement of instruction through standardized tests and inspection of teaching practices.

Classical organizational theory continues to impact schools. The "factory model" of education is highly engrained in schools' organizational structure and is evident in the language often associated with schooling. Phrases such as "producing students" and "measuring outcomes" illustrate an enduring mental model of school factories that produce a finished product of an educated youth. Specialization of labor continues to be practiced in schools, as teachers' roles are defined by their areas of expertise (art teacher, history teacher, special education teacher, fifth-grade teacher), and students are labeled and pigeonholed by their abilities (gifted student, honors student) and, unfortunately, also by their so-called disabilities or handicaps (learning disabled, behavioral disorder, mentally challenged). The basic school structure of grade levels, with students grouped according to their age, and the departmental structure of secondary schools, with curriculum and teachers organized according to academic disciplines, exemplify the constructs of classical organizational thought that are deeply imbedded in our educational institutions.

Behaviorist Period

Classical organizational theorists viewed workers as part of the "machinery" or "technology" of the organization. Human needs, responses, and goals were not considered separately from the aims and objectives of the organization. The social sciences period, which emerged in the 1920s, changed the focus of organizational theory to the consideration of **human dynamics** and the impact of **psychological and social factors** on the effectiveness and efficiency of the organization.

Interestingly, a major impetus for the emergence of social science theory in organizational management stemmed from an investigation framed in classical organizational thought and scientific management. In the 1920s, **Elton Mayo,** a professor of industrial research at Harvard University, launched a study of the Hawthorne Works of the Western Electric Company in Chicago to investigate the effects of lighting on worker productivity. In setting up the **Hawthorne studies,** researchers hypothesized that productivity would increase with increased illumination. Using a control group and an experimental group, results of a series of experiments showed that both groups' productivity increased regardless of whether lighting was increased, decreased, or held constant. Follow-up studies continued in the Hawthorne plant over several years, in which different variables such as rest breaks, length of workday, and other working conditions were manipulated. Findings were similar to the original illumination studies.

In the final analysis, researchers concluded that the effects of increased productivity were not determined by physical manipulations in the work place but rather were the result of psychological and social changes in the work environment. The workers and supervisors involved in the experimental situations were the object of considerable attention. Consequently, self-images and interpersonal relations changed. Supervisors acted more informally and were less directive. Workers, knowing they were being studied, viewed themselves differently and began to develop a culture of friendship and an informal structure of rules and norms among themselves. An informal standard of output and levels of production emerged, often lower than management's expectations or physical capabilities. Thus, it was concluded that social and psychological variables were more important to effective management than the manipulation of physical and economic conditions (Pugh & Hickson, 1989).

Two themes developed and merged during the behaviorist period. One was the human relations orientation, which brought attention to the informal structures of organizations, social interactions, and worker satisfaction and morale. The **human relations approach**, perhaps too simplistically, proposed that people work harder when treated well. A second theme was the **behavioral science approach**, which focused on the behavior of individuals within the formal organization structure, and combined principles of classical organizational thought with principles of psychology, sociology, political science, and economics. **Chester Barnard** is often credited with providing the initial framework for the behavioral science approach through his analysis of formal and informal structures within an organization. Barnard (1938) conceptualized organizations through the interactions between formal and informal structures. **Herbert Simon** (1957) described organizations in terms of equilibrium, where individual needs are balanced with organizational goals. Taking a rational approach typical of behavioral scientists, Simon postulated that equilibrium in an organization was achieved through an exchange of inducements and work. Employees continue with an organization as long as the benefits to them outweigh the work they produce. When both individual needs and organizational goals are being adequately met, an organization achieves equilibrium. Contributions to organizational theory from the social sciences approach include a better understanding of motivation, communication, and situational leadership. These concepts will be more fully addressed in subsequent chapters.

Systems Theory

The application of social sciences to organizational theory brought a focus to the human factor in organizations. Organizational theories broadened their perspective regarding the dynamics of an organization and expanded notions about organizational leadership to include not only managing the operations and technology of the organization but also considered the psychological and social factors involved in motivating workers. However, organizational theories of the 1940s and 1950s did not consider the relationship of the organization to factors in its external environment. The social sciences era tended to conceptualize organizations as closed systems. In the 1960s, organizational theory began to incorporate the notion of open systems. Borrowing from theoretical concepts of the natural sciences, organization theories applied the analogy of **organizations as living organisms.**

Systems theory, discussed more fully in Chapter 3, postulates that organizations are dynamic systems involving constant interactions among the various **formal and informal systems** within the organization as well as exchanges **(feedback and input)** between the organization and systems outside the organization. Schools, as open systems, have various subsystems that operate within it. For example, teachers, students, and administrators might be considered as different subsystems within a school. Additional subsystems might include the athletic department, the leadership team, the student council, or Mr. Jones' fourth-grade class. Individuals can belong to various groups, and the interaction among the various subsystems is complex. Individuals and groups interact both through formal structures, such as faculty meetings, and informal structures, such as a conversation over lunch in the faculty lounge. In addition, the school receives input and feedback from the outside environment and produces output that is exported to the outside environment. Inputs into the system include community expectations, parental demands, teachers' expertise, and the students themselves. The school transforms the input through activities within the organization, such as classroom instruction, parent-teacher conferences, or a career fair. The school then exports a product—a high school graduate, happy parent, or disgruntled community member—into the environment. The school will subsequently receive feedback from the outside environment. For instance, local businesses that hire graduates complain of lack of skills, or colleges recruit students for science scholarships as a result of the preparedness of graduates taking advanced physics and chemistry courses. And, the cycle continues.

Leadership within an open system is very complex. Conditions within and outside the organization cannot be precisely predicted, because the conditions themselves change, such as new laws, economic downturns, or new hires. The interrelationships among various subsystems within the organization and between the organization and other systems are complicated, intertwined, and overlapping. Thus, a chief function of the educational leader is the management of information among the networks within and outside the school or district boundaries.

This conceptualization of schools as open systems is a natural evolution of organizational theory that more accurately describes organizations operating in a postindustrial society. However, it is important to remember that organizations evolve gradually; they do not transform suddenly. Organizational structure and cultural mental models of how we perceive organizations are products of historical development. Thus, classical organizational theory, behaviorist approaches, and systems theory all provide valuable perspectives for informing and guiding the practice of educational leadership.

Application of Theory to Practice

This brief overview of the development of organizational theories in the past century provides a framework for understanding the structure and operation of modern school organizations. In subsequent chapters, specific organizational theories, which have application to educational organization and leadership, are presented within the context of their historical development and their applicability to school leadership today. Influences from classical organizational concepts, social sciences perspectives, and open systems theory are revisited throughout this book, as each chapter explores a specific body of organizational theory.

Basic concepts of organizational structure are presented in Chapter 2, which focuses on the functions and goals of school organizations as well as the bureaucratic nature of schools. Chapter 3 more fully explains the concept of systems as a way to understand the complexities of schools and how schools interrelate to other systems and organizations. Chapter 4 explores organizational culture and introduces the notion of schools as learning organisms. In Chapter 5, theories of leadership are presented in terms of traits and behaviors of leaders. In addition, the bases of power, authority, and effectiveness of leadership are explored. Chapter 6 relates the concepts of leadership to organizational structures through the presentation of contingency theories. This body of organizational theory attempts to identify organizational and environmental factors and situations that impact leader effectiveness. Chapter 7 focuses on the concept of motivation. This chapter explores human behavior and its impact on the organization. Chapters 8 and 9 discuss two primary functions of organizations and leadership—communication and decision making. The complexities of communication and decision-making processes are presented in terms of their interrelationship with the values, norms, motivations, and goals of the organization. Finally, Chapter 10 pulls together the concepts of organizational structure and leadership through the presentation of organizational change theories.

In each chapter, major theoretical concepts are discussed through their application to school leadership practice. At the end of each chapter, a case study is provided along with a sample analysis illustrating the application of theory to practice. The sample analysis in each chapter represents only one of several ways to interpret and solve the situation. Although organizational theories provide school leaders a basic framework of knowledge and principles from which to work, the dynamics of organizations are too complex to assure absolute predictability. Further, a leader's values and orientation are also key aspects to one's analysis and approach to solving the problems presented in these scenarios. Readers are challenged to reflect on their own values, perspectives, and context in considering how they might respond as educational leaders in these instances. Toward that end, a second case study, without analysis, is presented for the reader's application. Questions at the end of the case are intended to guide the reader's thinking. They should not be considered an exhaustive list of inquiries that might be applied to the situation presented.

References

Barnard, C. I. (1938). *The functions of the executive.* Cambridge, MA: Harvard University Press.

Cubberly, E. P. (1916). *Public school administration: A statement of the fundamental principles underlying the organization and administration of public education.* Boston: Houghton Mifflin.

Cubberly, E. P. (1923). *The principal and his school: The organization, administration, and supervision of instruction in an elementary school.* Boston: Houghton Mifflin.

Fayol, H. (1949). *General and industrial management* (C. Storrs, Trans.) London: Sir Isaac Pitman & Sons. (Original work published 1916)

Gulick, L. (1937). Notes on the theory of organization. In L. Gulick & L. Urwick (Eds.), *Papers on the science of administration* (pp. 3–45). New York: Institute of Public Administration.

Pugh, D. S., & Hickson, D. J. (1989). *Writers on organizations*. Newbury Park, CA: Sage.

Simon, H. A. (1957). *Administrative behavior: A study of decision-making processes in administrative organization* (2nd ed.). New York: Free Press.

Taylor, F. W. (1911). *The principles of scientific management*. New York: Harper and Brothers.

2

Organizational Structure: Fundamental Constructs that Define Schools

Synopsis of Organizational Structures

Examining the organizational structure of schools provides a basis for understanding the fundamental concepts of organizational behavior and organizational leadership. Scholars of organizational theory have conceptualized organizational structure in several ways in an attempt to first classify and then generalize common properties of organizational systems. As was seen in Chapter 1, the historical development of organizational theory has paralleled cultural and economic shifts in society. Early organizational theorists studied organizational structure from the perspective of the industrial era. As social and economic forces have produced organizational and institutional changes, organizational theory has shifted to reflect these transitions. Organizations, however, are slow to change. Schools in particular are institutions that are inextricably tied to the culture in which they operate; thus, the organizational structure of schools is strongly influenced by its historical roots. Many of the constructs of organizational structure and behavior that correlate to an earlier industrial era are still operational in school organizations. It is important for educational leaders to understand these historical underpinnings as well as organizational structures that are more closely aligned with the cultural demands and expectations of a postindustrial society. Educational leaders today must understand that the schools they are leading are transitioning organizations.

This chapter discusses organizational theory related to conceptualizations of organizational structure. First, this chapter presents various typologies that have been developed to explain and conceptualize organizational structure. Second, bureaucratic theory in terms of both formal and informal structures is presented. Third, theories that describe specific components of organizations are reviewed. Finally, conceptualizations of organizational structure in terms of critical dilemmas provide a framework for considering the transitional nature of the organizational structure of schools.

Applications for School Leaders

Understanding organizational structures will help school leaders to:

♦ Analyze the fundamental structural components of a school district in terms of their functions, specializations, and interrelationships

♦ Better understand the formal organization and bureaucracies

♦ Understand conflicts inherent to organizations and the relationship of these conflicts to the larger cultural and political context

♦ Use the power of leadership in a way that best matches the educational aims and purposes of the school

---

Organizational Typologies

What is the role that schools play in American society? The answer to that seemingly simple question varies and has changed over time. Educators today often lament that their roles have expanded. Schools have been given more and more responsibilities—once reserved for families, churches, or community—such as drug education, sex education, athletics, and after-school day care. Knowing an organization's role in society is fundamental to defining its primary purpose, identifying its goals, and structuring the organization in a way that best matches its social function.

Talcott Parsons (1960) classified organizations based on the social function they perform. He identified four types of organizations by the general problem they served to confront for society. His organizational classifications are as follows:

- **Economic organizations** that serve to solve the problem of adaptation, or acquiring sufficient resources and adapting to environmental demands
- **Political organizations** that operate to achieve basic societal goals
- **Integrative organizations,** such as courts and social agencies, that serve to maintain solidarity and unity within the society
- **Pattern-maintenance organizations,** such as schools and churches, that operate to preserve and transmit a society's culture

Parson's typology suggests the importance of the relationship of an organization to its environment and the larger society. Although Parson's typology has been criticized because it failed to establish mutually exclusive categories (Carper & Snizek, 1980), Parson's proposal that organizations receive societal support relative to the value society places on the organization's primary function is a significant concept for educational leaders. A society's institutions are reflective of cultural values. Thus, if a society highly values education it will allocate more substantial resources to these organizations than it will to other types of organizations.

Peter M. Blau and **W. Richard Scott** (1962) classified organizations in terms of who benefits. They proposed four types of organizations based on their prime beneficiaries:

- Mutual benefit organizations where the prime beneficiaries are the members of the organization. Examples of mutual benefit organizations include labor unions, political parties, professional associations, and churches.
- Business organizations where the main beneficiaries are the owners. Such organizations include banks, manufacturing and service industries, and wholesale and retail enterprises.
- Commonweal organizations where the primary beneficiary is the general public. Examples of commonweal organizations are the military, police departments, and fire departments.
- Service organizations where the main beneficiary is the public being served by the organization. Schools, hospitals, prisons, and mental health clinics are examples of services organizations.

Blau and Scott contended that although each type of organization has a primary beneficiary, others also gain from their association with the organization. Blau and Scott further suggested that each type of organization faces specific structural issues or problems. **Mutual benefit organizations'** major problem is to maintain membership control. Apathy among the membership often results in a select group becoming an oligarchy. The main problem for **businesses** is maximizing profits through efficient use of resources. In contrast, **commonweal organizations** must balance efficiency with the goal of serving the best interests of the public. **Service organizations** confront the problem of maintaining a focus on the client as the main beneficiary rather than others associated with the organization. In schools, for example, the focus must remain on what is best for students, in spite of teacher demands or administrative expediency.

Although Blau and Scott classified schools as service organizations, schools also face dilemmas associated with other types of organizations. Politically, public schools operate as commonweal organizations, with an elected board to serve the public's interest in children's education. Furthermore, private schools and charter schools face conflicting interests by operating to a certain degree as a business. For that matter, public schools must be concerned with the effective and efficient use of resources, especially at times when public education in not adequately funded.

A third typology is offered by **Amitai Etzioni** (1961), in which he classified organizations based on the kind of power exerted by leadership. He identified three types of power:

1. **Coercive power:** Actual or threatened application of physical sanctions, such as detention, suspension, or expulsion

2. **Renumerative power:** Use of material rewards such as salaries, bonuses, or fringe benefits

3. **Normative power:** Employing symbolic rewards or sanctions such as recommendations, commendations, honors, or grades

He further identified three types of reactions to power along a continuum of involvement. Commitment is the most intensely positive reaction; calculation is either mildly positive or mildly negative; and, alienation is an intensely negative reaction.

Etzioni proposed that each type of power is most congruent with a specific type of reaction. The use of **coercive power** tends to result in **alienation.** He termed organizations that primarily threaten or apply physical sanctions as a means to control as coercive organizations. The use of **renumerative power** tends to result in mildly positive or mildly negative involvement, or **calculation.** He classified organizations that predominantly use renumerative power as utilitarian organizations. Finally, **normative power** tends to result in **commitment** to the organization, and he identified organizations that use normative power as the chief means of compliance as normative organizations (Figure 2.1).

Figure 2.1. Reactions to Power: Etzioni's Continuum of Involvement

Negative (−)   ⟵———————————————————⟶   (+) Positive

Reaction to Power	Alienation	Calculation	Commitment
Power Used	Coercive	Normative	Renumerative

Etzioni used the concepts of power, reactions, and organization types as a basis for presenting **compliance theory,** offering generalizations about organizational structures. Etzioni delineated four organizational variables: (a) goals, (b) elites, (c) communication, and (d) socialization.

A goal is what an organization is attempting to achieve. Compliance theory distinguishes three types of goals:

- Order goals attempt to control members through segregation or preventing members from becoming involved in deviant activities.
- Economic goals are those related to profit from the production of goods or services.
- Culture goals refer to intentions to create or preserve cultural symbols or artifacts.

Etzioni proposed that each type of goal was best matched to a specific type of organization. **Coercive organizations** tend to have order goals; **utilitarian organizations** are disposed toward economic goals; and, **normative organizations** are primarily concerned with culture goals.

The second organizational variable is elites, which refers to those persons who have power in the organization. Elites are categorized as (a) officers, (b) informal leaders, and (c) formal leaders. **Officers** derive their power exclusively from their position or office within the organization. **Informal leaders** have no position of power or authority but do possess personal power to influence others. **Formal leaders** are those who hold an office within the organization and also have personal power. Officers of an organization tend to control what Etzioni termed as instrumental activities, or those tasks related to achieving organizational goals. Informal leaders, conversely, are more likely to control expressive activities, those processes involved in maintaining values and encouraging social integration among members.

Coercive organizations are characterized by two separate elites, where officers control instrumental activities and informal leaders drive expressive activities. Informal leaders are subordinate to officers and there may even be open conflict between the two groups of leaders. Cooperation and collaboration among groups of elites characterize normative organizations. Leaders directing expressive activities tend to dominate leaders of instrumental activities, and there is a high level of integration between leaders and subordinates. Utilitarian organizations fall somewhere between coercive and normative organizations, where instrumental activities are primarily controlled by officers and expressive activities by informal leaders. Instrumental activities dominate the utilitarian organization, and there is some integration among leaders and subordinates.

Reflecting on compliance theory in relationship to schools as organizations, it is important to note the primary goal of schools. Using Etzioni's typology of organizations, if we conclude that schools are organizations where the primary goal is the transmission of culture, then the use of normative power is best fitted to school leadership. It would behoove educational leaders to remember that if order is placed as a primary goal, there may be a tendency to replace normative power with coercive strategies. When this occurs, alienation of faculty and students will follow as will division between administrators, teachers, and students. For normative power to be effectively used, it must be accomplished through collaboration among all school stakeholders (Figure 2.2).

Figure 2.2. Etzioni's Compliance Theory: Organizational Typology Based on Power and Organizational Goals

Primary Power Used	General Reaction	Type of Organization	Primary Goal	Elites
Coercive	Alienation	Coercive	Order	Separation of officers from informal leaders Informal leaders subordinate to officers
Renumerative	Calculation	Utilitarian	Economic	Mixed
Normative	Commitment	Normative	Culture	Cooperation among officers and informal leaders High integration between leaders and subordinates

Formal Organizational Structure: Bureaucracy

Bureaucracy, perhaps more than any other organizational term, is a word commonly used to describe large, formal organizations. Bureaucracy, often associated with government agencies and large corporations, is characterized by a hierarchy of authority, top-down decision making, and impersonal interaction.

Max Weber is the person most recognized for his work on the bureaucracy. Although Weber's (1910–1914/1947) work primarily focused on governmental entities, it certainly holds truth for all kinds of organizational structures, including schools. Weber was not only interested in determining and describing the various characteristics of a bureaucracy but also in how authority was developed and used in organizations.

Authority represents the concept that certain directions given to others will be followed. These directions are followed because the authority held is based on some kind of **legal** precept such as one determined by legal position within the organization (e.g., principal). Legal positions are highly formalized. **Charisma** may also result in a positive response to authority, which inspires a person to follow the directions. Charismatic authority endures best for a longer period of time when directly associated with positional authority. Weber identified a final type of authority as **traditional**. Simply put, traditional authority is the result of authority practiced over a period of time and recognized because others have traditionally recognized it. Traditional authority is also representative of position. A teacher is a traditional authority. A principal is one also because he or she is recognized to have authority by others. Of course, teachers and principals also have legal authority and in some cases charismatic authority. It is important to note that Weber's conceptualization of bureaucracy dealt only with the institutional, formal portion of an organization. Weber's view of a bureaucracy was highly formal and legalistic. Characteristics of bureaucracies identified by Weber include:

1. Division of labor and specialization
2. An organization guided by rules and regulations
3. Technical competence and a career orientation
4. Impersonal orientation
5. A well-defined hierarchy of authority
6. Separation of ownership from administration

Although these six general characteristics explain the efficient functions of bureaucracies, each has weaknesses that can interfere with organizational effectiveness.

Division of Labor and Specialization

A key characteristic of bureaucracy identified by Weber was the division of labor and specialization of tasks. This relates to the manner in which **roles** and **functions** are distributed within an organization and official duties as detailed in job descriptions, flow charts, and policy manuals. A teacher, for instance, has a primary duty to teach, but the role also includes other duties and functions that are often enumerated in the teacher's contract. Teaching is further specialized by elementary or secondary and by grades or subject. The role and specialization required of an advanced calculus teacher in a math and science magnet school is significantly different than the role and specialized knowledge of a second grade teacher. The practice of state licensure and certification of teachers supports this notion of specialization as an inherent component of the educational system.

In light of the above example, division of labor and specialization are apparent in that teaching calculus requires different specialized skills than teaching second grade. Specialization implies that a specific **expertise** is required for a particular position. Thus, a school district may seek to hire an individual with a doctorate degree in math to teach calculus and a person with an early childhood degree to teach second grade.

Understanding this idea of specialization and division of labor helps one to comprehend more clearly how schools have developed. As more and more states provided for free, public education and enacted compulsory school attendance laws at the beginning of the twentieth century, the size of public schools grew. Interestingly, this shift in public education came during the time of industrialization to keep children from taking jobs in factories. As the notion of "education for the masses" took hold, it is not surprising that schools began to develop organizational structures resembling the industry model of mass production. Schools began to develop bureaucratic structures where children were grouped by age. When public high schools began to develop during this period, because of a continued increase in the age for compulsory school attendance and the recognition that work in an industrial era required higher skill levels for workers, secondary schools developed an organizational structure with specialized departments based on academic disciplines. As specialization entered the school venue so too did an extensive bureaucracy with formal roles and expectations.

Historically, schools were headed by the senior, experienced teacher known as the lead teacher or principal. The rise of the bureaucratic organization also brought with it a need for more levels of management and supervision. Thus, the role of the principal began to change. Instead of taking the role of lead teacher, principals became managers of teachers, students, facilities, finances, and other operations of the school. Eventually, schools developed several layers of administration—superintendents, curriculum supervisors, and other central office specialists, as well as layers of building level administrators (principals and assistant principals). This division of labor provided greater expertise, and bureaucratic theory would suggest this would lead to better education for children.

On the downside, a division of labor and specialization tends to **isolate** people within an organization. That is why it is so difficult for secondary teachers to clearly understand the elementary teacher's world. An additional negative result of specialization is a sense of boredom and a lackadaisical approach to the job. Teaching seventh grade English for 30 years can be a daunting task, especially if one feels isolated and unclear of his or her role within the total educational organization.

Schools will undoubtedly remain specialized to some extent. A division of labor among staffs seems to be the operational norm for most schools. Certainly there have been attempts to break down the division of labor and overcome the negative aspects of specialization. Site-based management, teacher teams, and multigrade level teaching are all ways to address this issue. However, the level of success in any school depends heavily on the site leadership. The principal must continuously seek ways to open paths of communication, to create a sense of community, and to focus on faculty and student morale.

Rules and Regulations

According to Weber, rules and regulations provide employees a certain type of technical competence and supply them a set of rights and duties inherent in their position within the bureaucracy. Without rules and regulations, chaos would result and employees would not have goals or organizational identity. There would be an absence of **uniformity** in the application of organizational goals and an absence of organizational **continuity**. Rules and regulations are used to buffer layers of the organization from one another, and by doing so provide different degrees of authority to subordinates and superordinates within the organization. Rules and regulations also legitimize and impersonalize punishment. People are expected to follow the rules. The operating norm becomes: "Things are done a certain way because that is the rule." Enforcement of rules and sanctions for violating rules are imposed uniformly, not because of who you are but rather what rules are violated.

Of course, organizations cannot effectively exist without rules and regulations. The result of no control is obviously chaos and anarchy. Schools have rules and regulations, often represented by student or teacher handbooks or policy manuals, and these rules are designed to ensure the smooth operation of the institution. That is the function of rules and regulations—to set parameters and provide guidance for those who inhabit the organization. That is why administrators have a different set of parameters than do teachers or students, because their function in the organization is different.

However, all of us have encountered the bureaucrat who uses rules and regulations not to accomplish organizational goals but rather to punish, hinder, or disenfranchise others. Bureaucrats sometimes hide behind rules so that the "human" side of the story doesn't have to be considered. Some bureaucrats in schools use rules and regulations in such a way that rules are enforced with certain students but not with others. Walk into any school in the United States today and some groups of students feel singled out by the rules and regulations although other groups of students never have the rules applied to them. School leaders should be aware of how rules can be used inappropriately to create unequal classes of student citizens within the school. School leaders must consistently weigh human needs against the intention and need for rules and regulations. In addition, school leaders must be cognizant of how rules and regulations are applied to students and whether they are equitably enforced.

For instance, a school's attendance policy states that students can be absent only 10 days each semester. A straight A student misses 11 days because of illness and a family crisis. Should this student fail, as the rule so states? If a special consideration is provided this straight-A student, will it likewise be provided a student with D grades in a similar situation? Unusual situations and unique circumstances are what make rules and regulations difficult. Administrators struggle with these decisions on a daily basis. Rules provide guidance and direction for, not absolution from, making decisions that effect the lives and futures of students.

Technical Competence and Career Orientation

Weber's concept of career orientation implies that success based on **technical competence and knowledge** results in increased employee morale, organizational loyalty, and motivation. Using this as the foundation for promotion within the organization, then those who are "high-flyers" with the greatest technical knowledge should be promoted first. Although promotion may be the result of technical competence, the reality in many organizations is that promotions are based on seniority or one's connections with others in the organization.

This ongoing conflict between **achievement** and **longevity** exists in many organizations. It is also true that what is perceived as knowledge in some situations may in fact be false knowledge and bravado. The "high-flyer" may have surface organizational and technical knowledge but may lack the depth of knowledge that comes from experience, as one develops an historical sense of the organization. There is an additional issue to be considered regarding promotions based on technical competence. If someone is promoted too quickly over more senior colleagues, the result may be diminished loyalty and motivation from those who have been in the "trenches." This sometimes is seen in schools when people are promoted to department chair or administrative positions over those who have been loyal to the organization for many years and have aspired to these administrative positions.

The key for school leaders is to build relationships with subordinates and superordinates so that potentially demoralizing issues related to one's career can be handled in a sensitive manner. One must learn to consider the needs of all people within the organization. A negative impact on one's career often results in a negative impact on the organization and its effectiveness.

Impersonal Orientation

An impersonal orientation implies that decisions are made in a **rational** manner without regard to a person's position within or outside the organization. This impersonal orientation view espoused by Weber allows one to make decisions, enforce policies, and respond to appeals without undue pressure from those within or outside of the organization. However, two things hold true regarding impersonal orientation.

First, one's personal views do impact decisions and policy enforcement. If a student argues, fights, and rants about his or her rights and fails to accept responsibility for misbehavior, then an administrator's personal dislike or absence of sympathy makes the decision to enforce the policies an easier one. However, if a student exhibits remorse and accepts full responsibility for misbehavior, the requisite policy may be more leniently applied. It is extraordinarily difficult to keep one's personal likes or dislikes removed from most decisions.

Second, taken to the extreme, if one adopts a totally impersonal orientation toward others, then it is easy to see how organizational morale can be diminished. Because human interaction is minimized by this impersonal orientation, ultimately the efficiency and effectiveness of the organization suffers. Can you imagine working in a school where no one cares about others, and people respond only on a professional level with no regard for personal concerns or needs? Schools do not and cannot function in this manner because the very mission of school is to prepare students both academically and socially.

Hierarchy of Authority

Some manner of hierarchical authority exists in all organizations. The classical oriented model, with its **flow charts** and **organizational schematics**, is still prevalent in most organizations. Even those organizations that claim a flat organizational structure clearly designate the chief executive officer (CEO), and people certainly understand who is in charge. The communication networks, power structure, and decision-making processes may differ, but a hierarchy of authority still exists to some extent.

Weber believed that a hierarchy of authority enhances organizational **coordination** and creates a level of disciplined organizational **compliance**. The problem that inherently exists within a hierarchy of authority is that people can misuse their positional power, because they know appeals can be made up through the chain of command. Another inherent flaw of hierarchical organization structure involves communication. **Communication** often flows one way—from the top to the bottom. Subordinates may not have opportunities to communicate to superordinates or do so with a sense of apprehension. Employees often fear that to ask supervisors for help or clarification may be construed as incompetence. Furthermore, they do not want to be viewed by superordinates as malcontents who create discord within the organization. Thus, people may become isolated within the hierarchy and may choose to do less. Ultimately, this has the potential to impact the organization's effectiveness and productivity.

One simple way a school leader can counteract the problems associated with a hierarchy of authority is to actively seek input from subordinates. Creating a shared vision and operational teams will help those who tend to feel isolated to view themselves as useful members of the organization. Finally, a leader can use his or her knowledge of motivation and communication to develop a sense of belonging and higher morale among all subordinates. The effort expended on such activities creates a loyal, conscientious, and involved workforce in any organization.

Separation of Ownership and Administration

The concept of separation of ownership and administration according to Weber is tied to issues such as authority (charisma, tradition, and legal) and the competence of those who may own or lead an organization versus those who administer it. **Policies, rules,** and **regulations** represent the basic manner in which an organization receives input on how to respond to specific situations and events. Those who are in control (owners) often set policies that are difficult to carry out by those who are the managers and administrators of the organization. If there is too much distance between those who create the policies and those who carry them out, then the result is a type of policy dissonance. Policies may often be too broad, too specific, or too conflicting to allow them to be effectively implemented. When policies do not adequately address the specific functions of the organization, overcentralization of authority may occur as attempts are made to carry out policies.

Overcentralization is exemplified in schools when school boards adopt policies that are either impossible to apply or unclear in their intent. The result is that both teachers and administrators have no idea what is expected but diligently attempt to make things happen within the context of the policies. As resistance from the teachers increases (as it will), the administrator becomes more coercive to ensure the policies are followed. This is the reason that school administrators must serve as a buffer between what school boards frequently envision and enact. Superintendents must diligently seek to develop open, honest relationships with the school board and be willing to tell the board when something will or will not work. If a school board (owners in a sense) adopts policies that do not ultimately advance the mission and goals of the school, then the result is a demoralized staff that seeks to educate children in a morass of disequilibrium and confusion.

The Informal Organization: Human Elements

The greatest weakness of Weber's theory of bureaucracy lies in his failure to discuss the **informal organization** and the power of **individual needs**. Weber focused on authority, which he classified as traditional, legalistic, or charismatic but did not discuss informal power structures which impact an organization.

It is important to understand Weber's concepts as a school leader because such knowledge assists one in responding to the issues of rules and regulations, seniority, and span of control. However, in working with human beings, knowledge of why and how people respond to issues and events is just as important. A school leader will not be successful if he or she focuses solely on the bureaucratic elements of the school; however, a school leader will fail if the bureaucracy is not considered.

Another criticism of Weber's theory of bureaucracy was expressed by Blau and Scott (1962) who indicated that there is a significant difference between **bureaucratic behavior** and **professional behavior**. Both represent a control of knowledge (how the system works) and both illustrate how decisions are made. The difference according to Blau and Scott is how one responds to organizational and human needs. Professionals, who are often functional members of bureaucratic organizations, seek to use both their professional training and bureaucratic knowledge to resolve issues. This implies a different way to seek solutions when compared to the bureaucratic employee who may use legalistic rules to legitimize decisions regardless of long- or short-term results.

Paul Adler and **Bryan Borys** (1996) attempted to reconcile the issues surrounding the informal and human elements within bureaucracies by examining the types of formalization found within an organization. Adler and Borys identified two types of formalization: (a) that which enables employees and (b) that designed to coerce compliance. They also considered the degree of formalization as the extent formal rules govern behavior and the extent to which rules are enforced. Using the concepts of type and degree of formalization, they proposed four types of bureaucracies, as outlined in Figure 2.3.

Figure 2.3. Adler and Borys Typology of Bureaucracies

Bureaucracy	Type of Formalization	Degree of Formalization
Organic	Enabling	Low
Autocratic	Coercive	Low
Enabling	Enabling	High
Mechanistic	Coercive	High

In a similar fashion, **Wayne Hoy** and **Scott Sweetland** (2001) used the Weberian concepts of formalization and centralization to describe four types of bureaucracies. Like Adler and Borys, they viewed formalization as either enabling or hindering, and they defined centralization as the degree to which employees participate in decision making. Hindering centralization refers to a hierarchy and administration that gets in the way of employees work, and, applied to school settings, would be characterized by administrators using power and authority to control teachers. Enabling centralization helps employees solve problems in their work; schools with enabling centralization are those where administrators view teachers as professionals and use their power and authority to protect teachers.

Using these two constructs from bureaucratic theory, they classified bureaucracies into four categories.

1. **Enabling bureaucracies** are organizations with enabling formalization and enabling centralization. Rules, regulations, and procedures are helpful and lead to problem solving, and hierarchical structure helps employees get their work done.

2. **Hindering bureaucracies,** with hindering centralization and coercive formalization, are punishment centered, demand conformity, and thus are inefficient and ineffective.

3. **Hierarchical bureaucracies** (hindering centralization, enabling formalization) are characterized by the authority and recognition of those in positions of power. Rules apply only when an administrator finds them convenient, or there may be no rules because the administrator makes all decisions on a case by case basis.

4. **Rule-bound bureaucracies** (coercive formalization, enabling centralization) have administrators who are rigid bureaucrats, where rules are rules no matter what the circumstances.

The organizational contrasts previously described are similar to Burns and Stalkers' (1961/1996) conceptualization of organic and mechanistic organizations. **Organic organizations** focus on adaptiveness within the organization, whereas **mechanistic organizations** emphasize production. Applying these organizational categories to the world of public education, a mechanistic school is one that stresses rules and regulations, establishes specific and rigid roles within the school, and has a well-defined hierarchy of authority and span of control. Production of graduates, controlling cost, and maintaining order are important to the mechanistic school administrator.

An organic school, conversely, places great trust in the staff, practices shared decision-making, and adopts only those rules and regulations that are necessary. There is open, free-flowing communication within the school, because there is no rigid, formal organizational structure. Teacher morale is high, because teachers are viewed as experts in their areas. Quality is emphasized instead of production quantity.

In reality, schools are both mechanistic and organic and function best when aspects of mechanistic and organic organizations are integrated. Although extremes serve to illustrate fundamental concepts, they seldom occur in such pure form in practice.

Structural Constructs of Organizations

Another approach to conceptualizing organizational structure is through the fundamental components of an organization. **Henry Mintzberg** (1979) identified three basic elements of any organization. These are (a) the operating core, (b) the administrative component, and (c) support staff. The **operating core** is comprised of those people who perform the basic tasks of the organization. The administrative component contains three parts—the strategic apex, the middle line, and the technostructure. The **strategic apex** embodies the top administrators who ensure the organization operates consistently with its mission. The **middle line** consists of administrators who link the apex to the operating core. The **technostructure** is composed of administrators whose primary responsibilities are planning and training. **Support staff** are specialists who provide support services for the organization but operate outside the organization's operating workflow. Figure 2.4 illustrates the five components and associated positions that make up the organizational structure of a school district.

Figure 2.4. Elements of School Organization: An Adaptation of Mintzberg's Five Basic Parts of Organizations

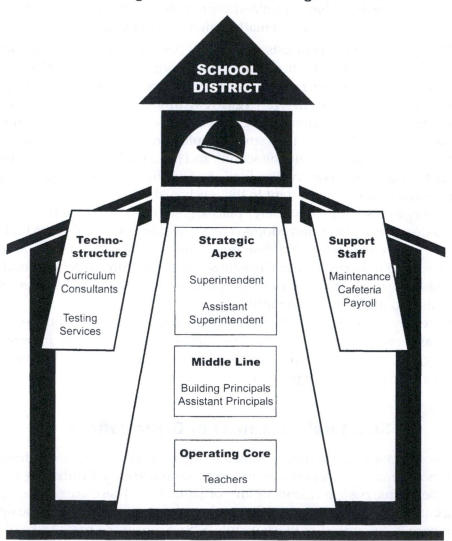

How various components in a school organization interact, and the mechanisms used to coordinate the five basic components, will determine the overall structure of the school. Different types of organizational structure lead to different results, some of which are more effective than others in educational organizations. Mintzberg identified five mechanisms that help coordinate what happens within an organization.

1. Mutual adjustment where coordination is achieved through informal communication among workers

2. Direct supervision where one person is responsible for monitoring and overseeing the work of others

3. Standardization of work where work procedures are prescribed and specifically outlined

4. Standardization of output where expectations of products and performance are specified

5. Standardization of skills where training, skills, and knowledge to perform tasks are uniform among workers in various specialized areas

The result of the interaction of the coordinating mechanisms with various key elements results in the creation of one of five types of organizations. They are (a) simple structure, (b) machine bureaucracy, (c) professional bureaucracy, (d) divisionalized organization, and (e) adhocracy.

The **simple structure** is one represented by a high level of direct supervision and a strong strategic apex (top administrators). Control is at the top, and communication is downward. The **machine bureaucracy** is a highly coordinated, planned organization. The organization is very formal. Rules and regulations are important. The machine bureaucracy represents, in many ways, the ideal Weberian bureaucracy. The **professional bureaucracy** is not as centralized but still has a well-defined bureaucracy. Standardized skills are very important, but the administrative control is more decentralized with power in the hands of the professionals.

In the **divisionalized organization,** the middle managers have a great deal of control. Outputs are standardized and viewed as essential for the successful operation of the organization. In the **adhocracy**, the support staff serves as the primary coordinating device. Of the five, simple structure, machine bureaucracy, and professional bureaucracy are more likely to be found in schools. These three organizational types represent a continuum from an organization that is highly structured and highly autocratic (simple structure) to an organization that is bureaucratically focused on the work and formality (machine bureaucracy) to one where the bureaucracy is decentralized and professionalization is critical (professional bureaucracy) (Figure 2.5).

Figure 2.5. Mintzberg's Organizational Typology

Type of Organization	Primary Coordinating Mechanism	Dominant Organizational Component
Simple structure	Direct supervision	Apex
Machine bureaucracy	Standardization of work	Technostructure
Professional bureaucracy	Standardization of skills	Operating core
Divisionalized organization	Standardization of outputs	Middle line
Adhocracy	Mutual adjustment	Support staff

In terms of schools, the simple structure is exemplified by a school where the administrator is in charge and teachers have as their primary job to see that students graduate. Problems in this type of school range from low morale to an absence of input from those in the classroom. The machine bureaucracy school is highly formalized; decision making is based on the hierarchical chain of command; and, authority and control of all aspects of the school are uppermost in the minds of administrators. Outcomes and cost effectiveness lend themselves to a type of machine oriented, industrial model. This model is characterized by producing graduates who meet established standards and by holding schools accountable. Some combination of these first two models represents what is found in most schools in this country.

The professional bureaucracy school with decentralized authority and power in the hands of professional educators is often talked about but more rarely found. The coordination of a shared vision with all members focused on educating all students to the best of their abilities represents this model. Although many aspects such as open communication, a flattened administrative structure, and professional norms can be found in schools, there remain too few schools that can meet the criteria of a professional bureaucratic organization as envisioned by Mintzberg.

Persistent Dilemmas that Define School Organizations

A final conceptualization for understanding the nature of school organization is the notion of persistent dilemmas, or paradoxes, that push against one another, causing tension or conflict within the organization. **Lee Bolman** and **Terrence Deal** (1991) identified 10 critical dilemmas that organizations attempt to balance for the effective operation and appropriate structure within a particular context. Figure 2.6 summarizes the ten dilemmas and the questions connected with each. School leaders play a critical role in seeking an appropriate equilibrium in each of these areas.

In examining school organization, **Rodney Ogawa**, **Robert Crowson**, and **Ellen Goldring** (1999) outlined internal and external dilemmas that schools face. They defined an organizational dilemma as a "fundamental dichotomy" that cannot be solved or resolved. Further, they asserted that organizational dilemmas imply "deep commitment to core values that are often found in conflict with one another" (p. 278).

Internal dilemmas identified were (a) organizational goals, (b) task structure, (c) professionalism, and (d) hierarchy. The dilemma of organizational goals refers to the relationship of, and possible conflict between, organizational objectives and the motives and interests of its individual members. Merit pay is cited as a reform exemplifying this conflict. Underlying values that may conflict here are competition versus equity. The task structure dilemma relates to the tension between the formal and informal systems within the organization. Conflicting values may emerge, for example, between mandated reform efforts (formal) and deep, cultural norms held about schools (informal). The authors noted that teachers' work is generally guided more by inherited practices and individual decisions than by any clear, common vision. The issue of professionalism pertains to the conflict between bureaucratic management orientations and professionalism. Professionalism implies specialization and may unintentionally contribute to a more bureaucratic structure. This dilemma may, in fact, go to the heart of schools' organizational structure and become the focus of redefining the institutional role of schools in a postindustrial society. The **hierarchy dilemma** is one of top-down versus bottom-up management. Reform efforts that grapple with this fundamental dilemma include standards-based curriculum reforms and the development of charter schools. Although the standards movement advocates a centralized structure of curriculum development and management, charter school proponents endorse decentralization and individual choice.

Figure 2.6. Bolman and Deal's Critical Dilemmas
of Organizational Structure

Dilemma	Questions
Differentiation vs. Integration	How can the work be divided, yet coordinated?
Gaps vs. Overlaps	Are all essential functions of the organization reflected in the organizational structure? Are there redundant efforts to accomplish the same thing?
Underuse vs. Overload	Are positions contributing to the organization? Are people being underused or over-burdened with responsibilities?
Clarity vs. Creativity	Do people understand their jobs and their purpose? Are they doing what is expected of them? Are people allowed enough flexibility and creativity in their job functions?
Autonomy vs. Interdependence	Are workers given autonomy to carry out their duties and responsibilities? Do workers collaborate with one another for the benefit of the organization?
Loose vs. Tight Coupling	Do procedures coordinate the services of the organization? Do rules and policies inhibit the effective functioning of the organization?
Centralization vs. Decentralization	Is power distributed appropriately? Does too much power and authority emanate from administration? Is too much power and authority delegated?
Goal-less vs. Goal-bound	Are goals relevant to the current conditions? Are goals revisited and revised or recycled?
Irresponsible vs. Unresponsive	Are people in the organization responding to students' needs? Is the organization responsible to the community and parents?
Conformity vs. Overconformity	Do teachers, administrators, and students conform to their roles? Is there an over-reliance on rules and regulations?

External dilemmas that school organizations face are (a) persistence, (b) organizational boundaries, and (c) compliance. Persistence refers to the fact that organizational structures remain remarkably stable over time despite efforts to change them. Ogawa, Crowson, and Goldring noted that reform is typically altered to fit the existing structures and practices of schools. The basic issue is to what extent organizations adapt to their external environment versus an organization's inherent function to reduce uncertainty and avoid destabilization. The dilemma of organizational boundaries relates to the issue of organizations as social systems that have boundaries. However, the location of boundaries is often ambiguous. Boundaries may be variously defined by an organization's membership, the social relation network, or the roles and activities of the members. The dilemma of compliance relates to whether a school complies with environmental demands in a technical or symbolic way. Technical compliance refers to a model of organizational structure that complies with national and state mandates and local expectations in a way that enhances the organization's core technology and primary mission. Symbolic compliance refers to organizational structures that exist to gain societal legitimacy. Graduation ceremonies illustrate the technical–symbolic issue. Does the ceremonial ritual of graduation represent the successful accomplishment of a school's primary mission (technical compliance), or is it a symbolic event to legitimize a school's purpose (symbolic compliance)?

This framework for considering organizational structures allows educational leaders to view schools and school districts in a broader context. It is essential that school leaders understand their organization's role within the larger culture and be aware of the contextual relationship of the school to the outside environment.

Summary

This review of theory related to organizational structures provides a foundation for understanding organizational theory and its practical application to school leadership. This chapter examined organizational structure in terms of organizational typologies, fundamental concepts of bureaucracy, components of organizations, and persistent dilemmas of organizational structure with which leaders must struggle in an effort to balance efficiency and effectiveness as well as the needs of the various school stakeholders.

The organizational typologies offered by Parsons and Blau and Scott provide a framework for understanding the functions and purposes of schools within the larger, cultural context. Parsons proposed that schools' primary function is to preserve and transmit a society's culture, and Blau and

Scott characterized schools as serving the public good. The identification of schools' primary purpose is essential to understanding how organizational structure supports or inhibits the attainment of fundamental goals. In that vein, Etzioni's conceptualization of compliance theory, based on the power structure of the organization, suggests that schools are normative organizations. This means that a school's primary goal is to preserve and reinforce culture. Thus, schools are organizations best suited to the use of normative power, which employs rewards and sanctions related to cultural norms such as honors, praise, and commendations. Such power tends to result in a positive commitment to the organization, which is characterized by a high degree of cooperation between school administrators and teachers.

This chapter reviewed basic constructs and elements of the formal organizational structure. Weber's theory of bureaucracy is fundamental to understanding the formal functions of an organization as well as discerning the weaknesses inherent in bureaucracies. Six basic characteristic of bureaucracy were presented along with their strengths and weaknesses. These are (a) division of labor and specialization, (b) rules and regulations, (c) technical competence and career orientation, (d) impersonal orientation; (e) hierarchy of authority; and (f) separation of ownership from administration.

Further, this chapter introduced the notion of the informal organization, taking into account the role of individuals. The concept of professionalism was contrasted with bureaucracy, providing a continuum to describe a range of organizational structures that emphasize one or the other to different degrees.

Finally, the organizational structure of schools was examined in looking at ongoing dilemmas related to core values that are often in conflict with one another. The core values that are modeled by teachers, administrators, parents, students, and other stakeholders form the basis of the of the school culture. It is perhaps the greatest challenge of leadership to guide a school or district toward a shared organizational vision that pulls together the various stakeholders through the recognition of common values and beliefs. This is accomplished through the actions and behaviors of leaders that mirror the espoused mission and vision of the school. When a school's organizational structure, operating policies and procedures, scheduling, and other coordinating mechanisms support organizational beliefs, the leader has succeeded in finding the appropriate response to the various dilemmas of organizational structure discussed in this chapter.

The concepts presented in this chapter are fundamental notions about organizational structure, in general. These concepts provide the building blocks for organizational and leadership theories that will be explored more fully in subsequent chapters.

Theory into Practice

The Case of the Missing Microscopes

John Richards, the principal of Matson High School, was thinking about his problem as he drove into the parking lot before school. He was frustrated because he did not know how to solve this problem. It was his first year as principal at Matson and his first year in the district. He had been successful as a principal at Belton Junior High in a neighboring community but had never run into this type of stone wall before.

Yet, he had promised his teachers he would handle the situation. As he walked toward his office, he thought about the teachers. They had been very supportive of him. Their requests were minimal. They seemed to like his style of leadership. He made sure he was in each classroom daily and visible during the day. He always stayed two hours after school, and several teachers had started dropping by to discuss specific students or concerns.

That's how the current dilemma came about. George Samson, one of the science teachers, stopped in to tell him how well the year was going. In passing, Samson had mentioned there was only one small problem. Richards smiled to himself as he thought how he had virtually leaped to solve the small problem. When he asked Samson what it was, he was advised that with the number of new students in science this year, especially biology, there simply were not enough microscopes for students to use, even in teams.

Richards knew that instructional supplies such as microscopes were allocated based on the number of students enrolled in classes. So, he felt there would be no problem fixing this, and he told Samson that given a few days he thought he could come up with the microscopes. As Richards reached his office, he realized that what was really bothering him was that he went a step further and promised Samson the microscopes. So, Samson had left a happy teacher ready to sing the praises of the new principal, and Richards had made himself a note to call the curriculum office the next morning.

The next day, Richards called Dr. Carol Smith, the assistant superintendent for curriculum, and advised her of his need. She agreed that microscopes were budgeted based on the number of students in science classes. In the course of the conversation, Dr. Smith even indicated that West High School's enrollment was down in science, and she was glad his enrollment had increased. She then advised him to contact Marjorie Withers, who handled curricular allocations. To this point in time, he felt this was going to be an easy problem to solve.

That, sadly, was before he talked with Ms. Withers. Marjorie Withers had been in charge of curricular allocations for 20 years. She was technically only a clerk but wielded great power. Principals feared her because of her knowledge of board policies and various district rules and regulations. One often had the impression that in providing materials to schools, she was paying for the supplies out of her own pocket.

Richards distinctly recalled his phone call to Ms. Withers. Yes, she indicated they should have more microscopes according to what he told her. But no, they could not have them. Her records indicated the school had all the equipment it needed. He inquired whether her records could be wrong, and she advised him that she meticulously kept track of all the curricular materials and enrollment figures for the district and had done so without a problem for many years. She told him she was offended by his implication that she was not doing a good job. Richards apologized and assured her that he did not mean to imply that she was not competent in her work.

Richards recalled what Dr. Smith had told him about West High School's dropping enrollment in science and decided to try another approach. He told Ms. Withers about the declining enrollment in science at West High School and asked whether he could have their unused microscopes. This seemed like a viable way around the issue to him. But, it did not seem so to Ms. Withers. She told him that the allocations were based on her records, and that West High School needed their legitimately assigned microscopes. He asked her what if Dr. Gonzalez at West agreed to let him have the excess microscopes. Ms. Withers responded by saying that was impossible because the allocations were based on her records and that to move materials around haphazardly would cause chaos and violate policy. She assured him there was no malice in her decision because she had heard good things about him "up until now" but that "the rules will be followed." She thanked him for his call and hung up.

Richards recollected how he felt after that conversation two days ago. It was still bothering him. He needed to solve this problem, not so much to be a hero to Mr. Samson, but for the good of his students. Withers had stopped him cold in his tracks, but he had to figure out a way to get the needed microscopes. As he left his office for his daily rounds, he knew he had to come up with a solution quickly.

Sample Analysis

John Richards can use his knowledge regarding Weber's theory of bureaucracy to help solve this problem. Without delving into issues related to his communication style with his teachers, suffice it to say his inclination to solve all problems without first checking out relevant data, such as district policies, will probably get him into trouble in the near future. But, it is obvious that he has developed a good rapport with his faculty and had done so in a relatively short period of time. He needs to be careful that his honeymoon, which most administrators experience, is not allowed to degenerate into something else.

Given those observations, the real problems are, first, a need for microscopes in the biology classes, and, second, how to deal with a long-term career bureaucrat who is using the rules and regulations for disbursement of curricular materials to justify her decision. She stated that her decision was made because of the rules, and that this impersonal orientation approach would be used no matter which principal called or what the needs were. In all probability, this is correct. Ms. Withers has the expertise to do her job, and it is the one that has been assigned to her for 20 years.

In this case, we see some of the major components of Weber's theory. These are a division of labor (her well-defined role); an impersonal orientation (a rational answer based on the rules); a hierarchy of authority (where she is in the chain of command); rules and regulations (the rules indicate whether you need or receive more supplies); and a career orientation (pride in doing her job as a senior level employee). The recognition of these aspects of the theory also provides Richards with a potential solution.

The choices are simple. He needs the microscopes. His request for microscopes was denied based on the reasons provided in the case. To continue to discuss this with Ms. Withers will get him nowhere. His first decision is whether or not he will move up the hierarchy of authority to Dr. Smith and ask for her assistance or seek another way to resolve the issue. Remember, when the need was originally brought to Dr. Smith's attention she referred him to Ms. Withers. Was it her intention to send him to Ms. Withers because she knew he would not get the microscopes or was it her intention to send him to Ms. Withers to get the materials? That is a question he may get answered by contacting fellow administrators and delicately asking questions regarding Dr. Smith's mode of operation. Once he has determined the answer, he can decide whether he wants to seek Dr. Smith's assistance or guidance in solving the problem. Seeking her guidance is a good way to get her support (she helps fix the problem). If he determines that going to Dr. Smith is not viable, then he should use the rules and regulations to get the microscope.

Collecting data from his school and other high schools regarding the need and use of the microscopes is an approach that will work if the data support his effort. In using supportive data, he supports Ms. Withers' impersonal orientation and reinforces her rational decision-making. By focusing on the rules and regulations, he helps Ms. Withers uniformly apply the rules and uses her expertise (outcome of division of labor) to resolve the situation.

If all else fails, he can use a little creativity and try to get the principal at West High School to loan him the extra microscopes at that school. He just needs to be sure the microscopes are returned to the correct place by the time an inventory is done. By doing this, Ms. Withers remains happy because she did her job and Richards is satisfied because his students will benefit from the borrowed microscopes. Good administrators solve the problem and do not "go to war" over something that can be handled in a more viable manner.

In this case, Richards must select his approach carefully. As a new administrator in a new district, his learning curve is very steep. If he elects to fight Ms. Withers directly, he will create problems for himself especially when other situations arise. It is always better to use your knowledge and solve the problem by trying to make everyone a winner.

The ultimate beneficiaries of this approach are the students. Do what is best for students and teachers so you can maximize the learning that takes place in a school on a daily basis. That is the sign of a good administrator.

Reader's Application

Rehab or Restructure?

In May, Jerry Burns, principal of Jefferson Elementary School, received notice from the superintendent's office that Jefferson would be one of the schools to be renovated and remodeled next school year. Jerry knew that the renovation project in Newkirk City Schools would involve a year of inconveniences in the schools marked for updating. A short-term bond issue had been passed to modernize about 15 of the city's oldest schools. All 15 schools were to be completed within a 3-year period; thus, each year 5 schools were targeted for intensive work.

Newkirk City School District was primarily an urban district, with the oldest schools located in inner city, low income areas. The district had a large facility and maintenance division that served more than 150 schools. The division employed various building and architectural specialists, and for this project set up a new unit to oversee the modernization project. Each school slated for renovation was assigned a planner from the unit whose responsibility was to oversee all aspects of the renovation and to coordinate all demolition and building activities with contractors, school facilities personnel, and the building principal.

Burns considered himself to be a very organized, detail-oriented person. Thus, he was confident that he could minimize disruptions for students and teachers by logically scheduling various moves required throughout the year and maintaining consistent communication with the renovation unit planner and his faculty, parents, and students.

The renovation unit informed Burns that reconstruction would begin June 15, during summer vacation, and that four phases for the project were planned. The first phase would involve major infrastructure rehab, including air conditioning and heating, duct work, and electrical work, such as preparation for dropping new wire for computer networking throughout the building and adding a security system. It was expected that this phase would be completed before school started on September 5. The second phase would involve the office areas and common use areas, including the library and computer lab. This phase would require the temporary relocation of these offices and classrooms and was expected to be completed during the first two months of school. The third phase involved the updating of classrooms and was to be done in sections, relocating six classrooms at a time, over a five-month period. The final phase would be to update the cafeteria.

Six portable buildings, each with space for two small classrooms, were to be delivered during July to accommodate the various moves that would be required throughout the year. The portables would have to be located on the edge of the playground area, thus necessitating a reduction in playground space. Using the four-phase renovation plan, Burns created a timeline for various moves and informed teachers and parents in June of the effects of the renovation and when and where classrooms and other areas would be moved.

The district offered Burns an extended contract so that he could work with the planner and be available on campus during July, when he was normally on vacation. He was delighted to do that, knowing that this would allow him more time to adequately prepare for the chaotic year ahead.

Work in June and July seemed to be proceeding as planned. Contractors showed up promptly on June 15 and worked diligently on the major projects of air ducts and electrical wiring. Burns met regularly with the planner, John Roberts. Roberts was always pleasant and always stopped by to chat with Burns about progress and walk with him through the site. However, by August 1, Burns was beginning to worry. Portables had not been delivered, and Roberts informed him that the delivery of air conditioning and heating units had been delayed until August 30 (only one week before school started). Deciding to be proactive, Burns contacted his area superintendent, Dr. Rowe, to check on the delivery of portables and to advise him of the air conditioning and heating delays. Burns had been told that any problems that the planner could not solve should be addressed to Dr. Rowe. Dr. Rowe assured Burns that portables would be there soon and that the area superintendent's office had control of this. He further advised Burns he would contact the facilities division director to make sure there were alternative plans for cooling until the new air conditioner units arrived.

A week later, Roberts stormed into Burns office demanding to know why he was interfering with the project and going over his head to "get things done your way!" Roberts informed Burns that his boss called him on the carpet for shirking his responsibilities. "Look, Burns," he said, "I don't have any control over the portables or the delivery of materials." Burns explained that he had only informed Dr. Rowe about his concerns about starting school. "Well," Roberts retorted, "we've been told to stop work on everything else so we can hook up portables that are being delivered tomorrow. That means we'll be another week behind." At that, Roberts left Burns' office, slamming the door behind him.

At that point, Burns decided to let Roberts cool off and see what would happen. Sure enough, the next week, three of the six portables were delivered and workers hooked up electricity to the buildings. However, there were no steps and no intercom system (including fire bells) for the portables. When Burns approached Roberts about these problems, Roberts simply said, "I'm doing the best I can. We'll get it taken care of. Give me a couple of days." Burns decided he should inform Dr. Rowe about the problems. Dr. Rowe responded by saying, "I can't do any more right now. The district has a lot of projects going, and we just have to be patient."

A week later, nothing had changed. It is now August 20, less than three weeks before school starts. Jefferson Elementary School has half the portables it needs (with no steps or communication), no air conditioning or heating, and no plan for temporary cooling. Frustrated, hot, and tired, Burns decides to take "the bull by the horns." He picks up the phone to call the facilities division director, Scott Sanders. His fingers poised to punch the number, Burns pauses and thinks, "Should I?"

Student Exercise: Case Analysis

1. Analyze this case in terms of organizational structure. How would you classify the district in terms of organizational types, as described by Adler and Borys, Hoy and Sweetland, Etzioni, or Mintzberg?

2. What organizational dilemmas, according to Bolman and Deal, are evident?

3. What would you do if you were Jerry Burns? How does knowledge of organizational structure and bureaucracy inform your decision?

References

Adler, P. S., & Borys, B. (1996). Two types of bureaucracy: Enabling and coercive. *Administrative Science Quarterly, 41*, 61–89.

Blau, P. M., & Scott, W. R. (1962). *Formal organizations: A comparative approach.* San Francisco: Chandler.

Bolman, L. G., & Deal, T. E. (1991). *Reframing organizations: Artistry, choice, and leadership.* San Francisco: Jossey-Bass.

Burns, T., & Stalker, G. M. (1996). Mechanistic and organic systems. Reprinted in J. M. Shafritz & J. S. Ott (Eds.), *Classics of organizational theory* (4th ed., pp. 209–213). Fort Worth: Harcourt Brace College Publishers. (Original work published 1961)

Carper, W. B., & Snizek, W. E. (1980). The nature and type of organizational taxonomies: An overview. *Academy of Management Review, 5*(1), 65–75.

Etzioni, A. (1961). *Complex organizations.* New York: Holt, Rinehart, and Winston.

Hoy, W. K., & Sweetland, S. R. (2001). Designing better schools: The meaning and measure of enabling school structures. *Educational Administration Quarterly, 37*(3), 296–321.

Mintzberg, H. (1979). *The structuring of organizations. A synthesis of the research.* Englewood Cliffs, NJ: Prentice Hall.

Ogawa, R. T., Crowson, R. L., & Goldring, E. B. (1999). Enduring dilemmas of school organizations. In J. Murphy & K. S. Louis (Eds.), *Handbook of research on educational administration* (2nd ed., pp. 277–295). San Francisco: Jossey-Bass.

Parsons, T. (1960). *Structure and process in modern societies.* Glencoe, IL: Free Press.

Weber, M. (1946). *Essays in sociology.* (H. H. Gerth & C. W. Mills, Trans.) New York: Oxford University Press. (Original work written between 1910 and 1914).

3

Systems Theory: Understanding the Dynamics of Schools as Open Systems

Synopsis of Systems Theory

Systems, as originally described in the biological sciences, have four basic components: (a) inputs, (b) processes, (c) output, and (d) feedback loops (von Bertalanffy, 1950). In schools as systems, inputs include information from the external environments such as laws, regulations, financial and human resources, and parent or community expectations. Processes include dialogue, teaching and learning, and problem solving. Outputs are the result of the system processes, such as student learning. Feedback is provided by external stakeholders as they judge the value or quality of the outputs.

System processes also include the internal organizational structure, technology, people, and communication patterns, which collectively make up the internal social infrastructure. People within a school include teachers, administrators, staff, and students. Individuals within the system take on prescribed roles defined by the school, such as teacher or administrator. Outside the school, these same individuals are participants in a larger social and political system; they are parents, taxpayers, church members, and so forth. Thus, to view the school as an isolated system is simplistic and does not take into consideration the complexities of the school as a system nested within larger systems.

The power of understanding general systems theory and its applications to organizations, in particular schools, was captured well by Peter Senge (1990) as "systems thinking." Senge proposed that systems thinking is vital to an educational organization, further noting that at any given time leaders must attend to many systems, see the interrelationships among the various systems, and understand that the whole is larger than the sum of its parts. Thus, the term "systems thinking" refers to a leader's ability to see the complexities and dynamics of many systems working simultaneously.

Applications for School Leaders

Understanding systems theory will help school leaders

- Identify and diagnose problems
- Make better decisions
- Balance organizational needs with individual needs
- Understand how to identify and respond to conflicts
- Understand the multiplicity of roles within a school
- Balance organizational needs with external community needs

Social System Theory

Social system theory was one of the first applications of systems thinking to schools, enlarging our picture of an organization beyond that of a linear, rational, and impersonal bureaucratic structure. Social system theory takes into account not only the formal organizational structure but also the people within the organization. Social system theory provides a way to view the interactions of the needs of people and organizational goals within an organization. The theory represents a constant interplay between the formal and informal organization and those who populate it as they seek to maintain an optimum level of equilibrium within the organization and between its various components. This ongoing tension is often a result of internal or external feedback that creates disequilibrium within the organization. Disequilibrium may potentially impact the culture and social structure of the organization. Social systems theory presents a dynamic picture of an organization where both the whole organization and its parts are equally important. This theory emphasizes to the practitioner how important it is to balance the formal, bureaucratic needs of the organization with those of individuals who populate the organization. Although the theory provides for some opportunities to predict, it more importantly illustrates the complexity of interactions and the relationships between human and organizational needs.

Fundamental Constructs of Social System Theory

Much of social system theory is the result of the work of **Jacob Getzels** and **Egon Guba** (1957). Their model provides an easily understood way to visualize the dynamic relationship that exists between the formal organization and those who populate the social system. Getzels and Guba proposed that organizations had five notable characteristics:

1. They are purposive—established to carry out certain ends.
2. They are peopled.
3. They are structural; that is they are organized into interrelated component parts with rules that define the functions of the organization.
4. They are normative, where tasks are assigned to specific roles which in essence serve as norms for behavior.
5. They are sanction-bearing, where positive and negative sanctions are used to ensure compliance with the norms.

Drawing on these basic premises and later work of Getzels and associates (e.g., Getzels, Lipham, & Campbell, 1968; Lipham, 1988), we can describe social systems as having six important constructs:

1. Boundaries
2. People
3. Open exchange of information between the social system and the external environment
4. Norms
5. Roles and expectations
6. Interdependence

All social systems have boundaries that separate them from the external environment. Those **boundaries** could be the school building or the walls of a classroom. However, social systems exist and function only because they are **peopled**. If a school site had no teachers, students, or administrators, it would simply be an empty building. Furthermore, social systems are essentially **open**. This means they are influenced by a constant exchange of information, resources, events, and values that enter from the external environment. Social systems have some type of output into the external environment, which may or may not result in some type of **feedback**.

For example, a group of students on their way home at the end of the school day, damage someone's property. Because of their actions, the students (output) will likely cause some type of feedback or reaction from the property owner, the police, or the central office. Feedback from the external environment enters as input and creates some type of reaction within the social system. In this case, the reaction may be to establish additional rules regarding student behavior or to place extra teachers on duty around the school at the end of the school day. The point is, a reaction takes place in the social system because of the input. All external input into the social system has the potential of creating a **disequilibrium** or imbalance within the social system. Input to the social system may come in the form of a reaction to output from the social system, as in the situation described above, or as something totally unrelated to the social system's output and which is outside the social system's control, such as legislative mandates or negative media coverage of educational issues.

Feedback also occurs as an internal process, as a result of actions within the social system itself. In this instance, the external environment is not involved. For example, a principal criticizes a teacher, and the teacher tells other teachers who become upset and confront the principal regarding the criticism of a colleague. This internal feedback clearly has the potential to create disequilibrium. In this situation, the principal needs to react to the teachers' concerns or the situation could worsen.

The intensity of both external and internal feedback varies, and feedback may be either positive or negative. Feedback of any kind always involves the perceptions of others. Whether or not perceptions are accurate interpretations of fact or misinformed opinions really doesn't matter. Feedback may cause disequilibrium within the social system, which results in a reaction from a few or all of the individuals within the social system.

In addition, social systems are basically **normative**. They have an established system of **sanctions** that can be brought to bear on those who do not behave in the manner which is expected of them. In viewing a classroom as a social system, this readily becomes apparent. Students and teachers are expected to exhibit certain behaviors and roles within the classroom. A teacher's role is different from a student's role. When a student does not behave in the manner ascribed to that role, sanctions are imposed on the student. If a student curses a teacher, behavior not expected of the student's role, the teacher might contact a parent, give detention, or send the student to the principal's office. Some type of sanction is employed to persuade the student to conform to expectations. Sanctions may be formal, such as referring the student to the principal's office, or they may be informal, achieved through verbal and nonverbal communication from the teacher to the student. The intensity of a sanction often depends on how far one deviates from the expected behavior.

Figure 3.1. A Social System in Action

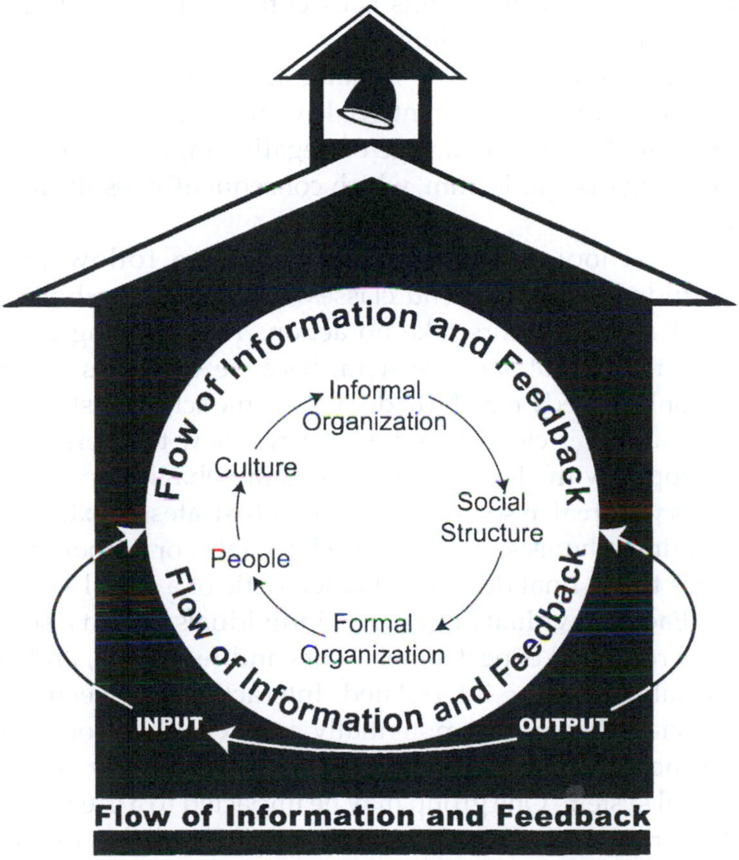

Flow of Information and Feedback

Flow of Information and Feedback

Informal Organization

Culture

Social Structure

People

Formal Organization

INPUT

OUTPUT

Flow of Information and Feedback

Each individual and group of individuals have specific **roles** within the social system, which contribute to the proper functioning of the whole system. Teachers, students, support staff, and administrators have different roles and expectations; they exhibit different sets of behavior; and participate in different activities that contribute to the totality of the school social system. Each element in the social system is important. When something happens that affects one element of the social system, the entire social system is impacted, creating an imbalance, or disequilibrium. There is a continual effort by those in certain ascribed roles in the social system to maintain equilibrium, or balance, within the social system. Balance among the various components of the social system represents stability within the social system (Figure 3.1).

Using the example of students who damaged someone's property on their way home from school, it can be seen that a complaint from the property owner or police will create disequilibrium that forces the principal and teachers to respond to resolve the situation. How the situation is resolved is not necessarily relevant to restoring equilibrium. However, the cooperation of the system's various components is essential. Synergy within the social system works to restore equilibrium.

Social systems are constantly seeking to maintain balance, or equilibrium, in response to external or internal events that create varying degrees of disequilibrium. A constant barrage of negative input into a social system can create ongoing disequilibrium, which consequently results in a dysfunctional system.

Envision a school where teachers refuse to follow appropriate curriculum, students do not attend classes or constantly exhibit disruptive behaviors, and administrators take no action. The resulting chaos will, in effect, destroy the school social system, because the parts cease to work together. The only remedy may be to do what some school districts have been forced to do, and that is close the school, recruit new teachers and administrators, and reopen with clearer expectations of behavior and performance. This scenario is very real in some settings and illustrates an extreme response to low performing schools sometimes used by states or school districts.

This relates to the final defining characteristic of a social system—**interdependence**. Each individual or group of individuals within a social system has prescribed roles and expected behaviors and responses, and all components of a social system are interrelated. Interactions between any components of a social system will potentially impact other components. For example, a principal's reaction to a particular situation may affect everyone within the social system. One group may be impacted to a greater extent than others, but everyone is affected in some way. The behavior of students (output) who damage property creates feedback (input), which forces those in the social system to respond in some manner. That response, such as establishing additional rules or placing more teachers on duty after school directly impacts all teachers and students in the social system.

A school as a social system is composed of individuals and subsystems and formal and informal structures in a complex network of interrelationships. As a social system is impacted by internal or external events, it responds. A social system seeks balance, or equilibrium, within itself as well as between the social system and the external environment. Sanctions are invoked to reinforce expected behaviors and actions and to restore equilibrium. In addition, individual needs and values are balanced with organizational goals.

Nomothetic and Idiographic Components

Getzels and Guba's initial model presented two broad constructs of social systems, termed the "nomothetic" and "idiographic" elements. These terms, which were derived from the Greek words, refer specifically to the formal organizational component of the social system, the **nomothetic**, and the individuals within the social system, the **idiographic**. Figure 3.2 illustrates the elements of the Getzels-Guba social system model in a school setting.

Figure 3.2. Adapted Getzels-Guba Model

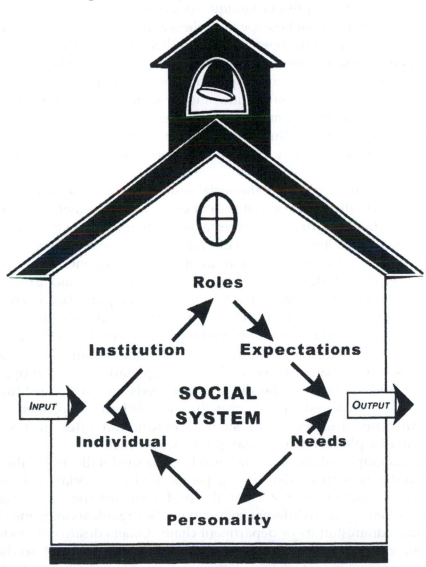

The nomothetic component of the social system represents the formal institution with its various prescribed roles, bureaucracy, and expectations. The idiographic component of the social system refers to the needs, wants, and personalities of those who populate the social system. The interaction between the broad institutional goals of the organization and the more specific needs of individuals results in various social behaviors that take place within the social system and that help to create the social system's organizational culture. The organizational culture also reflects the culture of the external environment surrounding the social system.

A school site may represent a unique social system with its own organizational culture, yet it cannot escape the beliefs and values of the surrounding community. Because of the open interchange between the school site and the external environment, community values and beliefs impact how a school's culture develops. Remember, people function not only within the school social system but also in a multitude of other social systems in the external environment. This amalgamated social system culture is very important, because it guides and influences a variety of reactions, activities, and behaviors (Deal & Kennedy, 1982; Schein, 1985; Sergiovanni & Corbally, 1984).

The nomothetic element of the social system is where the institutionally established activities of the social system exist. The nomothetic component represents established roles and expectations that guide formal, anticipated, and mandated activities of those within the social system. For instance, the role ascribed to a teacher is to impart knowledge to students. The expected outcome is that students will become knowledgeable and productive citizens. Aspects of the teacher's role include disciplinarian, curriculum developer, instructor, child psychologist, surrogate parent, and conflict manager. It is this variability within the broad construct of the role of teacher that creates differences from teacher to teacher and situation to situation. Variations in role manipulation and role interpretation provide opportunities for teachers to meet specific personal needs within the institutional confines of the social system. However, this can only be accomplished as long as organizational expectations such as graduation rates, test scores, classroom discipline, and curricular guidelines are met.

The idiographic element of the Getzels-Guba model illustrates the individual differences that exist among people within a social system. For instance, all teachers do not enter the profession for the same reasons. Teachers often aspire to different roles within the organization. Some desire to become administrators or department chairs. Others desire only to teach. Everyone enters the school social system with different sets of needs and different personalities which impact their responses to various situations. As an example, teachers differ in their responses to a fight in the classroom.

Some are cool and calm; some become upset and perturbed. Personality and individual needs shape individual behaviors.

Some dispositions are met by a desire to help the greater society (social system) by giving of oneself. Some meet their needs by being recognized for their hard work, others for the organizational power they possess. The important thing to remember for this chapter is that needs and personality impact the way one views the social system, the role in it, and how one chooses to behave in it. Getzels and Guba (1957) depicted an individual's behavior within a social system as the formula $B = f(R \times P)$, indicating that behavior in the social system is a result, or function (f), of the interaction between the roles (R) ascribed to one by the organization and the individual's personality (P). Individual needs are a component of one's personality.

The more formal the organization, the more powerful the roles are in influencing one's behavior within the organization. In a practical sense, this means that individuals balance their actions and responses (behaviors) between what they want to do and what the ascribed organization role says they should do. This balancing act is often complicated by the conflict that can arise between the multiple roles that an individual performs, because it is impossible to escape being part of multiple social systems and subsystems (Getzels, Lipham, & Campbell, 1968).

Role Conflict

Role conflicts are issues that everyone faces at one time or another in social systems. Getzels, Lipham, and Campbell (1968) noted various reasons for role conflict. The most prevalent conflicts relate to the inability to meet multiple role demands (such as parent, teacher, son, spouse) and the lack of time to meet the demands of any one role. Additional reasons for role conflict include discrepancies between an individual's needs and organizational needs. This is closely related to value conflicts, when the organization's demands are in opposition to one's personal values. An absence of role clarity also contributes to role conflict, because one is unsure of organizational expectations, and the result is often an uncomfortable degree of role ambiguity. Both adults and students may be confronted by one or more of these role conflicts. How role conflicts are handled reflects one's ability to analyze, adjust, and evaluate an existing situation in the social system.

Leadership-Followership Style

A major implication of Getzels and Guba's social system theory was that the interaction between individual (idiographic) and institutional (nomothetic) elements resulted in three distinct types of leadership-followership behavior, which they classified as (a) nomethetic style, (b) idiographic style, and (c) transactional style.

The nomethetic style is characterized by an emphasis on the organization, the role, and the expectations. Individual needs are minimized. The predominant behavior in such an organization would be to do things "by the book." The most likely conflict in this type of organization is role conflict, where organizational expectations of the role conflict with an individual's personality and needs. The idiographic style emphasizes individual needs and personality over the requirements of the organization. In this type of organization, it is assumed that more will be accomplished when people are contributing what is relevant to them rather than enforcing adherence to specific roles. In this type of organization, conflicts tend to be between individual personalities. The transactional style lies between the other two extremes. In this type of organization, roles are developed by the institution but are adapted to the personalities of the individuals assigned to these roles. Although role and personality conflicts will arise, they are handled through adjustment.

Max Abbott (1965) expanded on Getzels and Guba's concept of transactional level in his discussion of additional intervening variables and more clearly conceptualized internal and external feedback loops. Figure 3.3 is a graphic representation of Abbott's theory applied to schools.

The nomothetic component of the social system model envisioned by Abbott includes not only formal roles and expectations of the organization but also the organizational bureaucracy. The organizational bureaucracy involves a hierarchy of authority, highly specialized roles and rules, and organizational expectations. It is here where change often does (or does not) take place and where role conflict often emerges. This expansion of the nomothetic component more clearly uses Weber's and others' work on the bureaucracy. The role of bureaucracy is crucial in comprehending how a social system responds to disequilibrium resulting from internal and external feedback.

Abbott expanded the view of the idiographic component of the social system by emphasizing the importance of motivation as well as individual needs and personality. Motivation is discussed in greater detail in Chapter 7, but for the purposes of relating motivation to social system theory, it is enough to highlight two major concepts relative to motivation. First, an individual's ability and confidence in performing job tasks may impact motivation (Hersey & Blanchard, 1982). Second, people's behavior is motivated by personal and psychological needs (Glasser, 1986; Maslow, 1954). Understanding what motivates a person to perform within an organization is crucial to the success of a school leader. The motivation of individuals within a social system impacts subordinate-superordinate and peer relationships, which may directly influence the development of the formal and informal organizational culture within the social system. Principals need to use their

Figure 3.3. Elaborated Getzels-Guba and Abbott Adaptation: Social Systems Model Applied to Schools

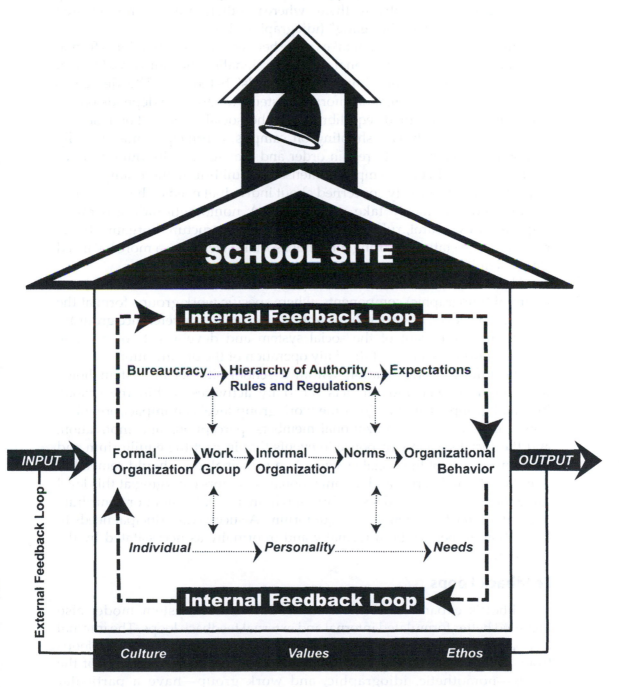

understanding of motivational theory to work with teachers and students. Some teachers, staff members, and students need to be treated more formally (nomothetically) to motivate them, whereas others are better motivated when treated as one of the "gang" (idiographically).

The constant interplay that takes place between the organization's formal and informal structures, personal and professional relationships, and formal and informal interactions impact individuals' behaviors. The degree to which a leader uses formal or informal systems to motivate depends on the cause and intensity of disequilibrium in the social system. For instance, during a crisis, such as a shooting on campus, a principal must initially respond nomothetically to regain order and manage the disequilibrium as well as possible. In this example of intense disequilibrium, there simply is no opportunity to be greatly concerned about individual needs when organizational needs obviously take precedence. A nomothetic administrative response uses control, rules and regulations, and structured organizational roles and expectations to bring the school social system into a more balanced state of equilibrium.

Abbott further discussed the interplay between formal (nomothetic) and informal (idiographic) components, where specific work groups form at the transactional level. A work group (Abbott referred to as a reference group) is a dynamic component of the social system and develops its own set of informal norms that impact the daily operation of the organization.

The informal organization within a school site social system holds tremendous power and impacts the daily activities within the school. Informal groups that emerge at the work group level can impact organizational cohesiveness, organizational members' perceptions and motivation, and the social system's response to events that impact the equilibrium and the homeostasis of the social system. As a principal, one should remember that the informal norms and organizational behaviors emerging at this level can either foster greater disequilibrium within a social system or contribute to greater interdependence and equilibrium. A successful principal needs to know how to behave both formally and informally as necessitated by the situation.

Feedback Loops

Abbott's expansion of the Getzels-Guba social system model also included better formulated internal and external feedback loops. The internal feedback loop represents an ongoing flow of multiple communication loops from any or all of the three components of the social system. Each of the levels—nomothetic, idiographic, and work group—have a particular purpose and organizational agenda which, when communicated through internal feedback loops, impacts the actions and behaviors of those within the social system. Everyone has experienced the effect of rumors and unilateral organizational edicts. These are prime examples of how such internal feedback can create disequilibrium within the social system.

Abbott's description of the external feedback loop is more powerful than Getzels-Guba's illustration. The expanded view of the social system's external feedback loop depicts a constant, ongoing response to output from the social system as the social system's output impacts and interacts with the culture, ethos, and values of the external environment. The external feedback loop also represents input into a school site social system that is totally outside the control or influence of the school site social system. Agendas established by federal and state agencies, news media, and local and national political, social, and economic groups impact the equilibrium of a school social system. The fact that schools are open systems means there is an ongoing avalanche of input from the external environment. This is an inescapable reality of school administration.

Leadership Style

Social system theory has a direct application to leadership style within a school setting. Although no leader will be exclusively nomothetic, idiographic, or transactional, it is certainly true that a principal's or superintendent's style of leadership may vary, depending on the situation, the level of disequilibrium, and personal proclivity.

An idiographic leader is one who expends a great deal of energy being concerned about individual needs rather than organizational needs. The idiographic leader is very laissez-faire and wants each individual to fit into the organization and takes a hands-off approach to problem solving. Idiographic leaders often delegate authority, fail to effectively use power, and believe that people should define their organizational roles in ways that are best suited for each person.

A nomothetic leader is a person who functions in a very formal manner, acting from a position of power and authority, and strictly enforcing organizational rules and regulations. A nomothetic leader is more focused on organizational expectations and prescribed roles. He or she is bureaucratically focused and seeks to maintain the social system equilibrium through formal mechanisms at all times. The nomothetic leader rewards conformity and consistency. People's needs are not nearly as important or relevant as organizational goals and procedures. A nomothetic leader applies the rules and regulations equally to all. This type of leadership style is particularly useful in times of crisis or when all other attempts to maintain equilibrium have failed. Do not believe that nomothetic leaders are unfeeling; they simply are focused on the formal organization and the bureaucracy more than on people.

The transactional leader functions more at the informal level of the organization but actually may exhibit characteristics found at the idiographic and nomothetic levels of the social system. A transactional leader receives power and authority from both the formal and informal organization. This style of leadership is a blend of the others and reflects an integrated approach to individual needs, the bureaucracy, organizational roles, and expectations. A transactional leader responds to specific situations and to the level of disequilibrium in the social system.

Finally, it is important to note that no leader functions solely at the nomothetic, idiographic, or transactional level. Rather, most leaders have a predominant style with which they are comfortable and toward which they have a proclivity. Good leaders recognize this tendency and are able to analyze the situation and adjust to it as necessary within the confines of the social system. Recognizing when to shift leadership styles and being able to do so are the results of applying social system theory effectively and productively.

Institutional Theory

Institutional theory expanded the model of open system theory by offering explanations for the environmental constraints that limit organizational change. **W. Richard Scott** (2008) defined institutions as "comprised of regulative, normative and cultural-cognitive elements that, together with associated activities and resources, provide stability and meaning to life" (p. 48). In unpacking this definition, Scott referred to the three elements of institutions as **pillars**. The **regulative pillar** involves rules and sanctions that govern behavior through both formal and informal mechanisms. The **normative pillar** includes both values and norms, where values are the desired standard and norms specify how things should be done. Further, values and norms may differ based on an individual's role within the institution. Roles may be formally assigned or informally ascribed. The **cultural-cognitive pillar** refers to the shared conceptions of social reality; that is, people's frames of reference from which they make meaning of the world around them. The three pillars draw forth different bases of legitimacy, and ultimately power. Regulative systems rely on conformity to rules; normative systems derive legitimacy from a moral basis; and cultural-cognitive systems depend on commonly understood roles and structures. The cultural-cognitive element represents the things we take for granted, or cultural assumptions. Every institution has a combination of all elements, but in any specific institution one element may dominate. In stable social systems, pillars may be equally balanced or one pillar virtually supports the social order.

Institutional theory further expands the notion of social systems by examining the networks that link various organizations, termed "organizational fields." **Organizational fields** are communities of organizations that are related and interact. For example, a school's organizational field would be other district schools, central offices, state and federal education and funding agencies, legislatures, parent associations, teacher unions, accrediting agencies, universities, and so on.

The networking and interrelationships among various organizations in the field tend to maintain the status quo and discourage change because of the tendency for organizations to reinforce other organizations in continuing to do things the way they have always been done—through cultural assumption, regulatory rules, or simply because it is "the right way" to do things.

However, organizational fields can also be the impetus for institutions to evolve as a result of pressures from other organizations. For instance, No Child Left Behind legislation (a force from Congress) has resulted in states and school districts redefining how student achievement is measured and reexamining school improvement processes. Whether one sees this as a good change or a bad one, it has resulted in change. However, the force for change from No Child Left Behind has not been isolated in federal legislation, but has been endorsed and empowered by others in the field of networked organizations responding to this mandate. For example, news media weighs in with reports of public opinion polls and editorials about student test scores and "grading" schools relative to student achievement. Professional educational associations have responded by developing standards for all academic areas. State and voluntary accrediting agencies have developed new processes for schools to use in working through school improvement efforts. These are but a few examples of the many organizations involved in a larger network that influences schools directly affected by this legislation.

Many, if not most, schools have responded to No Child Left Behind mandates in a regulatory way, simply complying to "the letter of the law." Some have responded more creatively to the forces from their network, by reconfiguring organizational structures or delivering curriculum in different ways. Examples of reconfigurations and curriculum modifications are virtual schools, K–12 schools within large, urban districts, and magnet schools that focus on specific themes such as aerospace or fine arts. To what extent these innovative approaches to education will actually result in altering deeply held assumptions about schooling is yet to be seen. However, it is important that we keep an eye on the impact of larger systems that are changing our social fabric and basic assumptions about ways of doing things. As the larger culture evolves, education and schools will also.

Summary

System theories demonstrate how schools are dynamic organizations where there is constant interplay between formal and informal systems; individual and organizational needs; and institutional goals and individual personalities. The interplay among the nomothetic, idiographic, and work group levels is complicated further by a dynamic internal feedback loop that contributes to or hampers organizational and individual efficiency. A social system strives to achieve a level of balance among its competing yet interdependent elements. An ongoing effort to maintain equilibrium exists within the social system for the social system to carry out its organizational mission. External feedback is continuous, and although often irrelevant, administrators must appropriately respond to feedback to maintain organizational balance and focus.

Thus, a school social system is a vibrant, consistently fluctuating organization where balance is sought so that the social system may perform at an adequate level. A viable response to disequilibrium is essential to the survival of the school social system. The desire to survive, represented by a quest for often elusive equilibrium, provides a catalyst for actions, reactions, and behaviors chosen both by the organization in totality and the individuals who populate it.

System theories explain the importance of educational leaders viewing their schools or districts as systems networked with other systems. Leaders must attend to both the people and the organizational structure (idiographic and nomothetic components). Further, leaders must understand that schools are open systems, where input is received from the outside environment and from other systems, and output to the external environment affects other systems, which results in feedback to the school. Effective school leaders pay attention to this constant cycle and complex interrelationships among networked systems, or organizational fields. School leaders do not make decisions in isolation; thus, it is important for leaders to employ systems thinking.

Theory into Practice

The Case of No Band Marching

Principal John Smithson sat in his office contemplating his conversation with high school band director George Anderson. He felt he was correct in telling Mr. Anderson that the high school band could only be dismissed from school for one parade downtown for homecoming. He believed that taking students out of school every day during homecoming week for a downtown performance was too much. Students often didn't make up their work, and, besides, he believed students should be in class.

After all, the School Board had told the principals when they adopted new attendance policies that students needed to be more academically oriented. Although students' scores on state-mandated tests were above average, everyone expected higher test scores this year, especially the board.

When Smithson returned from lunch, his secretary advised him that he had received several phone calls while he was away from the office. Most had been from parents, but one was from Sarah Ferguson, the school board president. She demanded to know why he had canceled all homecoming events and why he was not supporting student activities such as the band and the football team. The messages from various parents appeared to be in the same vein.

Smithson knew that these calls were the result of his conversation with Mr. Anderson. He also knew that he would probably receive a phone call or a visit from the superintendent before the day was over. As he got up from his desk and began to walk through the school, he reflected on how to address the current "mess." He decided he would first stop in at the band room before returning any phone calls.

Sample Analysis

This case clearly represents an example where disequilibrium is created within the social system because of a decision made by the principal. His decision reflected a nomothetic leadership style because there was no discussion with the band director but rather a statement to him that the band would only march one time, not every day of the week. This began the problem. The catalyst for the principal's decision was the increased emphasis by the school board on attendance and increasing test scores.

Evidently the band director either communicated the principal's decision to students, who relayed this information to their parents in the external environment, or the band director contacted some band parents directly. The result was output from the school-site social system and almost immediate feedback into the school system, which has the potential to create an increasingly disruptive disequilibrium within the school social system.

Surely the band director has many of his professional and personal needs met through his high school band. The band is a source of pride to Mr. Anderson, and its success motivates him to work hard. The problem is that Mr. Anderson's response to the principal's decision helped create the disequilibrium to which the school social system must now respond. Whether the interpretation of Mr. Smithson's decision was inadvertent or purposeful does not matter at this time, but its effect has been to upset parents and others in the external environment.

Mr. Smithson can resolve this problem by first determining what was said to the students and how the interpretation of his decision was conveyed to those in the external environment. He has several options on how to respond to the situation. Nomothetically, he can quote school board rules, regulations, and expectations. Idiographically, he can allow Mr. Anderson to do as he desires and allow him to have his personal needs met through the band's performance. What Smithson should do is to take a transactional approach by sitting down with Mr. Anderson to clarify the reason for the decision. He should explain how it fits with school board expectations and emphasize how one "great" parade still allows the band to be recognized and provides support to the community for homecoming. If Mr. Smithson had taken a transactional approach initially, he could have explained the necessity for changing the band's schedule and could have prevented some of the negative response now being received from the external environment. Mr. Smithson wants to be careful that his changes are clearly explained, so he does not differ radically from the external community or internal school culture. Mr. Smithson would have been wise to remember that changing the band's performances would likely cause some type of conflict and should have discussed his decision with others (central office personnel, superintendent, band director) prior to making it.

As can be seen from this case, even when one feels as if he or she has followed directives from superordinates—in this case the school board—problems can result if care is not taken to involve others in the decision. This is almost always the case, except in a crisis situation, and ultimately creates greater interdependence among the various parts of the social system. This case also illustrates the danger of a leadership style that is more directive than transactional.

Reader's Application

A New Discipline Approach for Old Ways

Principal Jane Bridgestone had attended a principal's conference during the summer. Specifically, she had been seeking a different approach to discipline. Up until this time, the primary way student behavior problems had been handled at Southside High School was through the use of after-school detention. Of course, other approaches such as counseling with the student and calling parents were also used. If the discipline infraction was related to drugs or weapons, students were suspended. It was the daily behavior problems that seemed to be resulting in detention being used for everything. And, it didn't seem to be changing student behavior. At the conference, Jane had learned about an approach to discipline that placed students in a "time-out" room so they could think about their behavior and make a commitment to behave appropriately and follow the rules.

On her return from the conference, Jane decided she would build a time-out room. She asked the custodians to create a small room in the corner of the office reception area. The room measured approximately six feet by six feet. It made the reception area crowded, but she thought it would work. She had three student desks placed in the room, even though Ms. Bridgestone could not envision a time when more than one or two students would be assigned there.

When the new school year began in August, she told the faculty about the time-out room and how she would assign students there who received too much detention. The faculty seemed supportive of this plan, but a few were unhappy with the crowded condition of the reception area. Some also questioned the supervision of the students and what would happen if three students were in the room at the same time. She assured them that all of this would be handled.

Four days later, Jane received a phone call from a local newspaper reporter asking for an interview regarding the school's new approach to discipline. The reporter indicated he had heard that Ms. Bridgestone had built a "box" that would be used for misbehaving students. Ms. Bridgestone assured the reporter that this was a small room—not a box—and tried to explain the concepts behind a time-out room.

Later that day, Ms. Bridgestone's secretary, Lori Little, asked to discuss the time-out room with her. She told Jane that she did not want to be responsible for supervising students in the room. Lori also indicated she was unhappy because the room took up too much of the space in the reception area, and she felt there was not enough room for visitors to be comfortable. Ms. Bridgestone was taken aback by her secretary's statements. Lori had said nothing negative to Ms. Bridgestone when the principal had come back from the conference and had told Lori of her decision to build a time-out room. Jane finally decided that Lori was concerned primarily about the supervision issue. Jane had never considered having Lori supervise students in time-out in the first place, and told her so.

The next morning, as she always did, Ms. Bridgestone picked up her newspaper and drove to school at 6:30 AM. She always arrived early so she could have some quiet time to read the newspaper. On arriving at her office, Jane sat at her desk and opened the paper. The headline told her this would not be a good day. It read: "School Principal Puts Unruly in Box." The subtitle stated, "A New Approach to Discipline." As Ms. Bridgestone leaned back and took a deep breath, her phone rang.

Student Exercise: Case Analysis

1. Analyze this case using system theories. Consider the inputs, outputs, and feedback that created disequilibrium.

2. How would you characterize Ms. Bridgestone's leadership style, and did it work?

3. Explain the situation in terms of institutional theory, especially in relationship to how the school is networked to other systems.

4. What should Ms. Bridgestone have done to avoid this situation?

5. If you were Ms. Bridgestone, what would you do now?

References

Abbott, M. G. (1965). Intervening variables in organizational behavior. *Educational Administration Quarterly, 1,* 1–13.

Deal, T. E., & Kennedy, A. A. (1982). *Corporate cultures.* Reading, MA: Addison-Wesley.

Getzels, J. W., & Guba, E. G. (1957). Social behavior and the administrative process. *School Review, 65,* 423–441.

Getzels, J. W., Lipham, J. M., & Campbell, R. F. (1968). *Educational administration as a social process: Theory, research, and practice.* New York: Harper and Row.

Glasser, W. (1986). *Control theory in the classroom.* New York: Harper and Row.

Hersey, P., & Blanchard, K. (1982). *Management of organizational behavior: Utilizing human resources.* Englewood Cliffs, NJ: Prentice-Hall.

Lipham, J. M. (1988). Getzel's model in educational administration. In N. J. Boyan (Ed.), *Handbook of research on educational administration* (pp. 171–184). New York: Longman.

Maslow, A. H. (1954). *Motivation and personality*. New York: Harper and Row.

Schein, E. H. (1985). *Organizational culture and leadership*. San Francisco: Jossey-Bass.

Scott, W. R. (2008). *Institutions and organizations* (3rd ed.). Thousand Oaks, CA: Sage.

Senge, P. M. (1990). *The fifth discipline: The art and practice of the learning organization*. New York: Doubleday.

Sergiovanni, T. J., & Corbally, J. E. (Eds.). (1984). *Leadership and organizational culture*. Urbana, IL: University of Illinois Press.

von Bertalanffy, L. (1950). An outline of general system theory. *British Journal for the Philosophy of Science, 1*(2), 134–165.

4

Organizational Culture: Schools as Learning Organisms

Synopsis of Organizational Culture

Organizational culture defines what a school stands for and how things are done. It is the shared values and beliefs, stories and heroes, ceremonies and rituals, and networks of people within the school and those who interact with the school. It may be the most important thing to which educational leaders attend, and it is fundamental to leadership. Those who manage schools may give little thought to the school culture, as management implies maintaining the status quo. However, one who leads a school must thoroughly understand its culture, and either commit to maintain the school's values and beliefs or work to change them.

Culture, like a tree, has deep roots which serve as the life force of the organization. A school's structure, rules and regulations, and systems of decision making and communication are reflections of the school's culture. A school is what it believes it is, and people in schools essentially do what they value. Thus, understanding and influencing school culture is the only way to affect any kind of meaningful change.

This chapter examines the concept of organizational culture and its relationship to organizational structure and social structure. Further, the idea of schools as learning organizations is explored. Finally, whether and how schools define themselves as communities extends our understanding of schools' functions within a diverse, multicultural, global culture.

Applications for School Leaders

Understanding organizational culture will help school leaders to:

◆ Align the goals, purposes, and functions of the school organization with the larger cultural and societal goals, norms, and values.

◆ Employ strategies to develop and clarify a school's values, norms, and vision.

◆ Develop purposeful communities engaged in continuous professional growth and student learning.

◆ Promote a school culture that embraces diversity and ideals of social justice.

Culture as a Defining Element of School Climate

Two theoretical concepts fundamental to understanding and leading organizations are climate and culture. Common usage often interchanges these terms, but they are two distinct concepts—culture being a subset of climate.

Climate is defined as the characteristics of the total environment in a school building and is composed of four dimensions—(a) ecology, (b) milieu, (c) organization, and (d) culture (Owens, 2004; Tagiuri, 1968). **Ecology** refers to the physical features of the school, such as the design, age, and size of the facilities and the equipment and technology used in the school's operation. **Milieu** is defined as the characteristics of the people and the social interactions that take place in a school. **Organization** denotes the structure of the organization, including communication and decision-making patterns and hierarchical relationships between administrators and teachers. **Culture** is the values, beliefs, norms, and behavioral patterns of the people who are members of the school community.

These four dimensions are intricately intertwined. Although ecology, milieu, and organization are overtly manifested, the culture of a school is not openly apparent. However, culture can be inferred by observing the artifacts of the organization and the behaviors of people in the organization. In other words, through observation and study of the milieu, ecology, and organization, one can gain an understanding of the school's culture by uncovering the patterns of thoughts, beliefs, and values that guide organizational behavior. Culture ultimately defines the essence of the organization, because it describes the "way things are done" in the school. People's actions and behaviors are based on underlying beliefs and values that are shared among the persons who are part of the school community, even though these beliefs and values may not be explicitly expressed. The underlying values and beliefs of culture are often described in terms of (a) assumptions and (b) norms. **Assumptions** are ideas and concepts that are accepted as true and nonnegotiable by the people in the organization. They are seldom discussed and inherently taken for granted. **Norms** are unwritten rules of behavior that arise from the cultural assumptions.

Edgar Schein (1985) proposed a model which explains culture at three levels.

Figure 4.1. Culture Is Like an Iceberg

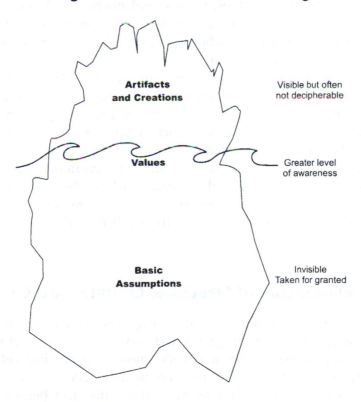

Using the analogy of an iceberg as depicted in Figure 4.1, artifacts and creations are visible manifestations of a school's culture. They include the school facilities, equipment, documents, and behavioral patterns which can be observed by a visitor to the school. Values lie partly above the surface and partially below the surface. Values may be overtly revealed through documents or other artifacts that describe the school's mission, vision, and philosophy. However, this is not always the case. Sometimes documents that appear to express a school's purpose may be misleading, as we often find written school philosophies that espouse certain beliefs and values, yet teachers and administrators act in ways contrary to what is written. This often occurs when building administrators and teachers create such documents solely to satisfy an external or central office mandate. Thus, the apparent mission or philosophy reflects nothing more than the fulfillment of an official reporting requirement. Basic assumptions are the part of the iceberg totally submerged below the surface of the water. Assumptions are the essence of the culture because they define the individuals' relationship to their environment and the realities on which the school is anchored.

Culture is closely tied to the history and traditions of the organization, and individuals who enter the organization are socialized to understand and accept the organizational values, beliefs, and norms. Such socialization is accomplished both through formal means, such as induction training, and through informal ways, such as when veteran teachers disregard or discount a new teacher's suggestion for change.

A school's culture is influenced and impacted by other elements of the organization, including the facilities, structural organization, purpose, leadership, and subcultures within the organization. For example, a typical high school departmental organizational structure tends to separate teachers by disciplines where each department may form its own subculture. In large high schools, it is not uncommon for faculty in a particular department to have little opportunity to regularly interact with teachers in other departments. The same is true in elementary schools, where one may hear such statements as "The primary teachers do things differently than we do in the intermediate grades."

Interrelationship of Structure, Climate, and Culture

Organizational structure ultimately impacts students. This is often apparent in areas of special programs and services. A most pertinent illustration is when teachers, legitimately concerned about the individual needs of a student, seek assistance from special education services. However, once the student is identified with a learning disability and begins receiving services, classroom teachers often distance themselves from the child and refer all concerns back to the special education department. This manifestation of "regular" versus "special" education subcultures is at the root of much of the controversy regarding inclusion and mainstreaming of special-needs children. Larger units of subcultures also exist within school communities based on a person's role and identity within the organization, such as that of teacher, student, parent, or administrator. Educational leaders can influence the collaboration and ultimately the identification with various subcultures through conscious manipulation of the organizational structure, scheduling, room assignments, procedures, and opportunities for dialogue and problem solving among staff, students, parents, and other stakeholders in the school.

School culture is also reflective of the larger societal culture in which it exists. John Goodlad (1984) and others (e. g., Cuban, 1984; Rowan, 1995) found that there is a routine and sameness in classrooms across the country. Additionally, social issues that impact the larger, national culture are mirrored within the school setting, such as divisions or subcultures that arise based on gender, ethnicity, or socioeconomic status. Although schools naturally reflect the larger, national culture, educational leaders also have the opportunity to reinforce or influence change in the school's culture through various mechanisms, such as organizational structure, decision-making processes, and inclusive dialogue among various subcultures and stakeholders.

Researchers have used instruments that measure teachers' perceptions of other teachers and administrators as a way to describe the climate of the school. Remember that climate is defined as the total environment of the school and reflects the totality and interdependence of the ecology, milieu, organizational structure, and culture of the school. **Andrew Halpin's** and **Don Croft's** (1962) **Organizational Climate Description Questionnaire** (OCDQ) was one of the pioneering and best known instruments to describe school climate. Several revisions and iterations of Halpin and Croft's original instrument have been made by other researchers (e.g., Hoy, Tarter, & Kottkamp, 1991). In general, the OCDQ instruments measure climate along a continuum from open to closed. An **open climate** is characterized by free-flowing communication between and among teachers and administrators. Teachers are highly committed to their work and are not directed or restricted by the administration. Administrators are highly supportive of teachers and respect their professionalism and competence. A **closed climate**, conversely, is highly restrictive, characterized by high levels of trivial busywork. Principals in closed climates lack concern for teachers and are controlling and directive. Teachers are frustrated, divided, and uncommitted.

School climate is an important construct in understanding organizations because of its apparent relationship to leadership for organizational change. Other chapters will more specifically address leadership, change, and motivation, but in general open school climates are more conducive to change and leadership that promotes effectiveness in teachers' professional development and student achievement.

Social Structure and Culture

Social system theory explains organizational dynamics in terms of social networks; that is the relationships and interactions of people within and outside the organization. **Blau** and **Scott** (1962) identified two fundamental principles that help define a social system. One is the **structure of social relations,** or patterns of social interactions within the social system. The other is the **culture**, or shared values of those in the social system. It is useful to remember that the structure of social relations and the culture of the organization can be viewed formally, informally, or holistically.

Social structure is determined by the types of social interactions among persons with varying status within the organization. **Social interaction** refers to the type and degree of interaction among those within an organization, whether they are superordinate, subordinate, or peer-oriented. For instance, it is important to note how often and how long people talk to each other within the organization and in what manner that discussion is conducted. Does the interaction represent an air of cooperation and collaboration, or is it done only to provide direction or criticize someone?

This interaction component leads to the second element of social structure, which relates to how **status** is viewed by those within and outside the organization or social system. Does the social interaction center around one's formal status within the organization, that is, principal to teacher, teacher to student, or is there an effort to avoid titles and formal position interactions? Status can be very formal, as described above, but status is also apparent within an organization's informal structures such as cliques, "insider" or "outsider" groups, or individuals who have marginal interactions and relationships with others. In some schools, for instance, there may be students who seem merely to "exist" in the school, rarely interacting or establishing relationships with others.

Both formal and informal social structures within an organization, or a social system, are important, because both operate simultaneously within the organization. Both formal and informal structures are relevant when determining how people function within the organization and how they interact with one another. An understanding of formal and informal structures is essential for educational leaders when they attempt to initiate programs or changes within the organizational social system.

The **culture** of an organization is equally important to the social structure of an organization. Culture impacts social structure and vice versa. Culture includes the **shared values, social norms**, and **role expectations** that exist within an organization. Shared values and beliefs may be manifested through the vision or mission of the organization or by the way in which an organization conducts its daily business (Chance, 1992). More broadly, values, norms, and role expectations are evident in the way people behave in an organization.

Each person who enters an organization brings his or her own set of beliefs and values. These personal values and beliefs then must be amalgamated with the values and beliefs of the organization. If an individual has difficulty balancing personal beliefs and values with organizational beliefs and values, the result is often a person who is unhappy. Such unhappiness causes personal reactions ranging from alienation to aggression to depression. Most people eventually conform to and support the organizational culture, either at a formal or informal level. In some cases, they may facilitate change in the culture so it better matches their personal values and beliefs.

Elements of organizational culture may be found at both the **formal** and **informal** levels of an organization. For instance, a school staff may have a shared value of certain school academic goals and outcomes. This shared value may be espoused formally through official school statements or documents, but at the informal level individual teachers may seek to achieve these academic goals and outcomes in different ways. Some may be more creative in their instruction whereas others may use more traditional instructional methods. Teachers may use sanctions and rewards differently in striving to reach similar goals. One teacher may be more inclined to use social sanctions such as criticism or public ridicule of students who perform or behave inappropriately, whereas another teacher may adopt a counseling approach and directly involve parents to help achieve a goal. Some teachers may rely exclusively on formally developed organizational sanctions and rewards, whereas others may create classroom sanctions and rewards.

It does not matter which approach to social sanctioning is taken to achieve organizational goals. These are personal decisions made by teachers and reflect their personal values, beliefs, and role expectations. The effect of any approach to social sanctioning is also reflective of the values, beliefs, and role expectations of individual students. So what does this mean? Simply put, some approaches work better with some students and some better with others. The desired result is to reach certain academic goals, and from an organizational perspective that is the ultimate measuring device.

The culture of an organization serves as a type of **normative compass** for those within the organization. An organizational culture provides a basis for agreement on the behavior, expectations, and roles of those who populate the organization. Remember, the essential purpose for looking at the social structure and culture of an organization is that it provides a way to analyze how people behave toward one another within both the formal and informal components of the organization.

The more formal the organization, the more formal the social structure and culture may be. Thus, a school that is led by a more formal principal will have a more articulated social structure and a more formal, discernible culture. A school that has a more laissez-faire leader might also have a less formal social structure and less pronounced formal culture. Generally, a family or social club organization will have fewer formal social structures and cultures. Of course, there can always be exceptions to this.

William Firestone and **Bruce Wilson** (1993) described the impact of school leadership in terms of bureaucratic and cultural linkages. Bureaucratic linkages are formal processes, whereas cultural linkages affect people's definitions of their tasks and their commitment to the school. Because schools tend to be loosely linked (see Chapter 6), focusing on bureaucratic links, or formal systems, is not adequate to shape a school's pattern of operation and effectiveness. Leaders' attention to culture is essential. Firestone and Wilson suggested that culture refers to what people believe and value and how these beliefs and values are communicated. Educational leaders link to the culture of the school or district through stories, rituals, and informal communication channels. Stories are much like Aesop's fables, in that they have a moral or illustrate something that is valued by the school culture. Rituals are ceremonial activities that reinforce values, such as graduation ceremonies or lunchroom procedures. How rituals are conducted makes a statement about what the school stands for. Assemblies that recognize academics communicate a message that student learning is valued. A lunchroom that plays soft music and dresses its tables with tablecloths and centerpieces sends a totally different message than a lunchroom where monitors are rushing students through lines and screaming for quiet. Further, informal communication channels can reinforce important stories and rituals. Teacher mentors for new teachers, for instance, serve not only to help new staff learn the bureaucratic, formal processes of the school but also serve as historians for new teachers. A mentor will explain to a new teacher "why we have homecoming the second weekend of October" or "how it came to be that there is a stuffed owl in the library." These symbols and rituals are a part of a school's history and provide linkages for developing a common cultural identity.

Schools as Learning Organizations

Intricately related to culture is the concept of organizations as learning organisms. **Chris Argyris** (1976) introduced the idea that learning processes play a role in organizational problem solving and decision making. Argyris proposed that organizational learning can be described as either single-loop learning or double-loop learning. **Single-loop learning** is that which involves changing processes or behaviors to solve routine or short-term problems, whereas **double-loop learning** requires changing the core values that govern an organization (Argyris, 1994; Hanson, 2001). Thus, true change (reform) will occur only if an organization evaluates and redefines the deeply held assumptions and values that guide the vision of what the organization desires to be and consequently how the organization does things. When this happens, cultural shift has occurred.

James G. March (1990) expanded on the idea of organizational learning by introducing the notion of organizational intelligence. March defined an intelligent organization as "one that adopts procedures that consistently do well (in the organization's own terms) in the face of constraints imposed by such things as scarce resources and competition" (p. 1). Although March framed organizational learning in terms of business, applications to school settings are valid. **E. Mark Hanson** (2001) described organizational knowledge as either hard or soft. Hard knowledge is recorded as procedures and rules, whereas soft knowledge is maintained by individuals within the organization or as prevailing beliefs and conventional wisdom. Over time, in smart organizations soft knowledge will inform hard knowledge (and vice versa). Thus, some schools may be smarter than others.

Schools that do not keep careful records or that routinely transfer teachers or administrator will likely have poorer organizational memory, thus leading to ineffective or inefficient decision making and problem solving and consequently lower performance. Smart schools rely on double-loop learning—that is learning associated with core values and focused on long-term solutions. While recognizing the value of individuals and single-loop, or short-term, learning, smart schools understand that even brilliant individuals cannot singlehandedly do all that is necessary to achieve high performance. Everyone must understand the core values and work together as a unit. This, in essence, demonstrates that organizational culture (shared values, beliefs, and assumptions) is at the heart of how well schools do or do not operate as learning organizations.

Peter Senge (1990) described five disciplines of learning organizations as (a) personal mastery, (b) mental models, (c) building shared vision, (d) team learning, and (e) systems thinking. **Personal mastery** involves the continuous clarification of personal vision, focus of energy, and viewing things realistically. It refers to a commitment to life-long learning. Thus, learning organizations encourage the growth of their people in this manner. **Mental models** are the deep assumptions and generalizations (often held as pictures or images) that shape our understanding of the world and how we behave. **Shared vision** is a picture of the future of the organization that is commonly held by all within the organization. Genuine vision causes people to excel and learn, because they want to and because they truly believe in the vision. Genuine vision is not simply a vision statement; it is individual visions translated into a shared vision and becomes the principles and values that guide practice. **Team learning** involves dialogue where members of a team suspend assumptions and quick judgments and engage in thinking together. Teams are the fundamental learning unit of an organization. Finally, **systems thinking** is looking at the complex interrelationships among various systems that impact the organization. Systems thinking requires one to look for patterns in a holistic sense, rather than focusing on isolated pieces. Senge termed systems thinking as the fifth discipline, because it provides the vehicle to integrate the other disciplines and fuse them into a cohesive ensemble of theory and practice. In Senge's view, learning organizations are those that practice the five disciplines and consider their organization in light of its place within a myriad of networked systems. In essence, learning organizations recognize (and act in such a way) that the whole is greater than the sum of its parts. And, at the heart of organizational learning as systems thinking is the attention to deeply held assumptions and beliefs that define the organizational culture within a larger cultural system.

Culture and Community

Thomas Sergiovanni (1994) considered the concepts of formal organizations and communities as well as the concepts of rational connections and cultural connections. Organizational structure, rules, and regulations are familiar mechanisms of the formal organization and serve to legitimize schools as having the proper tools to accomplish their purpose. Community, conversely, is not necessarily formal, but rather a collection of individuals bonded together by shared values and ideas. Connections among people in formal organizations are based primarily on the rational pursuit of self interests and legitimacy. Connections in communities are cultural and are based on loyalties, purposes, and beliefs.

Rational and cultural connections are competing forces. For instance, we want community but are taught the value of individualism. In examining differences between rational connections for self interest and cultural connections based on common purpose, Sergiovanni identified the following ways of satisfying our needs.

- Self-reliance ("I")
- Dependence on another ("I to I")
- Dependence on norms, customs, and mores built into a social structure ("We")

It is the third way that represents community, and one that humans are naturally inclined to favor. Thus, Sergiovanni suggested that schools must purposefully work to become communities. This requires schools to explore and define core beliefs and values that bind them and to develop norms and structures that guide decisions and behaviors. Until a school becomes a purposeful community, it cannot be a caring community, a learning community, a professional community, or an inclusive community. First, people in the organization must agree on a common set of values and beliefs that explain their direction and defines relationships within the organization.

Core beliefs and assumptions are central to the culture of a school and also reflect the broader local and national cultures. Thus, changing culture is difficult and slow, because people are intricately attached to values, rituals, ceremonies, stories, and heroes that define their school. However, **Terrence Deal** (1993) offered some concrete examples of how school leaders can work to effect change in school culture. These are

- Recreate the history of the school.
- Articulate shared values through slogans and symbols.
- Anoint and celebrate heroes.
- Reinvigorate rituals and ceremonies.
- Tell good stories.
- Work with the informal network.

Considerations for Diversity and Social Justice

An underlying principle of organizational culture is shared values and beliefs. However, from the perspective of postmodernist theory, this is paradoxical to the notion of diversity. Postmodernism refers to a concern for conditions that are becoming prevalent in the world, including such trends as global information, instantaneous communication, increased mobility, and the emergence of a multicultural, global culture. Shared values in a postmodern world does not mean sameness, but rather "acceptance of otherness and cooperation within difference" (Furman, 1998, p. 307). She further noted that if sameness is the basis for community, then some values and people are marginalized.

James Banks (2004), a noted researcher in the area of diversity and multi-cultural education, has challenged us to consider how multicultural nations can balance unity and diversity.

> Unity without diversity results in cultural repression and hege-mony. Diversity without unity leads to Balkanization and the fracturing of the nation-state. Diversity and unity should coex-ist in a delicate balance in democratic, multicultural nation-states (p. 298).

Banks further identified this balance, or dilemma, as one of constructing communities that incorporate the diversity of citizens yet maintain a set of shared values and ideals (Banks, 2008). This dilemma is becoming increas-ingly critical because of worldwide migration and the effects of globalization on local and national communities.

Banks approaches this dilemma through his stages of cultural devel-opment typology, in which he proposes that cultural, national, and global identifications are developmental. He contends that people cannot develop a clarified national identity until they have a reflective, clarified cultural identity, and they further cannot develop a global identification until they have acquired a national identity.

Applying the concept of diversity within unity to schools, Banks and associates (2001) offered twelve principles to which schools should attend.

1. Professional development programs should help teachers under-stand the complex characteristics of ethnic groups and the ways in which race, ethnicity, language, and social class interact to in-fluence student behavior.

2. Schools should ensure that all students have equitable opportuni-ties to learn and to meet high standards.

3. The curriculum should help students understand that knowl-edge is socially constructed and reflects researchers' personal ex-periences as well as the social, political, and economic contexts in which they live.

4. Schools should provide all students with opportunities to partici-pate in extracurricular and cocurricular activities that develop knowledge, skills, and attitudes that increase academic achieve-ment and foster positive interracial relationships.

5. Schools should create or make salient superordinate or cross-cut-ting groups to improve intergroup relations.

6. Students should learn about stereotyping and other related bi-ases that have negative effects on racial and ethnic relations.

7. Students should learn about the values shared by virtually all cultural groups (e.g., justice, equality, freedom, peace, compassion, and charity).

8. Teachers should help students acquire the social skills needed to interact effectively with students from other racial, ethnic, cultural, and language groups.

9. Schools should provide opportunities for students from different racial, ethnic, cultural, and language groups to interact socially under conditions designed to reduced fear and anxiety.

10. A school's organizational strategies should ensure that decision making is widely shared and that members of the school community learn collaborative skills and dispositions to create a caring learning environment.

11. Leaders should ensure that all public schools, regardless of their location, are funded equitably.

12. Teachers should use multiple culturally sensitive techniques to assess complex cognitive and social skills.

In terms of educational leadership, the notion that leaders must be activists in developing democratic schools and promoting equity and diversity has been framed within the concept of leading for social justice. Leading for social justice implies a conscious and deliberate attempt to influence the organizational culture and to change deeply held assumptions. Some have suggested that leaders should reflect on their decisions by asking: Who is being included and excluded? ; Who is being marginalized?; and, How will this decision lead to a just, democratic, empathetic, and optimistic organization? (Shields, 2004). Others have contended that an orientation toward resistance is necessary to actively engage in changing culture (Theoharris, 2007).

Theories framed within a social justice context are concerned with redefining the central values that bind an organization, suggesting the need to revisit the basic elements that define culture: (a) assumptions, (b) values, and (c) artifacts (symbols, stories, and heroes). Thus educational leaders must actively engage multiple stakeholders in an inclusive process to dialogue about what they value and create a new vision for their school (Chance, 1992).

Summary

This chapter contrasted the concept of organizational climate with organizational culture. Climate is defined as the total environment of the school and is the result of the interrelationships between the physical, social, structural, and cultural components of the school. Culture is defined by the underlying assumptions and values of the organization. Open school climates, characterized by high levels of communication among teachers and administrators and by teachers who are highly supported by administration and generally committed to the goals of the school, are more conducive to change and manifest leadership that promotes educational effectiveness.

The concept of social structure explains how formal and informal social interactions and patterns reflect a school's culture. In addition, the status of various individuals within the organization and the extent to which status is gained through formal or informal roles, is indicative of underlying assumptions that define the school culture. Further, this chapter discussed the role of symbols, stories, heroes, rituals, and ceremonies in defining school culture. Deal's work on school culture provides leaders with concrete examples for using these cultural artifacts to influence change.

The concept of schools as learning organizations was explored, beginning with Argyris' seminal scholarship regarding single-loop and double-loop learning, where double-loop learning represents the redefinition of deeply held assumptions and values. Senge's conceptualization of learning organization provides a model for the consideration of five disciplines—personal mastery, mental models, shared vision, team learning, and systems thinking—that are necessary to develop a school into a learning organization. Finally, the concept of community as a desired construct for school culture was explored. Leaders in public schools must surely be concerned with how to incorporate diversity into a community's shared values and beliefs that define a cultural unity and promote a climate of social justice.

Theory into Practice

Big Horn and Deep Creek Come Together: A Case of School District Consolidation

Big Horn School is a small district located approximately 50 miles from the nearest metropolitan center. The district consists of one site with three buildings serving 150 students in grades K–12 from a 140-square mile area. The student population is primarily white, with 14 percent Native American.

More than 60 percent of Big Horn's students receive free or reduced lunches, and last year's state report indicated an 11 percent drop-out rate.

Big Horn employs nine secondary teachers (grades 7–12) and six elementary teachers (grades K–6). A basic curriculum is offered along with academic elective courses in computer applications and Spanish I. The school is not served by any vocational-technology school or other regional services. Big Horn has cooperative programs with its neighboring school, Deep Creek, five miles away. Students participate in foreign language, drivers' education, and higher-level math classes through a cooperative arrangement between the two schools.

Deep Creek School has 400 students in grades K–12, 34 percent of whom are Native American. The remainder are white. Sixteen secondary teachers serve grades 7–12, and 17 elementary faculty teach grades K–6. Deep Creek School District encompasses 206 square miles and is served by an area vocational-technical school, which high school students can opt to attend during their junior and senior years. The Deep Creek School District reported a 2 percent dropout rate last year. In addition to core curricular classes, Deep Creek offers academic electives in basic computer applications, German I, Spanish I, drama, and speech. Beyond classroom teachers, Deep Creek employs a counselor and a librarian. The district consists of two buildings at two separate sites, one that houses grades K–8 and the other grades, 9–12. The elementary building is crowded, and classes meet on the stage and in parts of the media center.

Two months ago, voters from Big Horn and Deep Creek voted to consolidate the two districts. Members of both communities had realized that they did not have the financial resources to continue to operate their own school; they had to pool their resources and have one community house the elementary students and the other the high school.

Mrs. Jane Peterson was appointed as the superintendent of the newly formed Big Horn–Deep Creek School District. Mrs. Peterson had served as the superintendent of Big Horn for the last 11 years. Today is the first Saturday of December, and Mrs. Peterson is in her office putting together the agenda for the joint board meeting scheduled for Tuesday. She will be presenting a six-month transition plan for the voluntary consolidation. She feels fortunate that her appointment as superintendent was an amicable process, supported by both school boards. Mr. Jameson, the superintendent of Deep Creek for 18 years, decided to retire and agreed to work with her during this transition year. Even though the consolidation of the two districts was voluntary and was happening under the best conditions that could be expected, Mrs. Peterson knew there were many issues and hurdles ahead.

A major concern was the reduction in teaching staff that was inevitable. In addition, there was the issue of each community's pride and identity. Both communities had operated a high school for more than 60 years, and traditions and community activities at the high schools were a big part of each community's culture. She was also cognizant of the differences in leadership style and organizational structure that had operated at the two schools. Mrs. Peterson had received her bachelor's degree in elementary education from an out-of-state university and had begun teaching 25 years ago. Her master's degree was in remedial reading, and through the years she had taught kindergarten through eighth grades. She began her administrative career as a principal of a small, rural K–8 school, where she served for seven years before taking the superintendency in Big Horn. Mr. Jameson, conversely, began his teaching career in Deep Creek 32 years ago after spending 5 years in military service. He had taught high school math and coached boys' and girls' athletics prior to becoming the high school principal at Deep Creek and five years later took over as superintendent.

Sample Analysis

Perhaps the biggest issue facing Mrs. Peterson is the amalgamation or assimilation of two school cultures. This consolidation involves more than simply merging two school districts; it involves bringing together two entire communities. That is because in these two small, rural districts, the organizational culture of each school is intricately tied to the culture of the larger community. Community members, whose sons and daughters, grandchildren, and great grandchildren have graduated from their local high school, are greatly tied to "their" school. Local high school sporting events, graduations, and proms are a part of each community's way of life. School colors, mascots, and traditions are examples of some of the artifacts that reflect the values and basic assumptions underlying the community and school culture.

Mrs. Peterson faces the challenge of leading toward change in both communities. Her best opportunity to do this would be through an open climate where there would be a free flow of communication and a high level of stakeholder involvement. Open communication and involvement of teachers, students, and community must be encouraged. She would be wise to plan for open community forums as well as teacher, student, and community committees to decide on such issues as the new school colors, names, and mascots.

She should remember that the primary goal of the "new" school is one of creating and transmitting culture. Drawing on Bank's work on multiculturalism and diversity, Mrs. Peterson should consider the notion that persons cannot identify with a larger community until they reflect on and clarify their own cultural identity. Thus, a part of her open community forums should include activities where participants from each community identify their values and define the characteristics of their community that distinguishes it. Through this process, members from both communities will undoubtedly discover values and beliefs they share in common. These will serve to bridge the gap and provide a foundation from which to unify the two communities. In addition, they can then begin to decide together those rituals, stories, and symbols from their schools that they wish to keep, and how these may be combined in some way to represent an amalgamation of new traditions.

As much as possible, Mrs. Peterson should allow teacher input regarding any necessary staff reductions and reassignments. Additionally, members of both boards should be involved in working through the consolidation and ultimate membership reduction of the existing boards. The more Mrs. Peterson can encourage open communication, the greater the chance there is for consensus and cohesiveness. Ultimately, final decisions about staff reduction and board reorganization may have to be put to a vote of the new board or old boards, but if open communication precedes this action, there is a greater likelihood that teachers, students, and community members will respond with commitment.

Reader's Application

Everyone's Kids

Four years ago when Cheryl Brooks accepted the principalship at Hoover Elementary School, she knew she faced many challenges. Hoover had been designated as a "school in need of improvement" for the previous two years, according to state guidelines that administered No Child Left Behind policy. Only 25 percent of students were proficient in reading, writing, and math. The 800 student population was primarily minority, with 30 percent African American, 45 percent Hispanic, and 25 percent white. The school received Title I money and qualified for free lunch and breakfast programs for all students. Approximately 45 percent of Hoover students were classified as homeless, meaning they lacked a "fixed, regular, and adequate nighttime residence" according to government definition.

On that first day of the new school year, four years ago, Principal Brooks walked into the cafeteria at lunchtime and noticed that children were stuffing their pockets with ketchup packets. The cafeteria supervisor explained to Brooks that they were taking ketchup home so they would have something to eat tonight. At that moment, Brooks vowed she would do something. She would tell people about her kids; she would be their voice.

Now, after four years at Hoover, Brooks had succeeded in finding business and non-profit partners to provide students with back packs filled with supplies, food baskets for the weekends, and on-campus health and dental clinics. She had even talked her own hairstylist into volunteering to give kids haircuts. In addition, the school staff often spent their own money for food, shoes, and other necessities for the children. Student test scores in reading, writing, and math are continuing an upward trend, with 55 percent of students now proficient in these basic skills.

Student Exercise: Case Analysis

1. How would you describe the current culture at Hoover Elementary School?
2. How did the principal lead for social justice?
3. How is this case an example of systems thinking?
4. Analyze Hoover Elementary School using Sergiovanni's concept of community.

References

Argyris, C. (1976). Single-loop and double-loop models in research on decision making. *Administrative Science Quarterly, 21*(3), 363–375.

Argyris, C. (1994). Initiating change that perseveres. *Journal of Public Administration Research and Theory, 4*(3), 343–355.

Banks, J. A. (2004). Teaching for social justice, diversity, and citizenship in a global world. *Educational Forum, 68*(4), 296–305.

Banks, J. A. (2008). Diversity, group identity, and citizenship education in a global age. *Educational Researcher, 37*(3), 129–139.

Banks, J. A., Cookson, P., Gay, G., Hawley, W. D., Irvine, J. J., Nieto, S., Schofield, J. W., & Stephan, W. G. (2001). Diversity within unity: Essential principles for teaching and learning in a multicultural society. *Phi Delta Kappan, 83*(3), 196–203.

Blau, P. M., & Scott, W. R. (1962). *Formal organizations: A comparative approach.* San Francisco: Chandler.

Chance, E. W. (1992). *Visionary leadership in schools: Successful strategies for developing and implementing an educational vision.* Springfield, IL: Charles C. Thomas.

Cuban, L. (1984). *How teachers taught: Constancy and change in American classrooms, 1880–1980.* New York: Longman.

Deal, T. E. (1993). The culture of schools. In M. Sashkin & H. J. Walberg (Eds.), *Educational leadership and school culture* (pp. 3–18). Berkley, CA: McCutchan.

Firestone, W. A., & Wilson, B. L. (1993). Bureaucratic and cultural linkages: Implications for the principal. In M. Sashkin & H. J. Walberg (Eds.), *Educational leadership and school culture* (pp. 19–39). Berkley, CA: McCutchan.

Furman, G. C. (1998). Postmodernism and community in schools: Unraveling the paradox. *Educational Administration Quarterly, 34*(3), 298–328.

Goodlad, J. (1984). *A place called school.* New York: McGraw Hill.

Halpin, A. W., & Croft, D. B. (1963). *The organization climate of schools.* Chicago: Midwest Administration Center of the University of Chicago.

Hanson, M. (2001). Institutional theory and educational change. *Educational Administration Quarterly, 37*(5), 637–661.

Hoy, W. K., Tarter, C. J., & Kottkamp, R. (1991). *Open schools/healthy schools: Measuring organizational climate.* Beverly Hills, CA: Sage.

March, J. G. (1990). *The pursuit of organizational intelligence.* Malden, MA: Blackwell.

Owens, R. G. (2004). *Organizational behavior in education: Adaptive leadership and school reform* (8th ed.). Boston: Pearson.

Rowan, B. (1995). Institutional analysis of educational organizations: Lines of theory and directions for research. In R. T. Ogawa (Ed.), *Advances in research and theories of school management and educational policy* (Vol. 3, pp. 1–20). Greenwich, CT: JAI Press.

Schein, E. H. (1985). *Organizational culture and leadership.* San Francisco: Jossey-Bass.

Senge, P. M. (1990). *The fifth discipline: The art and practice of the learning organization.* New York: Doubleday.

Sergiovanni, T. J. (1994). *Building community in schools.* San Francisco: Jossey-Bass.

Shields, C. M. (2004). Dialogic leadership for social justice: Overcoming pathologies of silence. *Educational Administration Quarterly, 40*(1), 109–132.

Tagiuri, R. (1968). The concept of organizational climate. In R. Tagiuri & G. H. Litwin (Eds.), *Organizational climate: Exploration of a concept.* Boston: Harvard University.

Theoharris, G. (2007). Social justice educational leaders and resistance: Toward a theory of social justice leadership. *Educational Administration Quarterly, 43*(2), 221–158.

5

Leadership: Influencing Behavior, Relationships, and School Effectiveness

Synopsis of Leadership Theories

Leadership theories attempt to explain the role leaders play in influencing others and the relationship between leadership and organizational effectiveness. Studies of leadership have been approached in a variety of ways with the ultimate goal of identifying variables that impact leadership and affect organizational performance. Historically, research has tended to focus on one aspect of leadership and a limited number of variables, and the resulting leadership theories are often categorized according to the researcher's focus. In this chapter, leadership theories are classified into four categories: (a) trait theories of leadership, (b) power approaches to leadership, (c) behaviors of leaders, and (d) transformational, visionary, and moral leadership. Contemporary research on leadership provides more robust theories that frame leadership behaviors within various contexts and demonstrate a number of ways leaders influence organizational processes and systems. This chapter introduces the notion of leadership viewed from the lens of critical theory and explores integrated theories, such as flexible leadership and distributed leadership.

Definitions of leadership vary widely, tending to describe leadership in terms of a particular orientation or approach to leadership study. Yukl (1994) proposed that one commonality of the various definitions of leadership is that leadership "involves a social influence process whereby intentional influence is exerted by one person over other people to structure the activities and relationships in a group or organization" (p. 3).

In terms of organizational leadership, it is of particular importance to differentiate between leadership and management (or administration). Writers often distinguish these differences by the person (manager versus leader), rather than the process (managing versus leading). For instance, Bennis (1989) stated that "the manager does things right; the leader does the right thing," and "the manager focuses on systems and structure, the leader focuses on people" (p. 45). However, as Yukl cautioned, stereotypical labeling of people as managers or leaders is too simplistic. Yukl contended that if distinctions should be made, it is between the processes of managing and leading; however, there is no conclusive empirical research that would demonstrate that these processes are mutually exclusive or that they should be performed by different people. Schein (1985) proposed that leadership is distinguished from management in that the principal function of leadership is to shape and direct the organizational culture. Hanson (1996) characterized management as focusing on the "nuts and bolts of making the organization work," whereas leadership concentrates on strategic vision and skill in drawing followers into actively pursuing the vision (p. 155).

Applications for School Leaders

Understanding leadership theories will help school leaders:

- Assess personal strengths and weaknesses related to skills necessary for effective leadership
- Use power appropriately to positively influence and gain commitment from others
- Examine personal values and beliefs in relationship to assumptions about leadership and followership
- Understand the various roles of leadership
- Recognize the relationship between task-oriented and people-oriented leader behaviors
- Realize the importance of moral purpose and ethical values for leadership

---

Trait Theories of Leadership

Early studies of leadership sought to identify traits and characteristics that distinguished leaders from nonleaders. This approach paralleled Carlyle's conceptualization of the "great man" theory in history, in which he proposed that historical events were largely attributed to the individual accomplishments of great men. Yukl (1994) summarized the major findings from leadership research that attempted to identify traits and skills related to organizational effectiveness. He identified the following broad personality traits that contribute to leadership effectiveness. These were

- Energy and stress tolerance
- Self-confidence
- Internal locus of control
- Emotional maturity
- Integrity
- Power motivation
- Achievement orientation
- Need for affiliation

The leadership traits listed above are generic descriptions that might characterize any leadership position. They are indeed applicable to positions of school leadership. **High energy level** and **stress tolerance** are needed to cope with the hectic pace associated with school leadership, especially at the building level. The daily routine of the principal is one of constant interaction, moving incessantly from one incident to another. Studies have found that principals spend about 50 percent of their time in direct contact with teachers and students, and the job of the principal is characterized by decision making on the move (Sergiovanni, 1991). A principal's ability to engage in effective problem solving requires a capacity to remain calm when dealing with stressful interpersonal conflicts and crisis situations. **Self-confidence** is necessary for educational leaders to take risks and accomplish high goals. Self-confident leaders encourage and reassure teachers and other staff. Furthermore, leaders who are self-confident tend to deal immediately and directly with problems or conflicts, rather than procrastinating, ignoring, or passing problems on to others. **Internal locus of control** refers to the belief that events in one's life are determined by one's own actions rather than by outside events or circumstances. Leaders with an internal locus of control orientation take responsibility for their own actions and exercise more initiative in solving problems. **Emotional maturity** is defined as being well adjusted and being aware of one's own strengths and weaknesses. Educational leaders with high emotional maturity generally care about others in their schools, maintain self-control, and are receptive to constructive criticism.

Integrity denotes honesty, ethical behavior, and trustworthiness. School leaders who are deceptive lose credibility with teachers, parents, and colleagues, as do leaders who break promises or agreements. Teachers lack trust in administrators who exploit or manipulate others for the administrator's own self interests. Furthermore, leaders who try to blame others for their mistakes are seen as weak and untrustworthy. **Power motivation** refers to one's internal drive or need for power to influence others. A strong need for power is associated with effective leadership. However, how power is used is also relevant to whether or not power leads to effective leadership. Exercising power for the benefit of the school organization results in effective leadership, whereas power used to satisfy one's own personal gain or status is ineffective for the organization. **Achievement orientation** refers to a desire to excel and a drive to succeed. Like power motivation, achievement orientation can be either positive or negative in terms of a leader's effectiveness. An achievement orientation contributes to leadership effectiveness only when it is combined with a need for power associated with benefiting others and the school. A high **need for affiliation** means that a person has a strong desire to be liked and accepted by others. Leaders with a high need for affiliation tend to avoid conflicts and avoid making decisions that may be unpopular. They may show favoritism and seek approval rather than effective performance. On the other hand, a leader with a very low need for affiliation may fail to develop effective interpersonal relationships necessary to exert influence.

Skills relevant to leadership identified by Yukl (1994) included: (a) technical skills, (b) interpersonal skills, and (c) conceptual skills. **Technical skills** involve a knowledge of the specialized activities of the organization or unit which the leader supervises, gained through formal education and experiences. **Interpersonal skills** include an understanding of human behavior and group processes, the capability to discern others' feelings and motives, and the ability to effectively communicate and persuade. **Conceptual skills** include logical thinking, inductive and deductive reasoning, analytical ability, and creative thinking.

All three types of skills are necessary for leadership, but the relative importance of each set of skills varies with the situation. Conceptual skills are more important at top executive levels. In the case of schools, these skills would be important at the superintendent's level because of the need for a broad, long-term perspective and the need to understand complex interactions among a variety of variables affecting the district. Middle management roles, such as those held by building principals, require an equal mix of all three skills because of the fact that leaders at this level are in a position of implementing existing policies established at higher levels. Technical skills are most important for low-level managers responsible for direct supervision of specific tasks and activities. In a school district, these would be administrative positions such as curriculum coordinators or program specialists.

Power Approaches to Leadership

An essential function of leadership is influencing others in ways that effectively meet organizational goals. One facet of leadership that attempts to explain influence is the concept of power. **John R. P. French** and **Bertram Raven** (1968) developed a taxonomy that classifies interpersonal power according to its source. They identified five types of power, as follows:

- Reward power: Compliance is achieved by a leader's use of rewards for desirable behavior.
- Coercive power: Compliance is achieved by a leader's threat of punishment for undesirable behavior.
- Legitimate power: Compliance is achieved because of the leader's formal position. The subordinate complies because he or she believes the leader has the right to issue a directive, and the subordinate believes he or she has the responsibility to comply with the order.
- Expert power: Compliance is achieved because the follower believes the leader possesses specialized knowledge and expertise on the best way to do something.
- Referent power: Compliance is achieved because the follower admires the leader and seeks to gain the leader's approval.

Reward, coercive, and legitimate power emanate from the leader's position within the organization. Expert and referent power are more closely associated with personal attributes of the leader. The effect of power in terms of influence and compliance is complex. The potential for influence is ultimately dependent on the perception and consent of the follower. All five categories of power as described by French and Raven's typology refer to compliance through the beliefs of the follower.

In summarizing research based on French and Raven's power typology, Yukl (1994) noted that studies tend to suggest that effective leaders rely more on expert and referent power to influence followers. In terms of school leadership, teachers are more apt to be committed to principals who are viewed as competent, masterful teachers in their own right. A common complaint voiced by teachers regarding instructional supervision is that teachers feel that principals often do not exhibit a strong understanding of instructional issues and do not provide teachers with suggestions for growth. Principals who promote best practices based on a thorough understanding of the curricular, instructional, and developmental needs of children are more likely to gain a following of teachers who admire and support the principal's efforts. However, Yukl further commented that methodological limitations of the research might have biased results toward these sources of power. Additionally, studies did not attempt to separate effects of different types of power or examine interactions among these variables. Yukl surmises that further research would confirm that expert and referent power are emphasized by effective leaders, but that other types of power are also used and are important to effective leadership.

Behaviors of Leaders

Another approach to the study of leadership has been to examine the behaviors of leaders. **Douglas McGregor** (1960) explained that leaders' actions are based on their beliefs and assumptions about people at work. He described leadership behavior in terms of two opposing sets of beliefs, which he called **Theory X** and **Theory Y.**

Theory X leaders believe:

- ♦ The average human being has an inherent dislike of work and will avoid it if possible.

- ♦ Most people must be coerced, controlled, directed, and threatened with punishment to get them to put forth adequate effort toward achievement of organizational objectives.

- ♦ The average person prefers to be directed, wishes to avoid responsibility, has little ambition, and wants security above all (p. 33–34).

The actions of Theory X leaders reflect these assumptions. Theory X leaders believe that they must organize, direct, and control workers through persuasion, rewards, punishment, or coercion.

Theory X management can take either a **hard or soft approach.** A hard approach is characterized by close supervision, tight controls over behavior, coercion, and veiled threats. The soft approach involves permissiveness to satisfy people's demands in an effort to barter for their compliance. McGregor (1960) also identified a third approach, which combined both hard and soft modes of operation, which he referred to as the "carrot and stick" approach to leadership (p. 41).

In introducing Theory Y, McGregor (1960) conceded that "the human side of enterprise has become a major preoccupation of management" (p. 45). He cited policies and practices that stressed equity, humanitarianism, and safe, pleasant working environments. However, he concluded that these things had been done "without changing...fundamental theory of management" (p. 46). Thus, McGregor based his notion of Theory Y management on the following assumptions:

- The expenditure of physical and mental effort in work is as natural as play or rest.
- People will exercise self-direction and self-control in the service of objectives to which they are committed.
- Commitment to objectives is the function of the rewards associated with their achievement, specifically ego and self-actualization.
- The average human being not only accepts but also seeks responsibility.
- People are generally creative, imaginative, and possess ingenuity.
- In most work environments, the intellectual potential of the average person is only partially utilized (p. 47–48).

Theory X and Theory Y are important to school practitioners in their explanation of how leaders' actions relate to their understanding of human behavior. McGregor noted that Theory X management does not work "because direction and control are of limited value in motivating people whose important needs are social and egoistic" (p. 42).

Take for example how Theory X and Theory Y might be applied to a principal's supervision of classroom instruction. A Theory X administrator might closely monitor teachers to insure that lesson plans, instruction, and classroom management complied with specific organizational expectations. The teacher would be allowed little or no input into curriculum and would be constrained to conform to specific instructional strategies. Theory X management operates on the assumption that decisions about the school's operation, curriculum, and instructional philosophy are made at the administrative level and the role of the principal is to ensure teachers' compliance with all rules, regulations, and operating procedures including methods of classroom instruction and content of lesson plans. Teachers who deviated from expected norms would be punished through reprimands and poor evaluations. They might be threatened with dismissal or persuaded to comply by being rewarded with satisfactory performance evaluations. Teachers who comply with the established instructional norms may be rewarded through superior performance evaluations and less administrative intervention.

A Theory Y principal would take a more collaborative approach to supervision and would engage teachers in dialogue about how to make learning effective for all students. Believing that teachers are internally motivated, the Theory Y principal would involve each teacher in self-reflection and self-improvement goals. Creative and innovative approaches to classroom instruction would be encouraged to increase student achievement and enhance learning. Each teacher would be considered individually, because the Theory Y principal acts on the assumption that teachers' internal motivation will differ.

Two perspectives have been taken in research associated with leadership behavior. One focus involves the identification of the roles and nature of leadership. Another major research focus has attempted to differentiate between effective and ineffective leader behaviors.

One prominent theory developed from descriptive research on the nature of managerial work was Mintzberg's (1979) taxonomy of managerial roles. He identified the following roles in which all managerial activities could be classified. Specific activities involved one or more of these managerial roles:

- **Figurehead role:** Involves duties that are symbolic, legal, or social in nature, such as presiding at ceremonial events or signing documents

- **Leader role:** Involves activities where the purpose is to integrate the organization toward achieving the primary purposes of the organization, such as hiring, training, and promoting

- **Liaison role:** Includes activities intended to establish and maintain relationships with individuals outside the manager's organizational unit

- **Monitor role:** Activities that involve seeking information to identify and analyze problems and opportunities and understand events and processes within and outside the organizational unit

- **Disseminator role:** Activities involved in the interpretation and disbursement of information not directly accessible by subordinates

- **Spokesman role:** Activities involved in the transmission of information outside the organizational unit

- **Entrepreneur role:** Activities that initiate and control change toward improvement in the organization

- **Disturbance handler role:** Involves activities to deal with sudden crises, unforeseen events, or conflicts

- **Resource allocator role:** Activities that involve the allocation and use of money, personnel, material, equipment, facilities, and services

- **Negotiator role:** Activities which involve the bargaining for transactions requiring a substantial commitment of resources, such as collective bargaining, contracts, grievances, or employment of key personnel

The first three roles—figurehead, leader, and liaison—are associated with interpersonal behaviors. The next three—monitor, disseminator, and spokesman—involve information-processing activities. The last four—entrepreneur, disturbance handler, resource allocator, and negotiator—are related to decision-making behaviors of the leader. According to Mintzberg, manager's roles are primarily based on the specific nature of the managerial position, but mangers have flexibility in how each role is performed. At times, role conflicts may occur because of pressure from supervisors and followers regarding relative importance of different roles or the manner in which roles are carried out.

Other studies focused on the identification and differentiation of effective and ineffective leader behaviors. Fundamental and influential research in this regard was initiated at Ohio State University in the 1940s by John K. Hemphill and Alvin Coons (1950) and later continued by Andrew Halpin and B. J. Winer (1952). In the **Ohio State studies,** the primary form of data collection and research was the Leader Behavior Description Questionnaire (LBDQ) administered to managers and their superiors and subordinates. The **LBDQ** asked respondents to describe a leader's behavior and measured two basic dimensions—initiating structure and consideration. **Initiating structure** refers to the leaders' behavior in delineating the relationship between the leader and subordinates and in establishing patterns of organization, channels of communication, and methods of procedure. **Consideration** refers to leader behaviors indicative of friendship, trust, warmth, interest, and respect between the leader and subordinates.

Initiating structure and consideration were found to be independent behaviors. Thus, a leader might be high in consideration and low in initiating structure, although another leader might be high in both consideration and initiating structure. The resulting model from the Ohio State studies was a two-dimensional matrix with four quadrants describing four distinct leadership styles, as depicted in Figure 5.1.

Figure 5.1. Two-dimensional Leadership Behavior Matrix from Ohio State Studies

		Consideration	
		Low	High
Initiating Structure	**High**	**Quadrant II** Low consideration High initiating structure	**Quadrant I** High consideration High initiating structure
	Low	**Quadrant III** Low consideration Low initiating structure	**Quadrant IV** High consideration Low initiating structure

Early studies using the LBDQ to investigate leader behaviors of aircraft commanders, higher education administrators, and school superintendents suggested that "effective leadership is characterized by high initiation of structure and high consideration" (Halpin, 1966, p. 127). Halpin further noted that there is a relationship between leader behaviors and the organizational values. In other words, leaders in organizations that emphasize and place value on initiating structure tend to exhibit fewer behaviors associated with consideration and vice versa.

At approximately the same time of the Ohio State studies, researchers at the **University of Michigan** carried out similar research on leadership in insurance, manufacturing, and railroad industries. Their research found three types of behaviors that distinguished effective from ineffective leaders (Yukl, 1994). These were (a) task-oriented behavior, (b) relationship-oriented behavior, and (c) participative leadership. Effective leaders concentrated on task-oriented activities such as planning, scheduling, coordinating, and providing resources. In addition, effective leaders guided their followers to set high, yet realistic, goals for performance. However, effective leaders were not single-mindedly focused on task behavior. They also exhibited positive human relations with followers. Relationship-oriented behaviors associated with effective leadership included showing trust, acting friendly and considerate, exhibiting understanding of subordinates' problems, being supportive of followers' careers, open communication, and recognizing employees' accomplishments. Furthermore, effective leaders practiced general supervision rather than close inspection of employees' work. Finally, the Michigan studies found that employee participation in decision making resulted in higher satisfaction and performance.

Research on leader behavior led to a variety of models and theories that conceptualized leadership in two dimensions. Hanson (1996) noted that in comparing and contrasting various leadership behavior models, there appeared to be a surprising similarity of variables that corresponded to the notion of initiating structure (task behavior) and consideration (relationship behavior). The behavioral approach to leadership theory tended to focus on a universal model of leadership effectiveness. **Robert Blake** and **Jane Mouton** (1964), for instance, developed a managerial grid theory that described leaders in by their concern for people and concern for production. They identified the most effective leaders as having both high concern for people and high concern for production. However, they further noted that the "high-high leaders" do not simultaneously exhibit two different behaviors reflective of people and production nor do they alternate between people-oriented behaviors and production-oriented behaviors. Rather, these leaders choose specific behaviors that reflect both concern for people and production. Blake and Mouton (1982) recognized that the behaviors selected by a leader must be relevant to the situation to be effective. The specific behavior chosen varies from situation to situation and from one follower to another. The two-dimensional conception of leadership led to a variety of research and theory based on contingencies and variable situations. Contingency theories are explored more fully in Chapter 6.

Transformational Leadership

More recent theories of leadership attempt to describe the effectiveness of leadership by how leaders transform or change organizations. **James MacGregor Burns'** (1978) research on political leaders laid the groundwork for this recent body of leadership theory, which can be broadly described as transformational leadership theory. Burns proposed that leadership is inseparable from followers' needs and goals and is a result of the interaction between the leaders and followers. Burns distinguished between two fundamental forms of leader-follower interactions: (a) transactional and (b) transformational. **Transactional leadership** involves influencing followers through an exchange of something valued by both the leader and follower. For example, one good or commodity is traded for another, votes are pledged to a legislator who promises to support voters' interests, or a principal receives teachers' support for after-school meetings in exchange for giving teachers a duty-free lunch.

Transformational leadership, conversely, involves an engagement between leaders and followers bound by common purpose, where "leaders and followers raise one another to higher levels of motivation and morality" (Burns, 1978, p. 20).

Bernard Bass and **Bruce Avolio** (1994) defined the effects of transformational leadership as

- ◆ Stimulating others to view their work from new perspectives
- ◆ Knowing the organization's mission or vision
- ◆ Developing other's abilities to higher levels of performance
- ◆ Motivating others beyond self interests toward the benefit of the group or organization

Bass and Avolio explained transformational leadership by a leader's behavior, stating that transformational leaders employ one or more of the following behaviors:

- ◆ **Idealized influence:** Leaders act as role models and are admired, respected, and trusted. Ways in which leaders accomplish this are considering others' needs ahead of their own, sharing risks with followers, being consistent rather than arbitrary, and demonstrating ethical and moral conduct.
- ◆ **Inspirational motivation:** Leaders motivate and inspire by giving meaning and challenge to followers' work and a team spirit is developed. Leader behaviors that contribute to this include involving others in visionary activities, clearly communicating expectations, and demonstrating commitment to shared goals and vision.
- ◆ **Intellectual stimulation:** Leaders stimulate others to be innovative and creative. Leaders promote innovation and creativity by soliciting new ideas from others, not publicly criticizing followers' mistakes, and encouraging others to try new approaches.
- ◆ **Individualized consideration:** Transformational leaders attend to individual needs for achievement and growth by acting as mentor or coach. Leadership behaviors that promote individualized consideration include accepting individual differences and supervising according to individual needs, encouraging two-way communication, listening, and delegating.

An underlying principle of transformational leadership is the concept of a leader's **commitment to moral purpose** and **personal values** as essential to bringing about organizational change. Bennis and Nanus (1985) found innovative leaders had a vision for the future of their organizations; developed trust and commitment by communicating the vision and reinforcing the vision through their own actions; and facilitated continuous learning within the organization.

Kenneth Leithwood (1994) described transformational leadership in schools as having eight dimensions. These are (a) building school vision, (b) establishing school goals, (c) providing intellectual stimulation, (d) offering individualized support, (e) modeling best practices and important organizational values, (f) demonstrating high performance expectations, (g) creating a productive school culture, and (h) developing structures to foster participation in school decisions.

Recent theory regarding educational leadership has built on the notion of moral purpose, commitment to personal values, and vision as concomitant to effective school leadership. **Thomas Sergiovanni** (1992) proposed that there are five sources of authority on which leadership is based. These are (a) bureaucratic authority, (b) psychological authority, (c) technical-rational authority, (d) professional authority, and (e) moral authority. **Bureaucratic authority** is rooted in mandates, rules, regulations, job descriptions, and expectations of the organization. Sergiovanni described this as authority based on reasoning that one should "follow me because of my position." Psychological authority is illustrated by the rationale of "follow me because I will make it worth your while" to do so. **Psychological authority** assumes that teachers will respond to rewards given for desired behaviors. **Technical-rational authority** approaches leadership from the perspective that teachers will comply because the leader knows "what is best, as determined by research." This approach assumes that teachers will respond to logic and follow the prescriptions of scientific evidence of effective practices. Sergiovanni described these three approaches to leadership as being something that is external and imposed on the teacher.

He contrasted these approaches to professional authority and moral authority, which elicit teacher behaviors driven internally rather than as a response to something imposed on them. **Professional authority** refers to craft knowledge and personal expertise as these relate to the particular context in which teachers practice. **Moral authority** is defined as obligations and duties emanating from shared values and ideas.

Figure 5.2 outlines the assumptions, strategies, and consequences of the five sources of authority.

Figure 5.2. Sergiovanni's Sources of Leadership Authority

Source of Authority	Assumptions	Leadership Strategies	Consequences
Bureaucratic	Teachers subordinate and untrustworthy	Inspection and close monitoring	Teachers are technicians and do the minimal expected
Psychological	Meet teachers' needs. Harmony increases performance	Develop congenial atmosphere. Reward teachers for expected behaviors	If rewarded, teachers will perform. If not, performance is minimal
Technical-Rational	Teaching is a science. Facts rule over values and beliefs	Standardize teaching based on research. Monitor compliance	Teachers are technicians. Performance conforms to minimal expectations
Professional	Teaching is situational and contextual. Professional knowledge based onexperience	Dialogue about professional practice. Encourage peer accountability. Assist, support, and provide professional development	Teachers comply with professional norms. Performance is expansive, but uniform
Moral	Schools are professional learning communities with shared values and beliefs	Values and beliefs made explicit. Promote collegiality	Teachers conform to community values. Performance is expansive and sustained

Adapted from *Moral leadership: Getting to the heart of school improvement*, by T. J. Sergiovanni, 1992, San Francisco: Jossey-Bass.

Sergiovanni argued that although bureaucratic, psychological, and technical-rational authority have their place, the primary bases for leadership should be professional and moral authority. Similarly, Deal and Peterson (1994) contrasted two traditions of organizational theory, which they termed "rational-technical" and "symbolic." Rational-technical approaches to leadership are based on assumptions that organizations are primarily rational entities that exist to accomplish explicit and measurable objectives. Symbolic approaches emphasize the normative and social dynamics of organizations and stress the importance of core values and shared beliefs of people within the organization. They propose that effective leadership represents a balance of both approaches, observing that, "high-performing organizations have both order and meaning, structure and values" (p. 9).

Critical Theory Perspectives on Leadership

Critical theory has been defined as a "formal attempt to analyze social relations and the impact of class, power, and ideology on these" (Foster, 1989, p. 11). Critical theory conceives leadership as contextual; that is, situations in which leaders find themselves are not predictable. Critical theory uses narrative and discourse as means to view leadership from an historical context. Discourse, or the use of language, provides clues to underlying assumptions and beliefs that define culture. For example, feminist theorists and researchers have noted that the male voice has dominated leadership theories, whereas scholars researching minorities have argued that leaders are needed who understand children of color and who can think beyond conventional ways of involving parents and community (Larson & Murtadha, 2002).

Recent literature in educational leadership has more broadly conceptualized critical theory as **leadership for social justice.** Changes in school demographics, school governance structures, and policies that focus on accountability and assessment are contextual factors that shape the conceptualization of social justice leadership. Leadership for social justice has been likened to transformational leadership (Foster, 1989), moral stewardship (Murphy, 2002), democratic leadership (Furman & Starratt, 2002), and locally contextualized (Foster, 2004). Social justice leadership is concerned with the nature, culture, and structure of schools.

William Foster has been recognized as one whose work expanded critical theory's place in educational leadership theory (Lindle, 2004). Foster (1989) advocated activism in school leadership and viewed the resolution of moral dilemmas as the heart of school leadership. Further, Foster noted the importance of language, or discourse, in constructing social reality. This is why he suggested reconceptualizing schools as communities, rather than as organizations. Such rethinking impacts how we view classroom organization, the role of administration, and relationships among stakeholders. Foster (2004) noted that the language used (whether community or organization) reflects the "deep structures of thought. . .that guides. . .our action" (p. 189).

Toward an Integrated Approach to Leadership Theory

Recently, more comprehensive approaches to leadership theory have begun to emerge. Yukl and Lepsinger's (2004) model of flexible leadership offers a framework that takes into account the complexities of organizational processes and the ways leaders influence these processes. The **flexible leadership** model describes an organization's performance through (a) efficiency and reliability, (b) adaptation to changes in the external environment, and (c) human resources and relations.

The model proposes that situational variables will determine which of these three components is most important at any given time and further suggests that direct and indirect forms of leadership are used to influence these three components. In schools, **direct leadership behaviors** that are **task oriented** influence organizational efficiency, including such efforts as clarifying roles and objectives or monitoring teacher performance. **Relations-oriented** behavior, directed at the human resources component, might include providing support, encouragement, or recognition to teachers, staff, and students; building trust; empowering stakeholders; or developing teachers' professional skills. **Change-oriented** leadership behaviors, which affect a school's ability to adapt and innovate, are actions such as monitoring the external environment, building internal and external support for needed changes, or encouraging innovative thinking.

In addition, **indirect leadership** influences the organizational components through the use of formal programs, management systems, and the formal organizational structure. Reconfiguring grade-level or departmental organization, such as using a science specialist in an elementary school, where science is typically taught by a teacher in a contained classroom setting, is an example of **altering organizational structure** to affect efficiency and performance. Professional development programs, teacher mentoring systems, or teacher recruitment programs are examples of **programs and management systems** that influence human resources. A school's innovation and adaptation efforts may be influenced by processes providing an award program for creative ways to meet the needs of students.

It is important to understand that both direct and indirect leadership behaviors are likely to have consequences for more than one area. Although some programs or leadership behaviors will improve more than one area simultaneously, it is also possible that leadership actions that enhance one area will be detrimental to another. For instance, using a science specialist in an elementary school (as described in the above example) may result in larger class sizes, thus negatively affecting teacher morale and satisfaction.

Thus, Yukl and Lepsinger (2004) cautioned that leadership is about "doing the right thing at the right time" (p. 19). The concept of flexible leadership requires skills in diagnosing a situation, evaluating the challenges, balancing the competing demands of the situation and solutions to the problem, and coordinating and integrating a variety of leadership activities to meet the challenges or solve a problem.

Although the model of flexible leadership originates from the perspective of business organizations, scholars of educational leadership are also introducing more comprehensive approaches to school leadership. One example is the concept of **distributed leadership**.

Peter Gronn (2002) observed that the concept of distributed leadership first appeared in the field of social psychology in the 1950s but was not incorporated into organizational theory until the mid to late 1990s. Gronn defined distributed leadership as **concertive action** where organizational structure influences members of the organization to act in concert. He refers to three types of concertive actions: (a) spontaneous collaboration, (b) intuitive working relations, and (c) institutionalized practice. Spontaneous collaboration refers to individuals from various organizational areas and levels pooling their expertise for a particular task, and then disbanding. Intuitive work relations has to do with two or more members of an organization who come to rely on each other and develop a close working relationship. The third type of concertive action, institutionalized practice, occurs when an organization provides deliberate structures for collaboration across levels and areas.

James P. Spillane (2005), writing about the Distributed Leadership Study conducted at Northwestern University (see http://www.sesp.northwestern.edu/dls/) cautioned that "[s]hared leadership, team leadership, and democratic leadership are not synonyms for distributed leadership" (p. 149). Rather, distributed leadership frames leadership in terms of the interactions of school leaders, followers, and their situations.

The first principle of distributed leadership is that interactions among people generally involve multiple leaders in both formal and informal roles. The numbers of formal and informal leaders will vary depending on the routine or area of concern. For example, areas such as evaluating teacher performance involve fewer leaders, who have formal roles (e.g., principals and assistant principals). Other areas, such as teacher professional development, may involve formal leaders such as the principal and district curriculum specialists as well as informal leaders such as master teachers with specific areas of expertise. Thus, the interactions among the various leaders in a given situation define leadership practice, as individuals play off one another. The model of distributed leadership identifies three types of interdependence among leaders—reciprocal, pooled, and sequenced—which is credited to Thompson's (1967) work in organizational theory. Reciprocal interdependence was illustrated in the previous example of professional development. The example of teacher evaluation might be illustrative of pooled interdependence if a principal and assistant principal combine and coordinate their information to develop a fuller understanding of teacher practice. Sequential interdependence typically involves multiple tasks to be completed by different leaders in a specific order over a period of time.

The second principle of distributed leadership concerns leaders' interactions with tools, routines, and structures, which are considered to be aspects of the situation. How tools, routines, and structures are used or followed may vary from school to school or even from time to time within the same schools.

In discussing distributed leadership, Leithwood and associates (2004) noted that we do not yet have adequate research to understand how different patterns of leadership distribution are associated with different levels of effect on students. Nonetheless, the notion of distributed leadership and studies such as those being conducted through the Midcontinent Regional Education Laboratory (McREL) on balanced leadership (Waters, Marzano, & McNulty, 2003) hold promise for better understanding the organizational complexities impacting leadership behavior.

Summary

This chapter presented four categories of leadership theory defined by the central focus of the theory's approach to leadership. These categories were (a) theories that described leadership traits; (b) theories that explained influence based on power; (c) theories that described behavior and roles of leaders; and (d) transformational leadership that inspires change.

The traits of leadership as summarized by Yukl offer the school leader a list of characteristics and behaviors that contribute to effectiveness. Educational leaders must possess a high energy level and tolerance for stress. Self-confidence, emotional maturity, and willingness to accept responsibility for one's own actions are also necessary attributes of effective leadership, as are a solid sense of values and integrity. Effective leaders also have a desire to influence an organization for the benefit of students and community. Finally, educational leaders must be willing and able to work with people and possess strong, interpersonal skills.

French and Raven's power typology informs educational leaders about the strength that comes from expert and referent power. School leaders are most likely to influence and gain commitment from others when they are seen as competent individuals who have a strong understanding and passion for the primary work of schools; that is, curriculum, instruction, and student development.

Behavioral theories of leadership examine two primary dimensions of behavior that define leadership. Studies conducted in the 1950s at Ohio State University and the University of Michigan provided fundamental concepts of leadership behavior that have strongly influenced subsequent research and theory in organizational leadership. Two basic dimensions of leadership behavior were identified: (a) task-related behavior and (b) relationship-related behavior. Effective leaders are concerned with both task and relationship and adjust their focus on one or the other from situation to situation.

Transformational leadership theories were discussed and broadly defined as leadership that effects change in an organization. Burns described transformational leadership as an engagement between leaders and followers, who are bound by common purpose. The notion of a leader's commitment to moral purpose and personal values undergirds the concept of transformational leadership. Sergiovanni conceptualized leadership as emanating from various sources of authority and contended that the primary bases of educational leadership should be professional and moral authority.

Further, leadership was explored from a lens of critical theory. From this perspective, leadership is concerned with the nature, culture, and structure of schools and calls for leaders to confront issues of class and power to ensure equity and to preserve democratic ideals.

Finally, more comprehensive conceptualizations of leadership theory were explored. Yukl's flexible leadership model explains how leaders directly and indirectly influence various aspects of the organization. Distributed leadership theory demonstrates that organizational structure influences how formal and informal leaders interact within the organization and how leadership should be more broadly defined as actions distributed throughout the organization.

Overall, leadership theories paint a picture of school leadership grounded in a social consciousness and focused on a school vision based on craft knowledge and expertise. School leadership has been contrasted to school management, where the primary function of leadership is to shape and direct a school culture toward a vision, whereas management focuses on maintaining the basic operations and sustaining the status quo. Yukl reminds us that management and leadership are both necessary processes. It is true that leaders sometimes manage, but managers do not lead.

Theory into Practice

Establishing Order at Jackson High

At 6:30 AM, Tom Clayton, principal at Jackson High School, was in his office going through mail and messages that had arrived yesterday afternoon while he had been at a meeting at the central administration office. "What a waste of time," he thought. Tom hated to be gone from school, because he never knew what would be waiting for him when he returned or what kind of problem he would have to clean up the next day. Tom had taken the reins at Jackson High School a year ago. The school was in one of the poorest areas of the city and for the past five years had been plagued by increasing student discipline problems and a lackadaisical attitude from teachers and staff.

Tom's previous administrative position, which he held for two years, had been as the assistant principal at Walter Junior High School. As a teacher and assistant principal, he had always had a reputation of being tough and demanding. He had gotten results, too. His honors math students had, for the most part, scored high on SAT tests, and he was proud of the no-nonsense approach he had taken as the primary disciplinarian at Walter Junior High.

He was pleased to have been appointed to lead Jackson High School. He felt sure that the district appreciated his efforts as Jackson's principal. Although he knew that other district administrators considered Jackson a less-than-desirable appointment, he was confident that he could make a difference and "turn things around."

On assuming the principalship at Jackson, he immediately established his authority and laid down his expectations to faculty and students. He told faculty that he wanted lesson plans handed in weekly and that he expected teachers to establish strict rules of discipline in their classrooms. Infractions of the rules were not to be tolerated, no matter how minor. He told students the same and began giving detentions and suspending students when necessary. And so far his approach had worked. Although test scores didn't show improvement last year, the orderliness of the campus did. Hallways were clean, students were in class, and there were fewer disruptions. He had expelled almost 30 of the most disruptive students last year, and they had not returned to Jackson. Approximately one-third of the teachers had left after his first year, because they were not willing to meet his high expectations. In his opinion, that was a good thing for Jackson High School. He was able to replace those teachers with young teachers, many in their first year, who were willing to learn and take direction. However, maintaining an orderly climate remained a constant, daily task. It seemed that any time he was out of the building, something happened. He just couldn't trust his teachers, or assistant principal for that matter, to take care of things appropriately. He had tried to explain to his assistant principal, Sam Johnson, that he must be more forceful. The teachers and students did not fear Mr. Johnson like they did Tom.

As he looked through his in-basket, he saw that yesterday was no exception. There had been a theft reported after school from one of the teacher's classrooms, a food fight in the cafeteria, and he found a notice of a parent meeting this morning that had not been put on his schedule. He decided he better make a walk-through of the school to see what else may have happened. As he walked into the cafeteria, he was disappointed to see that one table had not been put away and that dirty coffee cups had been left in the area used by the faculty. "Well," he thought, "I guess I have to do everything myself," and he proceeded to return the cafeteria table to its proper folded-up position and wash the cups that had been left out.

He returned to his office at 7:15 and saw that his secretary, Rita Worth, and Mr. Johnson had just arrived and were chatting over a cup of coffee. Tom railed at them. "Do you two have nothing better to do than chit-chat and drink coffee? Mr. Johnson, you are responsible for this school when I am gone, and when I got here this morning I found that we had two major disruptions yesterday and the cafeteria was a mess! Don't you know that you have to ride our custodian or he leaves his job half-done? And, Ms. Worth, why was I not apprised earlier of a parent meeting this morning? I expect you to keep better track of my appointment calendar."

Sample Analysis

It is evident that Tom Clayton holds the assumptions of a Theory X leader. His actions and thoughts indicate that he believes people must be coerced and directed to do their jobs. Although Mr. Clayton's Theory X approach has resulted in establishing order, compliance appears to be the result of fear rather than leadership. Staff have not been involved in developing the school's philosophy or goals and there is no common vision shared by faculty and staff. Mr. Clayton is the sole person responsible for determining and directing the goals and mission of the school. Faculty appear to have little commitment to Mr. Clayton's notion of orderliness as evidenced by his observation that others don't take care of things appropriately unless he is there to oversee and supervise.

In terms of Mr. Clayton's leader behaviors, his concern is exclusively on task and he exhibits little, if any, regard for people. Blake and Mouton's two-dimensional managerial grid theory would suggest that his sole focus on task to the exclusion of people-oriented behavior would not lead to his desired outcomes. Blake and Mouton noted that the most effective leaders are those who exhibit both concern for people and concern for task.

It can be surmised that Mr. Clayton desires to be a change agent based on his comment that he wanted to "turn things around" at Jackson High School. Applying Burns' theory regarding the interactions of leaders and followers, Mr. Clayton's leadership holds little promise for change. To transform an organization, there must be an engagement between the leaders and the followers bound by some common purpose. There is no evidence that Mr. Clayton has involved teachers or other staff in the development of a vision for this school. Rather, the principal's behavior is akin to a "my way or the highway" approach to leadership. Although Mr. Clayton did establish his authority, he did so through the use of mandates, rules, regulations, and expectations. According to Sergiovanni, the principal's source of authority would be termed bureaucratic, suggesting that the consequences will be minimal compliance where teachers' performance falls within a narrow range of prescribed duties. A status quo will be maintained, but only through a sustained effort of close supervision and inspection. Mr. Clayton may be able to "keep the lid on" Jackson High School, but only if he maintains constant pressure. Little change can be expected, and order will be sustained at the expense of staff and student morale. It is likely that Mr. Clayton will continue to have a high turnover of staff. Those who do stay will lack any commitment to the organization, and, as Sergiovanni noted, teachers would behave as technicians, executing predetermined scripts in their classrooms.

Reader's Application

What's Happening at Eastbrook?

Dr. Michelle Adams was concerned about Eastbrook Elementary School, one of 16 elementary schools that she supervised as Assistant Superintendent of Region 4 in Cottonwood County School District. Cottonwood County was primarily rural, and its residents were mostly poor. Many families in Cottonwood County barely eked out a living on small subsistence farms. Others earned little more than minimum wage as part-time, hourly employees in small town restaurants or retail businesses. Some had maintained their jobs at the local glass factory, but this once-major employer had downsized and ran only one small shift of workers.

Dr. Adams was concerned about Eastbrook because of the high turnover in faculty for the past three years, since Margaret Lee had assumed the principalship. Margaret had been an elementary teacher and counselor in

Marshall City Schools, about 30 miles away from Eastbrook. Dr. Adams had hired Margaret and thought she would be a great elementary principal. And, in fact, she seemed to be. Whenever Dr. Adams visited her school, it appeared warm and inviting. Teachers seemed to be happy, and Margaret always conveyed her concern for staff and students. She seemed to genuinely care. In addition to an unusually high turnover of teachers at Eastbrook, Dr. Adams was concerned about the drop in student test scores. Although the drop was not great, there had been a continuous decline the last three years.

Dr. Adams had decided to investigate things a bit further and had learned that teachers who left Eastbrook, for the most part, had not left the county district but had requested transfers to other district elementary schools. Other schools in the district were demographically similar, so Dr. Adams did not think teachers were leaving for reasons related to its location or student population. The assistant superintendent decided to interview some of the teachers who had left Eastbrook, and most had nothing negative to say about Ms. Lee. Instead, teachers told her such things as, "Ms. Lee is a really nice person. It wasn't because of her that I left. I just wanted a new challenge," or "I just needed a change." A few, however, had been more revealing. One teacher stated, "Although I like Ms. Lee—she's very personable and caring—I just need to have more organization and direction." Another stated, "It was like the faculty just came into teach and socialize. No one wanted to discuss the kids, curriculum, or new ideas for the classroom. I wanted to be in a school that was concerned about academics."

Perhaps, Dr. Adams reflected, there is a problem with Margaret's leadership. She decided to review some of the required reports turned in by principals. She first checked on the annual school improvement plans Margaret had turned in and found that each year Margaret had filed her reports a week or 10 days after the due date. Dr. Adams had never been a stickler for deadlines but was more concerned about quality. Ms. Lee's school improvement plans had always seemed to be appropriate and right on the mark. However, maybe there was some pattern here. She noted that the last two reports had been amended after they were turned in, to adjust personnel and test score data.

Dr. Adams decided to call human resources to see what the director, Dr. Lester, had to say about the high turnover at Eastbrook. Dr. Lester's secretary, Jean, answered the phone. Jean informed Dr. Adams she would have to leave a message, as Dr. Lester was out of the office the rest of the day. Dr. Adams explained to Jean that she was calling regarding the openings at Eastbrook Elementary. Jean replied with a laugh. "Which ones?"

Dr. Adams had known Jean for many years and felt comfortable seeking a little more information, and asked, "What does that mean?"

Jean explained, "Oh, it's like this every year at Eastbrook. Ms. Lee never seems to know exactly what positions she has open from day to day, because she's always changing her mind or losing track of who she's moved where."

"You say it's always like this?" Dr. Adams inquired.

"Yes," Jean said, "and evidently it's not just personnel she's confused about. Laura, her secretary, is a friend of mine, and she tells me things are always in a state of confusion over there. It's driving Laura crazy, and, in fact, I think Laura has applied for a position at another school."

"Well, thanks for the information, Jean. Please ask Dr. Lester to call me tomorrow."

As Dr. Adams hung up the phone, she thought she was beginning to understand what was going on at Eastbrook.

Student Exercise: Case Analysis

1. What do the facts Dr. Adams has collected suggest about Margaret Lee's leadership?

2. What leadership theories presented in this chapter might be applied to assist Margaret Lee?

3. What are Dr. Adams' leadership roles and responsibilities regarding the school principals in her region?

References

Bass, B. M., & Avolio, B. J. (1994). *Improving organizational effectiveness through transformational leadership.* Thousand Oaks, CA: Sage.

Bennis, W. (1989). *On becoming a leader.* Reading, MA: Addison-Wesley.

Bennis, W. G., & Nanus, B. (1985). *Leaders: The strategies for taking charge.* New York: Harper and Row.

Blake, R. R., & Mouton, J. S. (1964). *The managerial grid: Key orientations for achieving production through people.* Houston, TX: Gulf.

Blake, R. R., & Mouton, J. S. (1982). *The managerial grid III.* Houston, TX: Gulf.

Burns, J. M. (1978). *Leadership.* New York: Harper and Row.

Deal, T. E., & Peterson, K. D. (1994). *The leadership paradox: Balancing logic and artistry in schools.* San Francisco: Jossey-Bass.

Foster, W. (1989). The administrator as a transformative intellectual. Peabody Journal of Education, 66(3), 5–18.

Foster, W. P. (2004). The decline of the local: A challenge to educational leadership. Educational Administration Quarterly, 40(2), 176–191.

French, J. R. P., & Raven, B. H. (1968). Bases of social power. In D. Carwright & A. Zander (Eds.), *Group dynamics, research and theory* (pp. 259–270). New York: Harper and Row.

Furman, G. C.,& Starratt, R. J. (2002). Leadership for democratic community schools. In J. Murphy (Ed.), *The educational leadership challenge: Redefining leadership for the 21st century*. Chicago: National Society for the Study of Education.

Gronn, P. (2002). Distributed leadership. In K. Leithwood & P. Hallinger (Eds.), *Second international handbook of educational leadership and administration*. Dordecht: Kluwer.

Halpin, A. W. (1966). *Theory and research in administration*. New York: Macmillan.

Halpin, A., & Winer, B. J. (1952). *The leadership behavior of the airplane commander*. Washington, DC: Human Resources Research Laboratories, Dept. of the Air Force.

Hanson, E. M. (1996). *Educational administration and organizational behavior* (4th ed.). Boston: Allyn and Bacon.

Hemphill, J. K., & Coons, A. (1950). *Leaders behavior description questionnaire*. Columbus, OH: Personnel Research Board, Ohio State University.

Larson, C. L., & Murtadha, K. (2002). Leadership for social justice. In J. Murphy (Ed.), *The educational leadership challenge: Redefining leadership for the 21st century*. Chicago: National Society for the Study of Education.

Leithwood, K. (1994). Leadership for school restructuring. *Educational Administration Quarterly, 30(4)*, 498–518.

Leithwood, K., Louis, K. S., Anderson, S., & Wahlstrom, K. (2004). *How leadership influences student learning*. (Learning from Leadership Project). Center for Applied Research and Educational Improvement, University of Minnesota, and Ontario Institute for Studies in Education, University of Toronto.

Lindle, J. C. (2004). William P. Foster's promises for educational leadership: Critical idealism in an applied field. *Educational Administration Quarterly, 40 (2)*, 167–175.

McGregor, D. (1960). *The human side of enterprise*. New York: McGraw Hill.

Mintzberg, H. (1979). *The structuring of organizations*. Englewood Cliffs, NJ: Prentice-Hall.

Murphy, J. (2002). Reculturing the profession of educational leadership: New blueprints. In J. Murphy (Ed.), *The educational leadership challenge: Redefining leadership for the 21st century*. Chicago: National Society for the Study of Education.

Schein, E. H. (1985). *Organizational culture and leadership*. San Francisco: Jossey-Bass.

Sergiovanni, T. J. (1991). *The principalship: A reflective practice perspective* (2nd ed.). Boston: Allyn and Bacon.

Sergiovanni, T. J. (1992). *Moral leadership: Getting to the heart of school improvement*. San Francisco: Jossey-Bass.

Spillane, J. P. (2005). Distributed leadership. *Educational Forum, 69*(2), 143–150.

Thompson, J. D. (1967). *Organizations in action: Social science bases of administrative theory*. New York: McGraw Hill.

Waters, T., Marzano, R. J., & McNulty, B. (2003). *Balanced leadership: What 30 years of research tells us about the effect of leadership on student achievement*. Denver, CO: Mid-continent Research for Education and Learning.

Yukl, G. (1994). *Leadership in organizations* (3rd ed.). Englewood Cliffs, NJ: Prentice Hall.

Yukl, G., & Lepsinger, R. (2004). *Flexible leadership: Creating value by balancing multiple challenges and choices*. San Francisco: Jossey-Bass.

6

Contingency Theory: Variables Affecting Organizations and Leadership

Synopsis of Contingency Theory

Contingency theory attempts to identify variables that impact the effectiveness of leadership. Approaches to contingency theory fall into one of two categories offering different perspectives from which to view variable conditions.

- Organizational perspective: Examines variables that impact the total system under various conditions.
- Leadership perspective: Analyzes variables that influence the effectiveness of leadership style.

Contingency theory, when approached from an organizational perspective, offers insight into how various factors in the internal and external environments impact the effectiveness of the organization. For the practitioner in school leadership, it points out the importance of planning for diverse situations and provides an understanding of how a school's organizational structure supports or hinders the organizational responses under varying conditions.

Contingency theory applied to leadership explores the relationship of a leader's style to the effectiveness of the organization. Although not definitive, this approach to contingency theory is useful to consider the connections among staff attitudes and personalities, a leader's relationship with staff, and the nature of the tasks in which staff are engaged. It points out that there is not one ideal style of leadership, and that the effectiveness of a leader's style will depend on the situation.

Applications for School Leaders

Understanding contingency theory will help school leaders

◆ Identify outside variables that impact a school

◆ Match leadership style with the needs of the school

◆ Consider the relationships among teachers' personalities and attitudes, work-related tasks, and leadership style

◆ Understand the importance of short- and long-term contingency planning

◆ Appraise the impact of a school's organizational structure on responses to external pressures and demands

---

The Uncertainty Factor: Contingency Theory Applied to Organizations

Contingency theory, when approached from an organizational perspective, is related to the concept of open systems and the notion of loose coupling.

Open system theory explains the relationships and exchanges between the organization and the external environment. Loose coupling refers to the connections among various units within the organization and describes units as interdependent, but at the same time each has its own identity, functions, and separateness. Contingency theory examines the internal adjustments of the organization as it responds to events in both the external and internal environments (Hanson, 1979).

Open Systems

Open system theory emanates from the analogy of organizations as organisms. Thompson (1967/1996), in writing about open systems, referred to organizations in Darwinian terms:

The complex organization is a set of interdependent parts which together make up a whole, which in turn is interdependent with some larger environment. Survival of the system is taken to be the goal, and the parts and their relationships presumably are determined through evolutionary processes. Dysfunctions are conceivable, but it is assumed that an offending part will adjust to produce a net positive contribution or be disengaged, or else the system will degenerate (p. 289).

Contingency theory expands on the notion of natural systems by focusing on the adaptation of organizations to their internal and external environments. **Tom Burns** and **George Stalker** (1961/1996) explained organizational adaptations to environment by their classification of organizations into two opposing categories: (a) mechanistic systems and (b) organic systems. **Mechanistic systems** were found to be appropriate to stable conditions and were characterized as having units with specialized functions, a hierarchic structure of control, authority, and communication with a tendency toward vertical communication, and a defined set of rules and regulations. **Organic systems** were found to be appropriate to changing conditions and were characterized by a collaborative approach to tasks, adjustments to individual responsibilities, a "community of interest" in the survival and growth of the organization, and lateral rather than vertical communication aimed at problem solving instead of directives. Burns and Stalker emphasized that these two systems were polar extremes and that organizations oscillated between the two forms depending on external elements of stability or change.

As Burns and Stalker pointed out, organizations respond and adapt to changes in environmental conditions. Katz and Kahn (1978) identified five major forces in the external environment that act as contingencies impacting an organization: (a) cultural, (b) political, (c) economic, (d) informational and technical, and (e) physical. They further described these forces as varying according to:

- The degree of stability or turbulence in the environment
- The degree of diversity or homogeneity in the environment
- The degree of structure or randomness in the environment
- The degree of scarcity or abundance of resources in the environment

Brian Rowan and associates conducted numerous studies over a 15-year period in an attempt to test the robustness of contingency theory in school settings. Results have been mixed and inconclusive. Studies on effects of organic systems on student achievement have generally showed small, positive effects or no effect (e.g., Miller & Rowan, 2006; Rowan, Chiang, & Miller, 1997; Rowan, Raudenbush, & Cheong, 1993; Rowan, Raudenbush, & Kang, 1991).

Loose versus Tight

An organization's ability to respond to external conditions is contingent on the organization's internal structure. **Karl Weick** (1982) characterized organizational structure along a continuum from loosely coupled to tightly coupled systems. Contrasting loosely and tightly coupled systems, Weick (1982) identified four characteristics of tightly coupled organizations as (a) the existence of rules, (b) agreement on the rules, (c) system of inspection for compliance, and (d) feedback to improve compliance. In more loosely coupled systems, one or more of these characteristics are missing. Weick proposed that schools are loosely coupled systems.

Loosely coupled systems contain units that are interdependent, yet are weakly connected. An advantage of the loosely coupled system is that departmental units can quickly adapt to environmental changes. Furthermore, problems in one unit are sealed off from affecting other parts of the organization. A disadvantage is that if a problem escalates, it is likely not to be communicated to other parts of the organization before a crisis occurs. Additionally, large changes are difficult to manage and sustain in loosely coupled systems.

E. Mark Hanson (1979) applied the notion of loose coupling to schools in terms of contingency theory. He identified five subsystems of the overall school system as (a) leadership, (b) students, (c) teaching, (d) guidance, and (e) maintenance. Each of these subsystems involves interactions among tasks, structure, technology, and people. He identified technical, cultural, political, and economic forces and institutions as impacting the total school system. Hanson indicated that educational institutions often "place tight constraints on the various subsystems by applying standard operating procedures" that result in responses that "ignore turbulent issues" (p. 108). He further recommended that schools practice **contingency planning** by identifying major contingencies and preparing various alternative strategies. Hanson (1996) suggested that, ideally, "as some aspect of the environment becomes turbulent...the appropriate subsystem is in place and can emerge to treat the issue. Thus, time and energy from the entire organization do not have to be diverted." (p. 140).

Hanson noted that variances in environmental needs and demands require varied organizational responses. In other words, organizational responses are dependent on the situation; programmed, standard operating procedures are not always effective in solving problems when the outside environment is changing or turbulent. In addition, Hanson suggested that the concepts of force, target, and source be considered when diagnosing environmental demands. **Force** relates to the intensity of the turbulence confronting the school. For example, are student behavioral problems isolated instances of fighting or have there been threats of violence and killing on campus? **Target** denotes the part of the school system that is affected by the turbulence. In this case, are behavioral problems occurring in classrooms or at athletic events? The **source** of the turbulence will also impact a school's response. For instance, are behavioral problems isolated incidents of individual students or the result of gang activity?

In planning for contingencies, Hanson suggested that schools use forecasting to identify constraints and opportunities in the external environment and apply long- and short-term planning as either proactive or reactive responses to the issues. Forecasting and subsequent planning may involve the consideration of several possible scenarios. Planning for contingencies allows a school to carefully consider the impact of external conditions on the system as a whole and identify the appropriate department or unit to respond. Additionally, contingency planning focuses attention on the interactions among the various departments within the school organization.

Contingency Theory Applied to Leadership

Fiedler's Leadership Contingency Theory

The foremost contingency theory of leadership was developed by **Fred Fiedler.** Fiedler's (1967, 1974) contingency model of leadership proposed that the effectiveness of an organization depends on two main factors: (1) the personality of the leader and (2) the degree of stability or uncertainty in the situation.

Fiedler defined two basic leader personalities as (a) relationship motivated and (b) task motivated. Leadership personalities are measured by the **least preferred coworker** (LPC) score, which is obtained by asking an individual to describe a person with whom the leader has been able to work least well. The LPC instrument asks leaders to rate their least preferred coworker on several items using an eight-point scale such as the following:

Friendly   8   7   6   5   4   3   2   1   Unfriendly

Persons scoring high on the LPC are considered relationship motivated, because they tend to see their least preferred coworker in positive terms. Low LPC scores indicate task-motivated leaders (Fiedler, Chemers, & Mahar, 1977).

In addition to categorizing leadership, Fiedler classified organizations based on how favorable the organizational situation is for the leader. Fiedler divided situational favorableness into eight categories that indicated the degree to which the situation gives the leader control and the ability to predict consequences of his or her actions. Three factors are used to define the situation: (a) leader–member relations, (b) task structures, and (c) position power. **Leader–member relations** refers to the support and acceptance of the leader by the work group. **Task structure** is the extent to which the group's task is clearly defined as to goals, procedures, and measures of success. **Position power** relates to the leader's authority to obtain compliance of the group through rewards and punishments. Fiedler defined Octant 1 as being the most favorable situation for the leader where leader–member relations are good, task is structured, and position power is strong. Octant 8 is considered the most unfavorable situation for the leader with poor leader–member relations, an unstructured task, and weak position power. Figure 6.1 summarizes Fiedler's definitions of the eight situation categories.

Figure 6.1. Fiedler's Categories of Situational Favorableness

		Leader–Member Relations	Task Structure	Position Power
Most Favorable	Octant 1	Good	Structured	Strong
	Octant 2	Good	Structured	Weak
	Octant 3	Good	Unstructured	Strong
	Octant 4	Good	Unstructured	Weak
	Octant 5	Poor	Structured	Strong
	Octant 6	Poor	Structured	Weak
	Octant 7	Poor	Unstructured	Strong
Least Favorable	Octant 8	Poor	Unstructured	Weak

Fiedler's studies of a variety of groups and leaders between 1951 and 1963 included military organizations, sales teams, factories, athletic teams, churches, and mental health organizations. His contingency theory was the outgrowth of these studies in which correlations between leader personality and situation were observed to be either effective or not effective in terms of a group's successful performance of the task. The resulting contingency model found that task-motivated leaders generally perform best in most favorable situations or least favorable situations. Relationship-motivated leaders were found to be more effective in moderately favorable and moderately unfavorable situations.

Fiedler later extended his contingency model of leadership in his formulation of cognitive resource theory. This theory set forth an explanation of how intelligence, stress, and experience are related to contingency theory. Fiedler suggested that intelligence contributes to successful performance only when the leader directs the group, the group is supportive, the environment is relatively stress-free, and the task requires intellectual effort (Fiedler, 1986). When stress is high, experience rather than intelligence is a more significant factor leading to successful performance.

Fiedler suggested that the contingency model of leadership has implications in three areas: (a) training, (b) selection, and (c) rotation of leadership. Fiedler argued that training would not affect a leader's basic personality or leadership style. Instead, training serves to increase a leader's expertise in how to handle various situations; thus, the effect of training is to increase the favorableness of the situation by teaching the leader how to structure tasks or gain support and compliance of employees. Following Fiedler's reasoning, leaders who are relationship-motivated will perform less well after gaining experience or training, and task-motivated leaders will perform better, because the situation has changed.

Furthermore, Fiedler proposed that his model would be most appropriately used in decisions concerning the selection and rotation of leaders. In other words, relationship-oriented leaders should be placed in moderately favorable situations whereas task-oriented leaders would be better placed in situations that are either extremely unfavorable or highly favorable. As conditions change, leaders should be rotated.

This might suggest that school districts rotate principals and other administrative personnel after some period of time in one school or department. In fact, many school systems do just that. However, Fiedler's contingency model must be examined more closely before considering its application to school settings. A highly unfavorable situation would be one in which leader–member relations are poor, task structure is low, and leader position power is weak. A school meeting these criteria could be characterized as one where teachers are unsupportive of the principal, where there is an unclear mission and direction for school curriculum or discipline, and where the principal has been unable to exercise position power to gain teacher compliance. In this case, a district might want to consider placing an experienced, task-motivated principal in this school "to gain control" and to establish some level of structure and order regarding curriculum or student behavior. The task-oriented principal may have success in moving this school to a moderately favorable situation, especially in terms of position power and task structure. However, at the point a school reaches a more favorable situation, the school may be better served by a relationship-oriented leader, according to Fiedler's contingency theory.

Even under the most unfavorable conditions, such as those in the school described above, the district may need to consider additional factors before deciding on the most appropriate leadership style. Fiedler's model does not account for factors in the outside environment that may be impacting the situation in the school. Considering schools in terms of loosely coupled systems, it is important that the external environment be examined. Under conditions of turbulence, diversity, or uncertain environmental forces, school leadership will be most effective using a collaborative approach, developing a feeling of community among teachers and other stakeholders, and emphasizing problem solving rather than directive, top-down conditions in which a relationship-oriented leader would be most effective. Thus, in the example of the unfavorable situation in the school described here, a task-oriented leadership style would probably have a better chance of succeeding if the outside environment were stable.

Path-Goal Theory

Another contingency theory of leadership is known as path-goal theory. This theory attempts to explain the effects of four kinds of leader behavior on subordinates' attitudes and expectations. Path-goal theory suggests that the relationship between leadership style and subordinate outcomes is contingent on subordinate and environmental characteristics.

The path-goal theory, as advanced by House (1971) and others (Evans, 1970; House & Dessler, 1974; House & Mitchell, 1974), differs from Fiedler 's contingency model in that path-goal theory postulates that individual leadership styles vary as situations within an organization change. Path-goal theory also differs from Fiedler's theory in its definition of leadership effectiveness, which path-goal theory defines as subordinates' job satisfaction, acceptance of the leader, and motivation. The path-goal theory has its roots in the motivational theory called expectancy theory (see Chapter 7). House and Mitchell (1974) stated that one function of a leader is to increase payoffs to subordinates for work-goal attainment by clarifying the path, reducing roadblocks, and increasing opportunities for personal satisfaction.

Path-goal theory identifies two categories of contingency factors. These are (a) **personal characteristics of subordinates** and (b) **environmental pressures and demands**. Regarding personal characteristics, path-goal theory contends that subordinate characteristics will partially determine their perception of satisfaction. Subordinate characteristics are determined through measures of three contingent variables:

- **Authoritarianism:** Subordinates' attitude toward directive and nondirective leadership styles
- **Locus-of-control:** The extent to which people believe they are in control of their environment (internal locus of control) or that events control them (external locus of control)
- **Ability:** Subordinates' perception of their ability to accomplish a given task

Environmental contingencies include:

- **Subordinates' tasks:** Level of complexity and ambiguity in task
- **Formal authority system of the organization:** Degree to which the system supports or inhibits the work behavior
- **Primary work group:** The degree of clarity and support of work-group norms

The path-goal theory identifies four types of leadership styles and offers explanations for when each leadership style is most effective.

- **Directive leadership:** In general, a directive leadership style is preferred when the task is ambiguous or when organizational policies are not clear. However, even when tasks are routine, a directive leadership style is preferred by subordinates who are closed-minded and dogmatic as measured by authoritarian scales.
- **Supportive leadership:** This style of leadership is characterized by friendly relationships, showing concern and trust for subordinates. This type of leadership style was preferred when tasks are stressful or dissatisfying.
- **Achievement-oriented leadership:** The leader using this style sets challenging goals, emphasizes excellence, and demonstrates confidence in subordinates. According to path-goal theory, workers performing ambiguous, nonrepetitive tasks prefer this leadership style.
- **Participative leadership:** Path-goal theory offers some tentative insights into subordinates' preference for involvement in decisions about the task. In general, participative leadership is preferred when the task is ambiguous and workers are highly ego-involved in the task, regardless of personality characteristics. However, when subordinates are not ego-involved in their tasks and when tasks are clear, personality characteristics make a difference.

Subordinates who have an internal locus of control and are not authoritarian still prefer a participative leadership style.

Path-goal theory's main contribution to the study of leadership is its use as conceptual framework for examining various contingencies that may impact leader effectiveness. However, as Yukl (1994) pointed out, the theory has "serious conceptual deficiencies that limit its utility," (p. 289), and he further noted that the theory has not been adequately substantiated through research. Key criticisms of the path-goal theory include its global categories of leadership that are not behavior-specific and that interactions among various leadership behaviors are not considered.

Situational Leadership

Another approach to contingency theory is the **situational leadership** model developed by **Paul Hersey** and **Ken Blanchard.** Based on the two-dimensional models of leadership that identified task and relationship as two primary concerns of leadership, Hersey and Blanchard added a third dimension related to the readiness level of followers.

Hersey, Blanchard, and Johnson (2001) defined **task behavior** as "the extent to which the leader engages in spelling out the duties and responsibilities of an individual or group" (p. 173). They further indicated that "task behavior is characterized by one way communication from the leader to the follower" (p. 173). **Relationship behavior** refers to leader behavior that involves interpersonal interactions with followers such as supporting and facilitating. In addition, relationship behavior is characterized by two-way communication. The two dimensions of task and relationship are formulated into a four-quadrant model with task displayed from low to high on a horizontal axis and relationship from low to high on a vertical axis.

The four quadrants represent four leadership styles identified as telling, selling, participating, and delegating. Each leadership style denotes the degree of interaction between relationship and task. Quadrant One, **telling,** denotes a style of leadership that has a high focus on task completion and a low concern for interpersonal relationships. Quadrant Two, **selling,** indicates a leadership style that has both a high concern for task completion and a high level of social-emotional support (relationship). Quadrant Three denotes **participatory leadership** behavior where there is a great emphasis on relationship and little emphasis on task completion. Quadrant Four is termed a **delegating** leadership style, which indicates a low need for emotional-social support, or relationship building, and little emphasis on guiding and directing (task behavior).

The third dimension of the situational leadership model is the **readiness level of followers**. In the case of schools, followers would be teachers, support staff, or students. Readiness refers to the extent to which a follower is willing and able to successfully accomplish a specific organizational task. **Ability** is defined as "the knowledge, experience, and skill that an individual or group brings to a particular task or activity" (p. 176). They further define **willingness** as "the extent to which an individual or group has the confidence, commitment, and motivation to accomplish a specific task" (p. 176). Thus, ability is whether one can complete the task; willingness is whether one has the desire to do so.

Four readiness levels are identified. Each of the four levels reflects a combination of some degree of willingness and ability. Each readiness level corresponds to one of the four quadrants of task and relationship, thus indicating the most appropriate leadership style to employ with a particular individual in a specific situation. Figure 6.3 summarizes the best match of leadership behavior with a follower's readiness level.

Figure 6.3. Hersey and Blanchard's Situational Leadership Model: Most Effective Leadership Behavior Based on Readiness Level of Follower

Leadership Behavior	Follower's Readiness Level
Telling	R1 (Low ability, Low willingness)
Selling	R2 (Low ability, High willingness)
Participating	R3 (High ability, Low willingness)
Delegating	R4 (High ability, High willingness)

Individuals who have low ability and low willingness to complete a specific organizational task are considered to be at the lowest readiness level, identified as R1. These individuals are not competent or confident, and unwillingness is often associated with their insecurity to accomplish the necessary task. The most effective leadership behavior in this situation is telling. This would involve a directive leadership style where clear, specific directions are given, and relationship building is deemphasized.

Persons at the R2 level are willing but unable to accomplish a specific task because of a lack of skill development at this particular time. A selling style of leadership is the best match for this situation. Selling involves directing and guiding the task while also reinforcing teachers' behavior through two-way communication and a high level of social-emotional support for their efforts.

Teachers who are able but unwilling fall into the R3 category. Their unwillingness may be related to a lack of self-confidence or to a motivational problem. A participatory style of leadership is most effective for this situation. This is characterized by a supportive, nondirective style in which the principal and teacher would share in the decision making. The principal is more concerned with relationship building than with task completion.

Finally, individuals who are both able and willing are classified at the R4 level. For these persons and these situations, delegating is the most appropriate leadership behavior. Teachers at this level of readiness require little direction or social-emotional support to accomplish a given task.

Application to School Leadership

The major contribution of contingency theories in educational settings is the identification of a variety of factors that interact with leadership style and the resulting effectiveness of the leader. Conditions related to task, teacher attitudes, and external factors must all be considered when determining the most appropriate leadership style for a particular situation. From a leadership perspective, Fiedler's contingency model and House's path-goal theory offer some insight into variables that impact leader effectiveness. In supervising teachers, school leaders should consider the structure of the task and teachers' attitudes. The business of teaching, in general terms, is an ambiguous task. Although schools may have clearly defined procedures and curriculum, the daily decisions connected to teaching are not clearly defined. Contingency theory suggests that under most circumstances, unless a school situation is extremely favorable or unfavorable, a relationship-oriented leadership style would be more effective than a task-oriented approach. Path-goal theory would tend to support this leadership approach, in terms less clearly defined as achievement oriented and participatory leadership styles. Path-goal theory's reference to effectiveness, of course, is in terms of employee satisfaction rather than task completion.

Fiedler's contingency theory and House's path-goal theory are most markedly aligned regarding conditions under which task-oriented or directive leadership is desired. Both models suggest that this type of leadership is desirable when organizational policies are unclear, and tasks are ambiguous. A directive, task-oriented style may be most appropriate, in terms of both organizational performance and teacher satisfaction, in schools that lack clear direction and strong leadership personalities.

From an organizational viewpoint, contingency theory is important for creating an organizational structure that is effective in responding to a variety of external environmental factors. Considering schools as loosely coupled systems, school leaders and policy makers should ensure that procedures and rules allow individual departments some level of autonomy in responding to particular situations. Because of the semi-autonomous nature of various subsystems in a school, principals must be alert to all departmental functions and decision making and be proactive in facilitating communication across departments. School leaders who apply contingency theory from an organizational perspective will actively plan for various contingencies and changing environmental conditions and will put into place response systems that will cause the least amount of disruption or disequilibrium to the entire school. For example, parental complaints about the reading selections in the English department can best be handled at the departmental level and will minimize impact and effusion into other curricular areas. This approach is poignantly encapsulated in the Nordstrom Department Store policy, which states: "We have only one rule: Use good judgment in all situations." The purpose of Nordstrom's single-rule policy is that all employees are empowered to make decisions without having to check with management first, thus providing a proactive and immediate response structure in their organization.

Summary

Contingency theory provides a basis for considering many variables related to leadership in the complex organizational systems of schools. This chapter has reviewed two applications of contingency theory: one from an organizational or systems perspective and the other from a leadership perspective. From an organizational perspective, contingency theory examines forces or variables that impact the effectiveness of various organizational structures. Contingency theory expands on the concept of schools as open social systems and explores the interrelationships among external forces and internal subsystems. Schools, as organizations, are loosely coupled systems, meaning their organizational structure is one of interdependent units that are weakly connected. Because schools are open systems, contingency theory suggests that schools should expect environmental changes to impact the school and should have in place various contingency plans for external conditions that may cause turbulence in the school.

Contingency theory as applied to leadership recognizes various factors that interact with a leader's style and contribute to a leader's effectiveness. Fiedler's contingency theory of leadership identified personality and attitudes of subordinates, task structure, and the leader's position power as variables influencing a leader's effectiveness. Path-goal theory further explored the concept of variables affecting leadership and identified personal characteristics of subordinates and environmental pressures and demands as two categories of contingency factors. Contingency theory offers some tentative explanations for why a particular leadership style is more effective in one situation than another. It explains that there is not one most effective or preferred leadership style, but rather that the effectiveness of leadership style is contingent on a number of other factors. Thus, the choice of leadership style, or leader, depends on the situation and organizational conditions.

Theory into Practice

A New Principal for Washington Middle School

James Anderson shook hands with Ronald Taylor, wished him the best, and quickly left the retirement party. As superintendent, James Anderson had mixed feelings about Ronald's retirement. Ronald Taylor was a good man, was truly concerned about students, and had been a good administrator in the past. But, frankly, the superintendent was relieved that Ronald had decided to retire this year. Ronald had served as principal of Washington Middle School for the last 15 years and had been a good leader for the school—that is until the last few years. Washington Middle School no longer served children from stable, middle-class homes that it had 10 years ago. Over the last decade, neighborhoods surrounding Washington had been transitioning to a more transient population as older, childless couples and upwardly mobile families moved to outlying sections of the city. Washington's student population now included approximately 40 percent Hispanic students, many of whom spoke limited or no English; 10 percent African Americans; 10 percent Asians (a mix of immigrants from Vietnam, Korea, India, and other countries); and 40 percent white students. Washington Middle School also experienced a high student transience rate, because families facing employment or other financial difficulties would often relocate to be closer to jobs or to find more affordable rent in other parts of the city. In fact, the entire district was facing economic challenges related to declining enrollment. The district, which served primarily the central metropolitan area, was losing population and businesses because new businesses were opening in suburban areas and many of the old, established firms were relocating outside of the city. This resulted in less state aid to the district and less financial subsidies from other sources, such as business partnerships, donations, and parental support for fundraising.

As Washington's population changed, Ronald's leadership had become less effective. Test scores had been declining, and teacher turnover had been high, especially in the last two years. Many teachers who had left Washington were experienced veterans and had complained that they felt ineffective in teaching the students who now came to their classrooms. They were frustrated with teaching students with limited English skills and whose parents often were not available to lend support to teachers' efforts. The teachers who were coming to Washington tended to be young and inexperienced, and many were first-year teachers. Unfortunately, they weren't staying either.

When the superintendent had met with Ronald about high teacher turnover and falling test scores, the long-time principal had replied that the factors were out of the school's control. He insisted that teachers just couldn't make a difference in these kids' lives: There were too many problems at home and in the community. Ronald pointed out to Mr. Anderson, "Look, James, it's not what we're doing—it's the community and homes these kids come from. We're not doing anything different than we did 10 or 15 years ago. The rules are the same, and our expectations for learning aren't any lower. What is different is the parents. If they don't care about getting their children to school and making sure they do their homework, there's not much we can do. We can lead a horse to water, but we can't make him drink." Then he added, "Teachers who leave are often not willing to comply with established procedures. They want to lower standards and give in to the kids. Frankly, I would just as soon they leave and go elsewhere."

As James Anderson recalled this conversation on the way back to his office, he thought to himself: "Yes, Ronald, there was the problem. You hadn't done anything different for 15 years!" Now with his retirement, the superintendent would have a chance to bring in new leadership. He was going to review those applications right now, but he had to give some serious thought to the type of leader Washington Middle School needed.

Sample Analysis

In seeking a new principal for Washington Middle School, the superintendent should look at a number of factors, both within the school and in the external environment. Using Fiedler's contingency theory of leadership, the superintendent might want to evaluate the favorableness of the situation at Washington Middle School, specifically regarding leader–member relations, task structure, and position power. The outgoing principal, Ronald Taylor, had been experiencing poor leader–member relations and weak positional power as evidenced by the high teacher turnover rate. Mr. Taylor's remarks to the superintendent regarding the operation of his school would suggest a structured task system in that the principal had continued to use a defined set of principles regarding curricular and behavioral expectations. His remarks to the superintendent also indicate that the principal's style of leadership is task-motivated. His comments about teachers who left signal that he does not view complaining teachers in favorable terms, stating he would just as soon see them go elsewhere. Given the situation, Mr. Taylor's task-motivated approach to leadership is not appropriate for achieving high teacher performance. Fiedler's contingency theory would categorize Washington Middle

School as moderately unfavorable; thus, a relationship-motivated leadership style would be more effective.

Factors in the external environment are also important in this case. The community that Washington Middle School serves is no longer stable. Washington's attendance zone is one where demographics are changing, the population is transient, and economic conditions are uncertain. From an organizational perspective, the new principal should be one who will be willing to adjust the procedures and policies that are currently in place and encourage collaboration, develop a sense of community, and emphasize lateral communication aimed at problem solving. Such an approach would serve to move the current, mechanistic system at Washington Middle School toward a more organic system, which according to contingency theory is more appropriate when conditions are changing or turbulent. In addition, the new principal should be someone who is prepared to empower teachers and other school employees to respond to needs and demands of the changing community. As Hanson suggested, loosely coupled systems such as schools should not constrain teachers through the ubiquitous use of standard operating procedures. Further, Hanson's application of contingency theory to schools suggests that the new principal should be one who uses forecasting tools to develop short- and long-term plans to respond to various possible futures that Washington Middle School may face.

Reader's Application

Changing of the Guard

It is July 1 and Carla Martinez's first day as principal of Washington Middle School. After Carla was hired in May, the superintendent, James Anderson, had shared with her his reasons for hiring her. He told her that her participative leadership orientation and her ideas for faculty collaboration were two of the qualities that he felt were needed at Washington Middle School. In addition, he had been impressed with her previous administrative experience, especially in terms of establishing goals and short- and long-term planning. Mr. Anderson had then gone into some detail about the changing nature of Washington Middle School and the economic and political issues facing the district. He explained to her his ideas about changing policies and procedures at Washington Middle School to be more responsive to issues that the school would have to deal with now and in the next few years. He had asked Ms. Martinez to develop an outline for what he termed contingency planning. Specifically, he wanted her to identify constraints and opportunities in the school's external environment, which were currently impacting the school or could impact the school in the future. Furthermore, he asked her to develop a plan for how the school could most effectively and efficiently prepare for or respond to these conditions with the least amount of disruption to the teaching-learning process.

Student Exercise: Case Analysis

1. Using contingency theory from an organizational or systems perspective, what external forces should Ms. Martinez consider?

2. If you were Ms. Martinez, what procedures and policies would you propose to maximize the effectiveness of interactions among internal subsystems and to minimize disruption to the total school system? Support your proposal on the basis of contingency theory and the concept of loosely coupled systems.

3. As Ms. Martinez begins her tenure as principal of Washington Middle School, what personal and environmental contingencies should she attend to in terms of her own leadership style?

References

Burns, T., & Stalker, G. M. (1996). Mechanistic and organic systems. Reprinted in J. M. Shafritz & J. S. Ott (Eds.), *Classics of organizational theory* (4th ed., pp. 209–213). Fort Worth: Harcourt Brace College Publishers. (Original work published 1961)

Evans, M. G. (1970). The effects of supervisory behavior on the path-goal relationship. *Organizational Behavior and Human Performance, 5,* 277–298.

Fiedler, F. E. (1967). A theory of leadership effectiveness. New York: McGraw-Hill

Fiedler, F. E. (1974). The contingency model: New directions for leadership utilization. Journal of Contemporary Business, 3(4), 65–79.

Fiedler, F. E. (1986). The contribution of cognitive resources and leader behavior to organizational performance. Journal of Applied Social Psychology, 16, 544.

Fiedler, F. E., Chemers, M. M., & Mahar, L. (1977). Improving leadership effectiveness: The leader match concept. New York: Wiley.

Hanson, E. M. (1979). School management and contingency theory: An emerging perspective. *Educational Administration Quarterly, 15*(2), 98–116.

Hanson, E. M. (1996). *Educational administration and organizational behavior* (4th ed.). Boston: Allyn & Bacon.

Hersey, P., Blanchard, K., & Johnson, D. E. (2001). *Management of organizational behavior: Leading human resources,* 8th Ed. Upper Saddle River, NJ: Prentice-Hall.

House, R. J. (1971). A path goal theory of leader effectiveness. *Administrative Science Quarterly, 16(3)*, 321–338.

House, R. J., & Dessler, G. (1974). The path-goal theory of leadership: Some post-hoc and a priori tests. In J. G. Hunt & L. L. Larson (Eds.), *Contingency approaches to leadership* (pp. 29–62). Carbondale, IL: Southern Illinois University Press.

House, R. J., & Mitchell, T. R. (1974). Path-goal theory of leadership. *Journal of Contemporary Business, 3(4)*, 81–97.

Katz, D., & Kahn, R. L. (1978). *The social psychology of organizations.* New York: Wiley.

Miller, R. J., & Rowan, B. (2006). Effects of organic management on student achievement. *American Educational Research Journal, 43(2)*, 219–253.

Rowan, B., Chiang, F.S., & Miller, R. J. (1997). Using research on employees' performance to study the effects of teachers on students' achievement. *Sociology of Education, 70*, 256–284.

Rowan, B., Raudenbush, S. W., & Cheong, Y. F. (1993). Teaching as a non-routine task: Implications for the management of schools. *Educational Administration Quarterly, 29*, 479–500.

Rowan, B., Raudenbush, S., & Kang, S.J. (1991). Organizational design in high schools: A multilevel analysis. *American Journal of Education, 99*, 238–266.

Thompson, J. D. (1996). Organizations in action. Reprinted in J. M. Shafritz & J. S. Ott (Eds.), *Classics of organizational theory* (4th ed., pp. 287–301). Fort Worth: Harcourt Brace College Publishers. (Original work published 1967)

Weick, K. E. (1982). Administering education in loosely coupled schools. *Phi Delta Kappan, 63(10)*, 673–676.

Woodward, J. (1965). *Industrial organization: Theory and practice.* London: Oxford University Press.

Yukl, G. A. (1994). *Leadership in organizations* (3rd ed.). Englewood Cliffs, NJ: Prentice Hall.

7

Motivation: The Human Dynamics of Leadership

Synopsis of Motivation Theories

The essence of leadership is motivating others to follow and achieve. Motivation theories help leaders understand why people behave and provide a framework for thoughtful reflection about one's own motivation, behaviors, leadership style, and values. Although there is not one single, definitive theory of motivation, there are common principles that emerge.

The preponderance of theories explain that motivation is a process that emanates from within the individual and generally explain behavior as the result of an individual's perceptions and interactions with their environment. Many theories examine basic human needs and the role these needs play in motivation.

For the practitioner, motivation theories call attention to the importance of environmental factors in schools and how leaders' behaviors influence teachers' and students' behaviors. Motivation theories are most useful when organizational philosophy and leadership style support and value open communication, feedback, and individual perspectives.

Individual and Group Perspectives: A Framework for Understanding Motivation Theories

Motivation Defined

Motivation theories explain why people behave as they do. Motivation is the reason or cause that produces some effect. Explanations of motivation, or human behavior, are rooted in the fundamental works of psychology and sociology. These two domains, while related, offer different perspectives about motivation. The psychological perspective is concerned primarily with an individual's behavior. Sociological studies, conversely, focus on understanding group behavior and the interaction of individuals in a group setting. Both perspectives are important for the school administrator who is concerned with leading and guiding individual teachers, and ultimately entire staffs toward effectiveness in educating students.

Individual Motivation

Psychological studies of human behavior can be classified into two distinct and opposing explanations of motivation. One is that people behave based on external stimuli. The other perspective explains human behavior in terms of internal conditions or processes within the individual. These two opposing perspectives are most easily understood by examining how the term "motivation" is used in each explanation.

Theories that explain human behavior as a result of external stimuli use motivation as something done to someone else, which causes that person to behave in a particular way. Those who believe that motivation is external would ask, "What can I do to motivate a person to work hard?" Conversely, those who believe that motivation comes from internal drives or needs would seek to understand motivation from the individual's viewpoint. They would ask, "What is the motivation that will cause a person to work hard?" Although the two questions may sound similar, the first question assumes that the leader can directly manipulate some external force, which will cause the person to work hard. The second question makes no such assumption. It seeks to find the cause of behavior that is a function internal to the individual and takes the perspective that there may be different reasons for different individuals to work hard. Those who believe that motivation to behave is an internal process do not assume they can directly cause a person to behave in a particular way. Instead, they attempt to understand what motivates an individual to work hard and then create conditions in the work place that the individual perceives as motivating an internal drive or desire.

External Motivation Theories

Perhaps the most influential psychological theory to explain human behavior in terms of external forces comes from the work of behaviorists such as Ivan Pavlov and B. F. Skinner. Pavlov's studies on classical conditioning and Skinner's experiments in operant conditioning were conducted to explain how humans learn. **Classical conditioning** theory explains human behavior as a response to external stimuli. Pavlov viewed stimuli and responses as either unconditioned or conditioned. Unconditioned responses were those that were automatic, or unlearned. Conditioned responses were those that were learned by introducing a neutral stimuli to an event that was considered unconditioned. Eventually, the neutral stimuli would elicit a conditioned response. In Pavlov's famous experiments with dogs, he taught dogs to salivate at the sound of a bell, because the dogs had learned to associate the bell with food. Before conditioning, a dog would salivate only when food appeared. During conditioning, every time the bell would ring, food was given and the dog would salivate. Eventually, the dog would salivate when he heard the bell (Papalia, Olds, & Feldman, 1989).

Skinner (1938) built on Pavlov's work by adding the concepts of reinforcement and punishment to shape behavior. Reinforcements are stimuli that are given for desirable behavior; punishments are negative stimuli given when behavior is undesirable. Pavlov's and Skinner's experiments and studies, which were conducted in the late nineteenth century and early twentieth century, led to stimulus-response theory to explain human behavior. Their works, in many ways, served to reinforce some of the earliest notions of explaining behavior, which date back to the early Greek philosophy of hedonism. Hedonism explained human behavior as directed toward comfort and pleasure and away from discomfort and pain.

Other early twentieth century explanations of human behavior involved the notion of instincts as the primary impetus for human behavior. Darwin theorized that much of animal and human behavior was determined by instinct. Freud's work, which laid the foundation for modern psychology, contributed to the instinct theories of human behavior by introducing the notion of unconscious motivation. Instinct theory dominated psychological studies during the early twentieth century, but, as Lawler (1973) noted, when the list of instincts totaled nearly 6,000 by the 1920s, this theory of human behavior began to be questioned. Russell (1971) pointed out that instinct theory had a great impact on the development of stimulus-response psychology and on the operation of schools. Behaviors viewed as favorable were believed to be rooted in positive instincts or learned behavior, and problematic behaviors were believed to be rooted in negative instincts. Thus, the notion of punishment was viewed as the necessary tool to prevent undesirable behavior. Russell (1971) further observed that "this focus has been extremely resistant to change…" (p. 9).

Internal Motivation Theories

The concept of internal **drives** and **needs** as motivators for human behavior began to emerge in psychological studies after World War I. Woodworth (1918) described the concept of drive as the impetus for behavior and noted that urges such as hunger and thirst drove people to behave to respond to these internal conditions. Allport (1937) classified drives as primary and secondary. Primary drives were considered to be biologically based, such as the need for food and comfort. Secondary drives, termed "motives," were linked to fulfilling basic drives.

The work of **Abraham Maslow** (1954) explained human behavior as satisfying a hierarchy of internal needs (Figure 7.1). Maslow categorized needs in five levels. The first, or lowest level, is the physiological, which consists of basic survival needs such as food, air, water, and shelter. The second level is described as safety needs that involve being protected against dangers and threats. The third level, social needs, was defined as the need for belonging and association with others. Fourth level needs were identified as esteem, which included both self-respect through achievement and knowledge, as well as respect from others through approval, status, appreciation, and recognition. The final, and highest, level of need was self-actualization, which referred to a person's achievement of potential and maximizing one's creativity and self-expression.

Figure 7.1. Maslow's Hierarchy of Needs

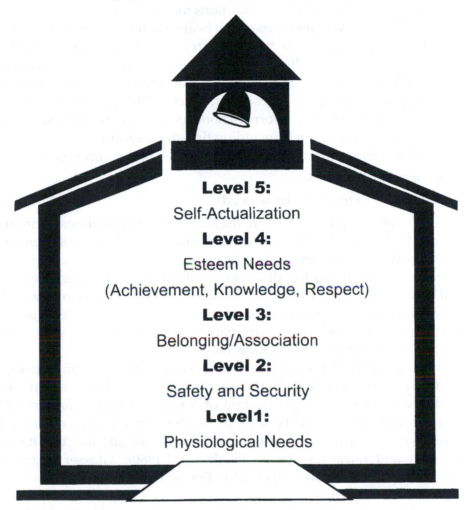

Level 5:

Self-Actualization

Level 4:

Esteem Needs

(Achievement, Knowledge, Respect)

Level 3:

Belonging/Association

Level 2:

Safety and Security

Level1:

Physiological Needs

Maslow believed that humans are motivated to behave to satisfy needs. As one level of need becomes satisfied, the next order of needs is activated as a motivator for behavior. The less a need is satisfied, the more it motivates behavior. Maslow (1954) pointed out that if a man has no bread, he lives for bread alone, but when his hunger is satisfied, new needs displace physiological needs.

Maslow contended that one need does not have to be entirely satisfied before the next level of need emerges. He further asserted that the first three levels of needs are regularly satisfied for the majority of people and thus no longer hold much significance in motivating behavior. The implication of Maslow's theory for educational leaders is that teachers' and students' needs for esteem and self-actualization are the primary motivators of their behavior. Thus, attention should be given to creating conditions that help individuals within educational organizations meet these needs.

In the mid-1960s, **William Glasser** first began writing about what he then described as a new approach to psychiatry, which he termed "reality therapy." Reality therapy challenged conventional psychiatric treatment and was the result of Glasser's disillusionment with the effectiveness of traditional therapy in helping people get better. Much of his original writing was influenced by his work at a reform school for adolescent girls who had committed serious criminal acts including first-degree murder.

Glasser's (1965) approach to therapy was based on two premises:

♦ All behaviors are chosen.

♦ People behave to satisfy basic needs.

Glasser's approach stemmed from the notion that mental illness, criminal actions, addictions, and other less serious emotional distresses were the result of individuals' unsuccessful attempts to fulfill their basic needs. Lacking effective strategies to fulfill their needs, these people begin to deny the real world and behave as if some aspects of the outside environment do not exist. Thus, reality therapy's approach to treatment was to lead people toward facing reality and, more importantly, to teach effective, or responsible, ways for people to fulfill their needs.

Through the 1960s, Glasser focused on the application of reality therapy to the treatment of juvenile delinquents, chronic mental hospital patients, and disturbed children. His publication of *Schools Without Failure* in 1969 applied the concepts of reality therapy to the management of student behavior with an approach to discipline that contradicted traditional punishment and reward systems. By the mid-1980s, Glasser began to develop a total theory of human behavior, first termed "control theory" and later renamed "choice theory."

Choice Theory describes all human behavior as the result of individuals' best attempt at fulfilling their basic needs of (a) survival, (b) love and belonging, (c) power and recognition, (d) freedom, and (e) fun. Unlike Maslow, Glasser does not place basic needs in a hierarchy. Choice Theory explains that people seek to keep all needs in balance, or a state of equilibrium. If a particular need is not being fulfilled, it places the individual in a state of disequilibrium and triggers the person to behave in some way so that the need will be met (Glasser, 1986, 1999). This is analogous to social system theory, which applies this same concept to an organization.

When needs are fulfilled and in equilibrium, people feel pleasure. When peoples' needs are frustrated, or in a state of disequilibrium, they feel pain. The pain associated with unfulfilled needs activates human behavior to satisfy the need. For example, hunger, thirst, and cold are discomforts related to the basic physiological need of survival. On feeling thirsty, a person normally behaves by drinking to satisfy a physical survival need.

The concept of equilibrium, however, is more complicated than behaving to meet one unsatisfied need. As people behave to fulfill one need, they may find this action conflicts with another need. Choice Theory further explains that people learn what is satisfying and what is not and mentally store these experiences. Events, places, and persons associated with these need-satisfying experiences are termed one's "quality world." Each person's quality world is unique and specific, which accounts for individual differences and preferences. For example, eating satisfies hunger, but one person may prefer vegetables and another meat. These differences are caused by individual experiences, some of which may be associated with one's early childhood experiences. The quality world represents what people want in their lives, because these things fulfill one or more basic needs. A person's quality world is the essence of motivation according to choice theory, because it defines why people behave. The quality world represents a kind of standard by which each individual judges and reacts to the external environment. As individuals perceive people, things, and events in the external environment, they compare these perceptions to things in their quality world that they want.

People perceive external events as neutral, positive, or negative. Neutral stimuli are simply processed as additional information, or knowledge. Positive stimuli are those things which people find satisfying to one or more needs and which evoke feelings of pleasure. People and circumstances associated with pleasurable feelings may become part of a person's quality world. Negative stimuli are external events that cause pain because they frustrate one or more needs. People behave as a result of their perception of external events and how these compare to what they want. Specifically, people behave in an attempt to control their external environment so that it satisfies their needs and better matches their quality world.

Some behaviors are effective, others less so. People may choose behaviors that are destructive to themselves or others, because they have learned that these behaviors help satisfy needs, even if only temporarily. To illustrate this process of motivation and behavior, consider the following example:

> In a faculty meeting, a principal tells her teachers that recent student achievement scores in reading are below average and that a school-wide "Drop Everything and Read" program will be implemented daily from 9:00–9:20 each morning. A 20-year veteran teacher protests that this time interferes with his scheduled science activities, and that besides, his students' reading scores are far above average. The principal restates that all

teachers must participate and that the teacher will just have to rearrange his science schedule. The teacher, now frustrated, feels out of control. He feels that his ideas and opinions do not matter. The teacher decides to comply with the principal's orders but also decides that he will no longer plan creative, fun science activities for his students because it just isn't worth the trouble, and no one appreciates the hard work he does anyway.

This behavior is his attempt to gain control over the situation and alter the external environment to better match his quality world and meet his needs. This teacher pictures himself as a professional who carefully plans lessons and instructions to maximize student achievement. This self-image is part of the teacher's quality world and is directly linked to his need for power and recognition. His perception of the principal's actions directly conflicts with his image of professional deliberation and collegial planning for instruction and frustrates his need for power over his own class-room instruction. His behavior, although compliant, may ultimately be detrimental to his students, but his behavior enables the teacher to meet his need for power through silent defiance.

Motivation in Organizations

The contrasting perspectives of internal and external motivation can be seen in organizational theories that attempt to identify management strategies for supervising subordinates. In the application of motivation theory to school leadership, it is critical to understand the relationship between strategies employed by the administrator and behaviors exhibited by staff, students, and others within the school community. To truly comprehend the concept of motivating others, the school administrator must examine his or her own orientation and beliefs about human behavior and must use strategies that are consistent with what is known about human behavior.

McGregor's (1960) Theory X and Theory Y, discussed more fully in Chapter 5, clearly captures the contrast between internal and external motivation theories as they relate to leadership behavior. Theory X and Theory Y explain that leaders' actions are based on their beliefs and assumptions about people at work. Theory X clearly rests on the assumption that behavior is motivated externally. Theory Y, however, operates on the premise that motivation is a function of people's internal needs.

Motivation-Hygiene Theory

Perhaps the motivation theory most emphasized in educational administration courses is Frederick Herzberg's motivation-hygiene, or two-factor, theory. Herzberg's theory of motivation specifically considered motivation in the work environment. The two-factor theory of motivation focuses on the identification of specific factors that influence behavior and is thus classified as a content theory of motivation (Hoy & Miskel, 1987; Steers & Porter, 1975), in contrast to motivation theories that consider the dynamics, or processes, involved in motivation.

The **two-factor theory** of motivation, based on **Frederick Herzberg's** (1966) research with accountants and engineers, proposed that motivation in the workplace was a function of two independent factors. Motivational factors contribute to job satisfaction, whereas hygiene (sometimes called maintenance) factors contribute to job dissatisfaction. Developed a little more than a decade after Maslow's work, the two-factor theory was based on two different sets of human needs—biological or physical needs and psychological needs associated with achievement and recognition.

Motivational factors that lead to job satisfaction are associated with the psychological set of needs. These include achievement, recognition, the work itself, responsibility, and advancement. **Hygiene,** or **maintenance,** factors reduce job dissatisfaction and are primarily related to physiological needs, but also include items that Maslow might have characterized as social needs. Hygiene factors are identified as salary, interpersonal relations, technical supervision, policies, working conditions, and job security.

Herzberg's theory asserts that hygiene factors do not motivate but rather reduce dissatisfaction. For example, increasing teacher salaries, developing a friendly school atmosphere, or reducing class size will abate teacher dissatisfaction and create a neutral environment wherein motivators can lead to greater job satisfaction. However, hygiene factors and motivation factors do not exist on a continuum. Rather, both sets of factors influence job satisfaction. Hygiene factors must exist in tandem with motivation factors. For example, teachers in a high-risk school who feel their safety is threatened may become so dissatisfied that they will disengage from students and put minimal effort into classroom and professional activities. In a more neutral environment, the work of teaching and collegial interactions would be motivating factors for teachers. However, leaders are cautioned not to focus solely on hygiene factors to effect change in school climate. Motivation for change will come from attending to factors such as recognition and responsibility. This means that a leader must involve teachers in the change process to garner any effect from hygiene factors. Thus, hygiene and motivational factors must be considered simultaneously.

Herzberg identified hygiene and motivation factors, which seem to support both external and internal perspectives on motivation theory. Hygiene factors such as salary, policies, and working conditions might be construed as external stimuli, whereas factors such as interpersonal relations and the work itself might be viewed as internal drives or needs. However, the motivation-hygiene theory actually falls short of explaining human behavior from either perspective, because it offers no interpretation of the process that gives rise to behavior. Herzberg merely identified work-related factors that were perceived as satisfying or not satisfying.

The application of Herzberg's motivation-hygiene theory must be considered in light of its basis on a study of accountants and engineers. Replications of Herzberg's study with teachers and school administrators found some differences in hygiene and motivational factors. Sergiovanni (1967) found that work in and of itself and advancement were not significant motivators for teachers, and Schmidt (1976) noted that for administrators, the job itself and responsibility were not classified as significant motivators. Additionally, both of these studies found that interpersonal relations could not be clearly categorized as either a motivator or hygiene factor. Interpersonal relations appeared to significantly impact both satisfaction (motivator) and dissatisfaction (hygiene). The fact that teaching and school administration are professions largely defined by interpersonal relations may account for these differences. Consequently, Herzberg's theory may have limited application in educational settings, although both Sergiovanni and Schmidt did concur with Herzberg's notion that motivators and hygiene factors tend to be exclusive of one another. That is, certain items or events tend to lead to satisfaction (motivators), whereas the absence of other factors (hygienes) tend to lead to dissatisfaction.

Expectancy Theory

Organizational theories referred to as process theories attempt to explain human behavior in terms of systems that take into account relationships among variables that impact individual behavior (Steers & Porter, 1975, p. 180). Process theories present a more complex interpretation of motivation in that they take into account how forces within the individual and forces in the environment interact to influence behavior. Process theories propose that human behavior is determined by an individual's beliefs, expectations, and anticipation of future events. Furthermore, such theories view behavior as purposeful and consciously directed toward goals.

One major body of theory that falls under the umbrella of process theory and has contributed to organizational theory relative to motivation is expectancy theory. **Victor Vroom** (1964) specifically applied the concepts of expectancy theory of motivation to the work environment. The Vroom model of **expectancy theory** defined motivation as the product of valence and expectancy. **Valence** is an individual's orientation toward a particular outcome. Vroom considered valence to be positive (a person prefers attaining a particular outcome), neutral (a person is indifferent to attaining it), or negative (a person prefers not attaining it). Expectancy is the individual's belief that a particular action will result in a particular outcome. Expectancy is described as strength on a continuum from 0 to 1, where 0 is minimal strength and 1 is maximum strength. Vroom stated that expectancy and valence combine to determine motivation, which he termed "force." Both valence and expectancy must exist to some degree, or there will be no force. For instance, if a person wants an outcome but does not feel his or her efforts will lead to the outcome, there is no motivation to act.

Edward Lawler (1973), building on Vroom's work, developed an expectancy model that he based on the following four premises:

- People have preferences among the various outcomes potentially available to them.

- People have expectancies about the likelihood that an action (effort) on their part will lead to the intended behavior or performance.

- People have expectancies (instrumentality) about the likelihood that certain outcomes will follow their behavior.

- In any situation, the actions a person chooses to take are determined by the expectancies and preferences that a person has at the time (p. 49).

Lawler (1973) attempted to clarify the concept of instrumentality, which Vroom (1964) had considered as "an outcome-outcome association" (p. 16). Lawler explained that motivation is influenced by a person's estimate of probability that he or she can perform at the necessary level to accomplish a particular task (effort-performance [E-P] expectancies). Furthermore, motivation is influenced by the person's estimate that successful performance will lead to the desired outcome (performance-outcome [P-O] expectancy or instrumentality). He further identified factors that determined or influenced expectancies. Factors that determined E-P expectancies include the actual situation, an individual's self-esteem, one's past experiences in similar situations, and communication from others. All of these factors, with the exception of self-esteem, also were seen as impacting P-O expectancies. In addition, Lawler identified the attractiveness of outcomes, one's belief in internal versus external control, and an individual's estimate of performance capability as other factors that influence P-O expectancies. Lawler cautioned, however, that the expectancy model of motivation can only predict behavior if one knows how an individual perceives the situation and how that person values various outcomes and pointed out that people rarely consider all the factors that may impact a particular outcome.

The following example illustrates how expectancy theory might apply in a school setting. In this example, **valence** refers to an individual's desire to achieve a goal; **instrumentality** refers to a person's estimate of the probability that specific actions will produce the desired goal; and, **effort** is the individual's belief that he or she can perform at the necessary level to achieve an outcome.

> Mrs. Jones, the high school band director, wants her marching band to perform at an out-of-state competition (valence). She believes she can convince the principal to approve this trip if she can garner the support of her students' parents (instrumentality). Mrs. Jones believes there is a high probability of gaining parental support (effort). As long as Mrs. Jones maintains high valence, instrumentality, and effort her motivation will continue to be high. If, however, she lowers her probability estimate of one of the factors, her motivation will diminish. For instance, if parents begin complaining about Mrs. Jones' direction of the band at football games, instrumentality will fall and motivation will diminish.

Expectancy theory points out that each individual will consider various alternatives to reach the desired goal and weigh the negatives and positives associated with each alternative (Porter, Lawler, & Hackman, 1975). Expectancy theory clearly presents the perspective that human behavior is internally motivated, yet acknowledges that those external events and variables influence individual's decisions through how one perceives the external environment. Although expectancy theory offers a model that explains motivation as the result of cognitive processing, it is limited in that it specifies no content factors, such as needs or drives, that affect motivation.

Goal Theory

Goal theory is another example of a process theory that explains motivation by a person's desire to achieve goals. **Goal theory** and its application to organizations resulted primarily from the works of **Edwin A. Locke**. Locke's (1968) theory of goal-driven behavior was based principally on controlled laboratory experiments using college students who performed simple tasks for short periods of time. Goal theory defines a goal as what an individual is consciously attempting to do. Goals contain two distinct components: content and intensity. Content refers to the desired outcome, and intensity describes the level of importance a person ascribes to the goal. Goal theory explains that a person gains knowledge about the external environment through perceptions and makes value judgments to determine what actions will enhance the individual's well being. The individual compares personal interests, or value standards, against perceptions of the environment. An individual anticipates how behavior will satisfy personal needs and estimates the probability that the behavior will lead to the desired outcome. If goal achievement is judged to be highly probable, anticipated satisfaction is high. Goal theory explains human behavior as purposeful and motivated consciously by goals and intentions. Although goal theory refers to personal needs, it provides no construct for understanding what human needs consist of, other than that they are shaped by individuals' experiences, knowledge, and understanding of the external environment.

Hoy and Miskel (1987) offered four generalizations drawn from research on the application of goal theory to organizational behavior. First, specific goals result in higher achievement than do general goals. Second, more effort will be exerted to achieve difficult goals, if an individual values the outcome. However, very difficult goals are often not viewed as acceptable. Third, individuals are more satisfied if they are involved in goal setting. Although participation does not ensure increased performance, it may result in more difficult goals and higher performance if the individual places value on the goal. Finally, goal setting combined with feedback enhances employee motivation (p.195–196).

The concepts of goal theory have particular relevance to educational practices because goal setting is commonly used in schools. For instance, student performance standards, curricular objectives, and teacher appraisal systems all use goal setting as a way to motivate achievement. Goal setting is also seen in the development of district missions, strategic plans, and site-based decision making models. Thus, the motivational effect of goal setting is an important consideration for educational leaders.

Building principals often use a leadership team, composed of teacher representatives such as grade-level or department chairs, and sometimes parent representatives, to develop short- or long-term goals for the school site. Members of each grade level or department then generate sub-goals or objectives that are compatible to site goals. Individual teachers subsequently define personal objectives or job targets for achieving department and school-wide goals. In addition, criteria for measuring attainment of goals and objectives are established.

In considering this goal-setting process, educational leaders should be aware of organizational practices that may impede its motivational purpose. First, a leadership approach that is not participatory in nature runs counter to the fundamental premises of goal theory. Second, if emphasis is placed on the formality of goal setting through meticulous documentation procedures, the paperwork becomes burdensome and inhibits performance. Third, putting undue stress on quantitative measures may divert a leader's attention away from important outcomes related to quality, which are often difficult to quantify.

Too often, the practice of goal setting becomes buried under a bureaucratic structure. This is the case when teachers receive directives to submit yearly goals, which must correspond to school or district goals that have been predetermined by either building-level or central office administration. When this happens, the process becomes merely a paper chase of documentation where both teachers and administrators simply "go through the motions," and there is little thought or commitment to what is written. Leaders' use of goal setting as a means to motivate relies upon leaders' commitment to the process, not upon the formality of the goal-setting structure.

Group Dynamics

Psychological explanations of human behavior, framed in terms of the individual, provide only partial insight into motivation. School administrators must be concerned not only with the motivation for an individual's behavior but also with factors that influence the collective actions of staff, students, and other groups involved in the school organization. Understanding behavior as it relates to group dynamics is essential to effective leadership.

The study of behavior within a group context offers a holistic perspective, which views the group as an entity unto itself. A group is more than the "sum of its parts." In this sense, a group operates as a separate organism, and behavior is a function of the group's dynamics.

Groups are like organisms in that they develop and change over time, and group development can actually be categorized into stages. **Bruce Tuckman** and **Mary Ann Jensen** (1977) identified five fairly predictable stages of group development, which they termed: (a) forming, (b) storming, (c) norming, (d) performing, and (e) adjourning. **Forming** is an orientation period characterized by polite conversation and tentative interactions. During this stage members exchange information, develop bonds, and identify common values. **Storming** follows the forming stage and is a period of conflict when ideas are criticized and hostilities are evident. Competition among members dominates this stage of group development. A group that works through the storming period enters the third stage of **norming**. At this point, roles and relationships are established and cohesiveness develops. The group comes to agreement about rules and seeks consensus. Members become supportive of one another and begin to think in terms of their identity as a group. The next stage a group enters is **performing**. It is in this phase that a group is most productive. There is a focus on achievement, performance, and productivity. Decision making, problem solving, and cooperation are the results of this stage. The final stage of group development is **adjournment.** This occurs when the group's task is complete. Members move away from the group, often with feelings of regret and high emotion, because the group no longer has purpose.

Specific elements associated with each of the stages of group development are important to leaders' effective facilitation of groups in the workplace. The formation of groups in the workplace may occur spontaneously, as in social cliques, or deliberately, as in committees or task forces. Leaders should be cognizant of the negative and positive aspects associated with group membership. Negative aspects of group membership may include tension, time investment, rejection, and loss of freedom, whereas more positive aspects of membership can be mutual support, social interaction, and attainment of desired goals (Forsyth, 1983).

Viewed in this light, leaders should facilitate groups so that positive aspects offset negative and equilibrium is achieved. A group will be effective only if each member perceives his or her association with the group as satisfying personal needs. Voluntary participation in committees or team activities will help ensure a successful beginning for any group. Leaders should also consider diversity in group membership. The initial involvement of a diverse population whose members represent various interests creates a stronger foundation for organizational support of decisions or recommendations made by the group. A leader should also consider the size of the group. The larger the team, the more difficult it will be to maintain focus and facilitate communication. The task to be accomplished may affect the size of the group. Complex activities may require greater numbers of people to be involved, and this large group may need to break into smaller subgroups to accomplish specific tasks.

After a group's initial formation, the leader should anticipate conflicts that may arise as the group enters the storming stage. It should be remembered that the variety of perspectives, knowledge, and experiences that individual members bring to the group serve to enhance productivity and improve the quality of desired outcomes, but it is inevitable that disagreements will arise from these differences. A leader should prepare for this by seeking the assistance of all group members in setting ground rules that facilitate task completion. Ground rules should include agreement on attendance, promptness, participation, agendas, and group behavioral expectations. The explicit rules will facilitate the group's development of implicit norms, which characterizes a group's movement into the third stage.

The following are some implicit norms that may develop:

◆ People should be listened to and recognized.
◆ Members may criticize ideas but not individuals.

◆ Objectivity and honesty are valued by the team.

A leader may facilitate the development of positive norms, which promote a group's effectiveness, through modeling desired communication strategies and interpersonal behaviors. If team coordination and facilitation is delegated to group members, the leader should provide training and direction to these individuals.

With the parameters outlined above firmly established, the group should be ready to enter the performing stage. At this point, the group's task should be clarified, and expected outcomes delineated. Questions to be considered at this stage might include:

◆ What is the problem to be studied?

◆ What standards or criteria must be applied to the problem?

◆ What are the group's boundaries or limitations, especially related to time, money, and information to be provided?

◆ What is the authority of the group? Will the group make recommendations to administration or will the group make final decisions that will be implemented? (Adapted from Scholtes, 1988)

A leader's successful direction of work groups and team activities can produce powerful results, and collaboration among teachers plays an important role in motivating effective performance and high achievement. The group processes involved in leading others toward organizational goals goes beyond facilitating teams and workgroups. School administrators must consider the group dynamics involved in larger group settings such as faculty meetings, PTA sessions, or community information gatherings. In any of these settings, as in small group activities, individual participants may take on specific roles that tend to facilitate or hinder the task at hand. It is incumbent on the educational leader to maintain the group's focus by nurturing those roles that support the group's and organization's efforts and by minimizing roles that hinder effective performance and divert the group's efforts. Figure 7.2 provides some examples of roles that may be manifested in any group setting.

Figure 7.2. Group Roles

Facilitating Roles	
Encourager	Friendly, supportive, praises others
Comromiser	Willing to yield in order for group to progreee
Harmonizer	Mediates differences
Clarifier	Probes for meaning; restates problems
Energizer	Motivates, encourages groups
Elaborator	Builds on others' statements
Summarizer	Reviews and synthesizes discussion
Procedural expert	Understands school policies, procedures, rules, and regulations
Hindering Roles	
Dominator	Asserts authority and manipulates group
Blocker	Rejects others views, returns to issues previously resolved
Lobbyist	Pleads for his/her special interests
Jumper	Changes the subject and group focus
Confessor	Talks irrevelantly about personal feelings
Retreater	Withdraws from group, engages in private conversations
Antagonist	Criticizes others; aggressively disagrees
Recognition seeker	Boasts; talks excessively; centers attention on self

Adapted from Collaboration, team building, and total quality philosophy for systemic change in education by E. W. Chance, 1995. In P. Jenlink (Ed.), *Systemic change: Touchstones for the future school* (p. 173), Palatine, IL: I RI/Skylight.

Leaders should be prepared to deal with individuals who take on hindering roles. Considering an individual's motivation for playing such a role may provide insight into diverting that individual to a more facilitative role. For instance, the parent whose only interest in attending a PTA meeting is to complain about the playground facilities might be asked to attend a focus group meeting to discuss that specific topic. This could provide the person the opportunity to be heard as well as involve the parent in learning more about finances, maintenance, and other issues associated with playgrounds. Although the parent's concern about playgrounds may continue to be voiced, it will be done in a more appropriate venue. The leader may also find that by recognizing the person and valuing his or her feelings, this parent will begin to take on more facilitative roles in future PTA meetings.

Summary

Motivation theories provide a framework for understanding human behavior. Motivation is inextricably tied to the tasks of educational leadership as school leaders strive to develop an effective learning environment where teachers are motivated to teach and students are motivated to learn. This chapter has examined motivation from both individual and group perspectives. Motivation theories help leaders understand that human behavior is not absolutely predictable and is dependent on a number of factors including individuals' perceptions of the external environment and basic human needs as well as personal goals and desires. Educational leaders must understand that they cannot directly manipulate others' behaviors, but they can influence teacher and student behavior by controlling and managing the school environment. In addition, motivation theories help explain the role of interpersonal relationships and the importance of two-way communication between a leader and followers.

This chapter also addressed motivation from the perspective of the organization and group behavior. School leaders should note that certain theories and strategies may be specific to particular work situations and thus they should consider the unique characteristics of the school environment and the nature of the teaching-learning relationship. Because of the widespread use of committee structures and faculty teams for planning and decision making in schools, educational leaders will benefit from understanding the effect of group processes on motivation. The latter part of this chapter provided specific leadership strategies for motivating teaching teams toward effective performance and goal achievement.

Theory into Practice

Low Morale at Lincoln

It had been a long day for Edith Jackson, principal of Lincoln Elementary School. As she drove home, she reflected on her first three months at Lincoln. Ms. Jackson had been a successful principal for six years at Washington Elementary, an exemplary school in the district. Washington had a high level of parental participation, a well-behaved student population, and many faculty members who had taught at Washington for many years. Teachers at Washington had emphasized basic fundamentals, and their approach had been successful. Students performed well; parents, teachers, and students were happy; and, the school climate was orderly and safe.

Lincoln was none of these things. Lincoln was in one of the poorest sections of the city. Students' skill levels and achievement were low, and students' general behavior was boisterous and disrespectful—of teachers and one another. It seemed that Ms. Jackson spent much of her day dealing with discipline problems. Today alone she had suspended two fifth-grade boys for fighting and doled out about 25 after-school detentions. Parents either didn't seem to care or didn't have time to help their kids. Worst of all, teachers' morale was low, and they didn't seem motivated to teach or help maintain order.

When the school year started, Ms. Jackson had devised a discipline program and duty schedule she felt were needed to create a safe school environment. She had made every attempt to make procedures easy for teachers and to develop an equitable duty schedule for playgrounds, hallways, and lunches. Her discipline plan, modeled after the program she had used at Washington, used a progressive approach with three steps:

1. First offense—teacher counsels with student
2. Second offense—teacher contacts parents
3. Third offense—refer student to office

She knew that some teachers were not following the process because so many students were being referred to her. She had implemented accountability procedures where teachers had to document their actions and contacts with parents. She truly felt that if parents became involved, student behavior would improve. But teachers simply complained that they could not reach parents, and they should not have to put up with continual disruptive behavior. Ms. Jackson had also tried rewards—for both teachers and students. She had implemented a "Caught Being Good" program where students were given tokens for good behavior that they could exchange for treats and prizes. During faculty meetings, she recognized teachers whose students had earned 100 tokens and were treated to a pizza party. At first, these programs seemed to work, but recently she had heard teachers complain that tokens were unfairly distributed and that students who were behavior problems were being bribed for acting like they should in the first place, whereas kids who were generally well behaved were ignored. As far as instruction was concerned, Ms. Jackson's classroom visits indicated that teachers were barely coping. Teachers seemed to rely on whole-class instruction and lots of paper and pencil worksheets to keep students busy.

Ms. Jackson felt overwhelmed and discouraged as she thought about the tasks ahead of her in leading this school. She sometimes just wanted to throw her hands up and quit, but there were some bright spots that gave her hope. Mr. Jordan, a fourth-grade teacher, was one of them. He seemed to work miracles with his students. When she visited his classroom, there was always fun and laughter. A veteran teacher of 20 years, he had spent 18 of those years at Lincoln. He was a strict disciplinarian and put up with no nonsense, but his students loved him and worked hard for him. She often saw him on the playground, refereeing basketball games with his kids during recess. He also spent time before and after school helping individuals or small groups of children. She knew that kids often confided in Mr. Jordan about problems at home, and he seemed to be more effective than the school counselor in resolving conflicts among students and finding health and welfare services for his students' families.

"Well," she thought as she pulled in her driveway at home, "tomorrow is another day. I think I will make an appointment with Mr. Jordan. Maybe he could help by sharing some of his secrets with me."

Sample Analysis

Ms. Jackson obviously faces a situation where neither staff nor students are motivated toward organizational goals. The principal's attempts to control behavior are not working because she has failed to examine underlying causes of behavior. She has assumed that rewards and punishment will be effective in changing behavior.

A first step for Ms. Jackson would be to consider the needs of her staff and students. She has focused on issues of safety and security, an obvious need but has overlooked psychological needs that motivate behavior. Students' disruptions and the prevalent use of instructional techniques aimed at keeping things under control are indicators that students' need for power and recognition are not being met. Nor does there appear to be any organized effort to fulfill students' needs for belonging and association, except perhaps in Mr. Jordan's classroom.

It is apparent that in Ms. Jackson's enthusiasm to establish a safe and orderly school climate, she implemented procedures and schedules with no input from teachers. In doing so, she failed to recognize the basic needs that motivate teachers' behaviors. Although teachers desire to work in a safe environment, their need for power and recognition is being thwarted. This is evidenced by their complaints that discipline programs aren't working and by their attempts to maintain control in classrooms through direct instruction that keeps students busy and quiet. Teachers appear to have little ownership in the plan that has been devised and feel little control over the process, so they behave in such a way as to try to gain some control.

Ms. Jackson's implementation of rewards and punishments is characteristic of the Theory X manager. She is acting on assumptions that teachers are lazy, self-centered, and do not want responsibility. In fact, in her words, she designed programs and schedules that would make it easy for teachers. Ms. Jackson hasn't realized that these assumptions and her subsequent actions are not truly congruent with her own beliefs about people. She stated that she truly believed if parents were involved it would make a difference in the school climate. Yet, she failed to recognize that the same is true for teacher involvement.

Ms. Jackson's actions appear to be a sincere effort on her part to create a safe environment that will motivate effective teaching and learning. However, looking at the situation in terms of Herzberg's theory, Ms. Jackson's focus has been fixed on hygiene factors, for example, policies and work conditions. She failed to consider motivational factors such as achievement, recognition, and responsibility. Herzberg's theory demonstrates that hygiene factors and motivational factors are not a continuum but must be considered together.

In this case, Ms. Jackson seems to have stumbled on a course of action that may ultimately help her solve the problem of motivation among her staff and students. Her decision to speak with Mr. Jordan represents an essential first step in leading others toward organizational goals. Although she may not consciously realize it, Ms. Jackson's plan to meet with Mr. Jordan denotes a leadership behavior that is congruent with the notion that motivation is an internal, not external, process. She is beginning to consider motivation from another's viewpoint rather than her own. Rather than asking, "What can I do to motivate others?," she is seeking to understand what motivates Mr. Jordan and what he believes motivates his students.

Ms. Jackson would be wise to follow this same process with other teachers. She should seek forums for listening to teachers' concerns and ideas. This can be done through a combination of individual conferences, grade-level meetings, and whole faculty gatherings. She might consider setting up one or more task forces or committees to make recommendations for improving school climate. By doing these things, she will be attending to teachers' needs for power, recognition, and involvement. At this point, Ms. Jackson needs to be careful that she adequately prepares committees by focusing their tasks, setting ground rules, and defining the parameters of their work. She must continue to remain cognizant of how her behavior will be perceived by teachers and consequently impact motivation. Teachers' input must be genuinely sought and considered. Anything less will be perceived as controlling and manipulating and will result in teachers reverting to old behaviors (i.e., complaining and maintaining) or manifesting new ones which may be even more destructive to the organization.

Reader's Application

Tensions in the Second-Grade Team

It was the third week of school, and things were definitely not off to a good start. Lois Fuller, principal at Lincoln Elementary, was very disturbed after the conference with Cindy Jones and Brenda Daily, two second-grade teachers who she considered to be among the most effective on her staff. They had come to complain to her about their colleague, Greg Peters, another second-grade teacher.

This was Mr. Peters' second year at Lincoln Elementary in Pleasantville. Mr. Peters had moved to the Pleasantville community from a neighboring state where he had taught third grade for four years. He came to Lincoln highly recommended by his previous principal who had indicated that Mr. Peters was enthusiastic, well liked by students and parents, and a willing team player who often volunteered for school committees and special projects. Mr. Peters was a newlywed when he moved to Pleasantville. He and his wife Peggy had decided to make Pleasantville their home because of Peggy's employment as a sales representative for Major Products, a local manufacturing company.

As Ms. Fuller reflected back on Mr. Peters' first year at Lincoln, she had to admit that these teachers' complaints did not really surprise her. Mr. Peters had seemed eager and enthusiastic at the beginning of last year. He had told Ms. Fuller that he was very anxious to implement some of his math and science units he had used in his previous school. He explained how his students worked together on projects and conducted experiments in which they measured, calculated, and even applied some geometry. He had followed her suggestion that he volunteer for the primary math curriculum committee, which had been formed to develop thematic units that integrated math concepts and skills.

When Ms. Fuller had visited Mr. Peters' classroom during the first few months of school last year, students seemed to be happy and on-task. However, she had been a little disconcerted to see that he was relying a great deal on drill and practice, recitation, and whole-class instruction. These instructional techniques seemed to oppose the philosophy of small-group instruction, center activities, and experiential methods employed by the other second-grade teachers. In fact, this teaching style contradicted what Mr. Peters himself said he believed in. However, Ms. Fuller's concerns had been dissuaded after conferencing with Mr. Peters. He had presented a thoughtful explanation for his instructional plans, and students appeared to be responding. He had admitted to Ms. Fuller that although he preferred a more experiential, hands-on approach to instruction, he found that students at Lincoln lacked so many basic skills that he had felt the need to alter his approach. Ms. Fuller had sensed at that time that Mr. Peters' previous experiences in an affluent suburban school had not fully prepared him for working with students whose families were barely making ends meet and many of whom came from dysfunctional situations. But, she felt confident that Mr. Peters had the ability and just needed some time to make the transition. She perceived that his involvement with the other second-grade teachers would provide a support system for him and help him become an effective teacher at Lincoln.

She decided, in fact, to ask Ms. Jones, the grade-level chair, to make a concerted effort to help Mr. Peters. When she spoke to Ms. Jones about this, the grade-level chair stated that she had already offered her help to Mr. Peters, as had the other second-grade teachers. She said that Mr. Peters had been polite about it, but acted as if he didn't really want their help. Ms. Jones had then asked if Mr. Peters would share some of his ideas for math and science that he had discussed with Ms. Fuller. He told her that he wasn't going to use any of those units at Lincoln. He had tried one the first two weeks of school and found the children were unable to do these activities. He went on to explain that the students became unruly, and they did not have the discipline or skills to deal with such high-level problem solving activities. Ms. Jones had decided to back off. If he wanted help, he could come ask. The principal encouraged Ms. Jones to try again and to be sure to include him in grade-level planning.

Ms. Fuller also recalled the primary math curriculum meetings she had attended later that fall. Mr. Peters seemed to be taking quite a leadership role. She remembered how animated he was as he described the units he had developed and implemented over the last two years and how proud he was of his students' achievement. She felt then that her earlier concerns had been unfounded. She gave little more thought to it despite the fact she saw no evidence of his using these ideas in his classroom. What he was doing seemed to be working, and she decided not to push too hard. As she remembered it, there were no other outstanding incidents with Mr. Peters until last March.

At that time Ms. Fuller met with Mr. Peters for the required performance review conference. Ms. Fuller had given him satisfactory ratings in all areas and had even commended him for his collaboration with other staff. She recalled thinking that this was the appropriate time to encourage Mr. Peters to be more creative, now that he was feeling more comfortable at Lincoln.

Ms. Fuller explained to Mr. Peters that a part of the district's performance review system required principals to set future objectives for teacher performance, which fit with district goals. Currently, one primary district goal focused on developing students' critical thinking and problem-solving skills. Ms. Fuller suggested that Mr. Peters' objectives should be related to this goal. Strategies could include the implementation of more hands-on experiences and other activities that required students to solve real-world problems. She suggested to him that he use some of the units that he had used successfully in his previous school and that he confer with the other second-grade teachers for their ideas as well. Although Mr. Peters formally agreed with these suggestions, he did not conceal his frustration. He told Ms. Fuller that he was very disappointed in her evaluation of him, as he had always received exemplary—not satisfactory—evaluations. He further stated, in a rather curt manner, "I am an experienced teacher, and I have found that the kids here need something different. However, if you want me to share my ideas with the second-grade team, I will be happy to do so."

During the last two months of the school year, the mood of the second-grade team had been tense. When Ms. Fuller met with these teachers in April to go over their supply orders for next year and to discuss the implementation of the new math curriculum, everyone was exceptionally quiet. A normally exuberant and enthusiastic group, the teachers seemed to be just "going through the motions" to turn in appropriate forms and documents. She later asked Ms. Jones what was wrong, and the grade-level chair responded that the teachers were simply tired and ready for a break. Although nothing erupted during the last month of school, Ms. Fuller observed that Mr. Peters no longer joined his colleagues for lunch in the faculty lounge. In fact, he spent most of his lunch times alone in his room. He also did not attend the year-end faculty party, giving the excuse that his wife was not feeling well, and he needed to spend that time with her.

Frankly, Ms. Fuller had hoped that the summer break would renew the second-grade teachers' spirits, and it seemed to have done just that. Ms. Jones had informed Ms. Fuller the week before school started that the second-grade team was meeting to discuss some ideas incorporating math skills into thematic units that would be a collaborative grade-level project. Ms. Jones was very excited and was hosting a lunch meeting at her home. During the first week of school, Ms. Jones shared their plan with the principal, and Ms. Fuller noted there was less enthusiasm. Ms. Jones' statement that "at least it is a beginning" indicated that something had put a damper on the team's excitement.

Now, after the conference with Ms. Jones and Ms. Daily, she knew what had happened and was beginning to see things more clearly. The teachers' complaints centered on Mr. Peters' lack of cooperation and attempts to block all ideas and suggestions put forth by the others. He had attended the lunch meeting at Ms. Jones' house, and according to Ms. Jones and Ms. Daily, had ridiculed almost every idea. He stated, "You can write up whatever you want, but it isn't going to work with these kids." The other second-grade teachers persevered and incorporated some of the things Mr. Peters seemed insistent on, such as drill and practice worksheets for addition and subtraction facts. He reluctantly agreed to participate in the collaborative grade-level project.

Today, after just beginning the project, a major disagreement and argument had ensued at the grade-level meeting. Mr. Peters had accused the other teachers of discounting him and his ideas and blamed them for his "poor evaluation" last year. He implied that they had been criticizing him behind his back and had influenced the principal's obvious dislike for him. He had informed the second-grade teachers that he would prefer to be left alone to do his own thing with his kids. As he walked out of the room, he turned around and said, "No one at this school cares about me anyway."

Student Exercise: Case Analysis

1. Analyze this case using motivational theories that might help explain Mr. Peters' behavior.
2. What assumptions, if any, did Ms. Fuller make about Mr. Peters' motivation?
3. What impact did Mr. Peters' behavior have on the other teachers?
4. What strategies did Ms. Fuller employ to motivate Mr. Peters?
5. What could Ms. Fuller have done differently which might have prevented this ultimate conflict?
6. What should Ms. Fuller do now?

References

Allport, G. W. (1937). The functional autonomy of motives. American Journal of Psychology, 50, 143.

Chance, E. W. (1995). Collaboration, team building, and total quality philosophy for systemic change in education. In P. Jenlink (Ed.), Systemic change: Touchstones for the future school (p. 167–177). Palatine, IL: IRI/Skylight.

Forsyth, D. R. (1983). An introduction to group dynamics. Monterey, CA: Brooks/Cole Publishing.

Glasser, W. (1965). Reality therapy: A new approach to psychiatry. New York: Harper and Row.

Glasser, W. (1969). Schools without failure. New York: Harper and Row.

Glasser, W. (1986). Control theory in the classroom. New York: Harper and Row.

Glasser, W. (1999). Choice theory: A new psychology of personal freedom. New York: Harper Collins.

Herzberg, F. (1966). Work and the nature of man. Cleveland, OH: World Publishing Co.

Hoy, W. K., & Miskel, C. G. (1987). Educational administration: Theory, research and practice (3rd ed.). New York: Random House.

Lawler, E. E., III. (1973). Motivation in work organizations. Monterey, CA: Brooks/Cole Publishing Co.

Locke, E. A. (1968). Toward a theory of task motivation and incentives. Organizational Behavior and Human Performance, 3, 157–189.

Maslow, A. H. (1954). Motivation and personality. New York: Harper and Row.

McGregor, D. (1960). *The human side of enterprise.* New York: McGraw Hill.

Papalia, D. E., Olds, S. W., & Feldman, R. D. (1989). *Human development* (4th ed.). New York: McGraw-Hill.

Russell, I. L. (1971). *Motivation.* Dubuque, IA: William C. Brown.

Schmidt, G. L. (1976). Job satisfaction among secondary school administrators. *Educational Administration Quarterly, 12,* 68–86.

Scholtes, P. R. (1988). *The team handbook: How to use teams to improve quality.* Madison, WI: Joiner Associates.

Sergiovanni, T. (1967). Factors which affect satisfaction and dissatisfaction of teachers. *Journal of Educational Administration, 5,* 66–82.

Skinner, B. F. (1938). *The behavior of organisms: An experimental approach.* New York: Appleton-Century.

Steers, R. M., & Porter, L. W. (1975). *Motivation and work behavior.* New York: McGraw-Hill.

Tuckman, B. W., & Jensen, M. A. C. (1977). Stages of small group development revisited. *Group and Organizational Studies, 2,* 419–427.

Vroom, V. H. (1964). *Work and motivation.* New York: John Wiley.

Woodworth, R. S. (1918). *Dynamic psychology.* New York: Columbia University Press.

8

Communication: The Impact of Organizational Structure on Information Flow and Perceptions

Synopsis of Communication Theory

Communication is an essential function of any organization. Schools, as organizations, rely on the cooperation and collaboration of many people to achieve their goals. In fact, educational institutions' primary function is communication, because learning is essentially receiving, processing, interpreting, and responding to information. People gather information from others and provide others with information through communication. Communication is a social force that facilitates cooperation and organization among individuals toward the pursuit of mutual goals (Kreps, 1990). To a great extent, the culture of an organization is defined by its communication structures. Beliefs, values, and norms are transmitted and interpreted through the process of communication.

Communication is a dynamic, ongoing process. Organizational communication involves not only communication between individuals but also is affected by the structure of the organization itself. Additionally, because schools are open systems, organizational communication involves the flow of information into and out of the external environment. As information is channeled out of the system, it is interpreted, acted on, and fed back into the system. The same is true of information channeled into the system.

This chapter discusses communication theory in terms of organizational leadership. The fundamental elements of communication are defined to form the groundwork from which to apply communication to schools as organizations. Processes of organizational communication are explored in terms of organizational structure, vertical and horizontal channels of communication, formal and informal systems, and the role of organizational structure and individuals within the organization in restricting and directing communication.

Applications for School Leaders

Understanding communication theory will help school leaders:

+ Understand the impact of organizational structure on communication

+ Use formal channels of communication more effectively

+ Identify key individuals who may hinder or facilitate communication

+ Facilitate communication so that a receiver's perception is congruent with the intent of the message

+ Understand that organizational communication is ongoing and dynamic

+ Prevent information overload that can inhibit the effectiveness of the school organization

---

Organizational Structure:
A Framework for Understanding Communication Theory

Basic Elements of Communication

Four main components commonly identified in communication models are the source, the message, the channel, and the receiver. A simple model of communication that references these four components is often referred to as the **S-M-C-R** model (Berlo, 1960). **Everett Rogers** and **Rehka Agarwala-Rogers** (1976) proposed two additional elements of communication—effect and feedback—as essential to defining the basic processes of communication. Figure 8.1 illustrates a simplified conceptualization of the fundamental communication process of Rogers and Agarwala-Rogers.

The **source** is the individual or group of individuals who originate the message. The **message** is the idea that is transmitted by the source. Messages are essentially symbolic representations of ideas that involve encoding by the source and decoding by the receiver. The source encodes meaning into symbols that can use language, hand or facial gestures, body movements, or pictures. **Receivers** decode symbols into meaning in the form of ideas, images, and thoughts. Meaning is assigned by the source and the receiver; thus, communication involves not so much the message itself but what is intended by the source and what is perceived by the receiver. A **channel** is the medium through which a message travels from the source to the receiver. The receiver is the most important element in the communication process, because it is the receiver's perception of the message that will define the effects of the communication process. Rogers and Agarwala-Rogers (1976) defined effective communication as "communication that results in those changes in receiver behavior that were intended by the source" (p. 13). Thus, **effects** are the changes in knowledge, attitude, or actions of the receiver that result from the message. **Feedback** is the receiver's response to the source's message, resulting in dynamic, two-way communication. Effective communication requires feedback (both positive and negative) and denotes the source's concern for whether the receiver understands the intent of the message.

Although the S-M-C-R model is useful in defining the basic elements involved in the communication process, it presents a static view of communication and does not fully capture the complexities of the communication process. Communication processes correlate to the structure and function of the organization.

Figure 8.1. The Communication Process
of Rogers and Agarwala-Rogers

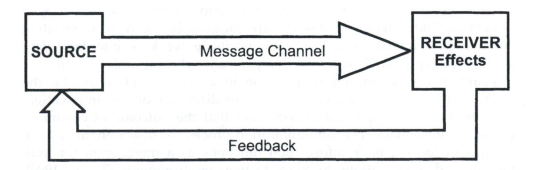

Katz and Kahn (1966) described communication as "the very essence of a social system" (p. 223). Rogers and Agarwala-Rogers (1976) noted that communication is the "lifeblood of an organization" that "pervades all activities" (p. 7). They further defined an organization as "an elaborate set of interconnected communication channels designed to import, sort, and analyze information from the environment and export process messages back to the environment" (p. 7).

The intractable connection between organizational structure and communication processes can be seen when examining the historical development of organizational theory. Classical organization theorists, in the era of scientific management, discussed communication as formal, vertical channels from the leader to the workers. The emphasis of communication was task-related, and its purpose was efficiency. The emergence of the human relations era, arising from the Hawthorne studies, recognized the importance of informal, interpersonal relationships. Barnard (1938) identified communication as an indispensable function of the informal organization and stated that "informal organizations are necessary to the operation of formal organizations as a means of communication, of cohesion, and of protecting the integrity of the individual" (p. 123). In fact, he identified communication as the first executive function. In spite of the fact that Barnard identified communication as a function of the informal organization, his discussion of communication principles focused on formal, top-down communication strategies. However, Harvard researchers who conducted the Hawthorne studies emphasized that organizational communication was informal and interpersonal and rarely, if ever, was the result of formal communication channels (Roethlisberger & Dickson, 1939). Managers were encouraged to use informal channels and intervene when rumors spread. Rogers and Agarwala-Rogers (1976) noted that even though the human relations ethic invited worker participation, the main objective was to attain higher performance levels, and they commented, "Unfortunately, there was an inauthentic quality to organizational communication" (p. 48).

The complexities of communication are evident when presented as the dynamics of open systems. Hanson (1996) defined communication in open systems as "the exchange of messages and meaning between an organization and its environment as well as between its network of interdependent subsystems" (p. 224). Two aspects of organizational communication that are relevant to understanding its function in an open system are (a) the restriction of communication and (b) the direction of communication. Furthermore, it is important to remember that the outcome of communication is information. The communication process of disseminating, gathering, and feeding back information functions as a mechanism for individuals and organizations to adapt to their environments (Kreps, 1990).

Kreps wrote that "communication is irreversible [and] is bound to the context in which it occurs" (p. 26).

The following discussion will examine specific elements and dynamics of organizations that impact or are impacted by communication, and will further explore the concepts of restriction, direction, and outcomes of communication within the context of schools as open systems.

Organizational Structure

Daniel Katz and **Robert Kahn** (1966) pointed out that organization requires that communication be constrained and restricted to reduce diffuse or random communication that would interfere with the accomplishment of organizational goals. Thus, channels of communication are designated and are manifested in organizational charts and hierarchical structures. These represent the formal structures of the organization. Two major forms of **formal communication** flow are (a) vertical communication and (b) horizontal communication.

Vertical communication consists of downward and upward communication. Downward communication generally involves directives such as regulations and procedures but can also include feedback on performance and messages intended to indoctrinate subordinates about the mission of the organization. Katz and Kahn observed that leaders often underuse downward communication channels for performance feedback and indoctrination. School administrators whose communications to teachers and staff are predominantly directive in nature miss opportunities to provide effective leadership toward desired goals.

The teacher evaluation process is a primary example of a formal communication channel that is underused by school leaders. Principals often provide little or no feedback to teachers regarding classroom instruction except through formal, written communication in the form of summative evaluations. Although the formal communication channel is intended to improve or reinforce effective instruction, when it is underused, teachers perceive that the principal does not value classroom instruction or does not fully understand what teachers are doing in the classroom. Directives, intended to improve teaching performance, are likely to result in resentment and opposition rather than positive changes in teacher behavior. Principals who frequently use the formal system of teacher evaluation to communicate with teachers through preobservation and feedback conferences will find that their intended message (to reinforce or improve effective instruction) is more accurately perceived by teachers, as there has been opportunity for feedback and two-way communication. Principals who appropriately use this formal channel of communication also use it to reinforce school goals and clarify the overall mission of the organization. Consequently, teachers are more likely to use the information received to make adaptations toward achieving specific goals.

Upward communication is less frequent in organizations. Additionally, the content of messages sent upward tends to be more positive than negative. Superiors are more likely to receive inaccurate information that is fed up the line, because subordinates tell their bosses what they think their bosses want to hear.

Formal communication systems also provide for **horizontal information flow.** In educational settings, formalized lateral communication occurs in department or grade-level meetings at the building level and in division head or cabinet meetings at the central office level. Katz and Kahn noted that communication among peers is critical for the effective operation of the system and provides a mechanism for task coordination and furnishes emotional and social support to the individual.

Equally important to the formal system of communication is the **informal communication** system. Informal communication uses primarily, but not exclusively, horizontal channels of communication. The informal network of communication, often referred to as the grapevine, does not follow the formal vertical or horizontal communication patterns. It develops its own structure based on informal relationship among organizational members. Information transmitted through the **grapevine** undergoes three types of changes, according to Lewis (1980). These are (a) leveling, (b) sharpening, and (c) assimilation (Lewis, 1980). **Leveling** refers to the dropping of details and the simplification of context. **Sharpening** involves embellishing a story with more vivid details and heightened drama. **Assimilation** is the tendency for people to modify rumors in a way that fits their needs. In spite of these changes, however, informal communication channels are less likely than formal channels to distort information (Kreps, 1990).

The grapevine can be a useful and powerful channel of communication and can be effectively used by the leader to disseminate information. For example, a principal or superintendent may want to provide informal leaders—key teachers, parents, or community members—with relevant, accurate information to suppress the spread of untrue or dangerous rumors and to augment formal communication channels. Efforts to restrict rumors through the informal communication system are usually futile and serve to further entrench the grapevine. Restricting informal information flow increases uncertainty in the system and promotes individuals' need for information. Kreps (1990) described an inverse relationship between formal and informal communication systems.

> The less the formal communication system is used to provide relevant information to organization members, the more they

depend on the grapevine for information, and the more power-ful the grapevine becomes. Conversely, the more the formal communication channels provide members with relevant orga-nizational information, the less these members depend on the grapevine for information. (p. 201–202)

Information Overload

Lack of communication is an often-cited complaint in organizations. In fact, the opposite is more likely the case. Principals and central office admin-istrators are deluged with volumes of paperwork, including local, state, and national reports, letters and other correspondence, as well as keeping up with professional reading. Computer technology contributes to the barrage of information through e-mail and instant accessibility to data through the Internet. The result can be information overload. Miller (1960) identified seven possible reactions to information overload, as follows:

- Omission—the failure to process some information
- Error—the incorrect processing of information
- Queuing—delaying responses during peak times
- Filtering—neglecting to process certain types of information
- Approximation—providing generalized or blanket responses
- Employing multiple channels—communicating through alternate channels, decentralization of communication processes
- Escape—turning away from task, ignoring communications

Katz and Kahn (1966) further distinguished these reactions to infor-mation overload as adaptive or maladaptive. They identified omission, error, and escape as inherently dysfunctional to the organization. Queuing, filtering, and approximation are legitimate ways to cope with information overload if they are used for a short duration, for the purpose of organiza-tional efficiency, and not for individual convenience. Katz and Kahn iden-tified the use of multiple channels as an effective response to information overload but considered it an organizational restructuring rather than an individual coping mechanism.

Networks

Patterns of communication are evident within organizations and between an organization and its surrounding environment as information is often channeled through networks of individuals. Rogers and Agarwala-Rogers (1976) defined a network as "interconnected individuals who are linked by patterned communication flows" (p. 110). They further identified associations that hold networks together as common work tasks, common liking or attraction to one another, or mutual interest in some topic.

Networks may be part of the formal organizational structure or the informal communication structure in an organization. Studies of networks in organizations analyze communication through interpersonal communications, formal communication structures, and cliques identified on the basis of individuals who communicate most with each other. **Rogers** and **Agarwala-Rogers** (1976) described four key roles that individuals play within communication networks. These are (a) gatekeeper, (b) liaison, (c) opinion leader, and (d) cosmopolite.

A **gatekeeper** is a person whose position in a communication structure is such that he or she controls messages flowing through a communication channel. For example, the principal's secretary often plays the role of gatekeeper by screening calls and visitors. The purpose of a gatekeeper is to decrease information overload and to filter out low-importance messages. This is a critical position to the effectiveness of the school and its leader, because the gatekeeper determines to a great extent what information the leader receives. Individuals may use informal communication channels to bypass the gatekeeper. In many ways, these informal bypasses enable the leader to keep a check on the formal gatekeeping function. In large organizations, several layers of gatekeepers may develop along the hierarchy, resulting in greater omissions and distortions of information as it filters to the top. For instance, a large city superintendent may deliberately insulate himself or herself from the day-to-day operations of individual schools. The superintendent relies on his or her cabinet or assistant superintendents to keep informed about important issues. Although this is a necessary mechanism to prevent information overload, the superintendent should remember that the information he or she receives has been filtered. Thus, there have been many opportunities for information to be distorted, and chances have increased that the superintendent is being given only information that others want him or her to hear.

A second role in communication networks is the **liaison.** A liaison is an individual who connects two or more cliques within a system but who does not belong to any clique. Similar to the function of liaison is what Fayol (1949) described as a bridge. Fayol's bridge differs from a liaison in that a bridge is formed between individuals at equal levels in different departments to facilitate horizontal communication and bypass the communication hierarchy. Liaisons play a crucial role in connecting subsystems within an organization or between organizations. When liaisons are removed, a system tends to disintegrate into isolated cliques. Liaisons play strategic roles in the organization and can either expedite or bottleneck the information flow. Liaisons may be characterized as having one foot in each of two different camps.

When no informal liaison emerges, it is often important for organizations to formally create such a position. Assistant principals often play the role of liaison between the principal and teachers. Teachers sometimes "test the waters" by communicating sensitive information to the assistant principal that they may be uncomfortable sharing directly with the principal. The assistant principal may be used as a sounding board for information a teacher wants the principal to know but feels that direct communication may violate an issue of trust with a colleague or student. This places the assistant in a situation where he or she must decide whether or not to communicate the information to the principal, and, if so, how to filter the information to the principal.

A third role that emerges in communication networks is that of the opinion leader. **Opinion leaders** are informal, rather than formal, leaders who regularly influence others' attitudes or behaviors. Opinion leaders generally have greater access to external and expert sources of information, and they connect the organization to that external environment. They also tend to be individuals who conform to the norms of the organization, thus giving them credibility with members of the organization. A teacher who is an opinion leader in a school may be one who is active in outside professional development activities but who is viewed as committed to the values and beliefs of the school. Other teachers rely on this person's opinion and the information he or she brings to the school. Teachers trust that the opinion leader will not promote practices or programs that are not compatible to the school's norms. The opinion leader will play a critical role in the change process and school improvement efforts. A principal wishing to introduce change into his or her school would be wise to first communicate and develop alliances with identified opinion leaders. If opinion leaders are convinced that a proposed change would benefit the school, they will influence others to accept the change.

A fourth communication network role is that of the **cosmopolite**. This is a person who has a great deal of communication with the system's external environment. In schools, cosmopolites may be administrators, teachers, or support staff. Their communications with the outside environment differ in that they are connected to different aspects of the environment. Administrators' contacts include leaders in community and professional organizations and other schools; thus, they are in a position to bring new ideas from these sources to their schools. Teachers and support staff are in a position to have greater contact with a variety of parents and students. These sources of information are vital links to understand the opinions and concerns of stakeholders as well as to disseminate information to the community.

The concept of networks also serves as a framework for systems thinking and is rooted in the mathematical and scientific principle of mapping. When mapped, relationships in a network are not linear, but they do involve cyclical paths that can generate feedback loops (Capra, 1996). Networks as described by physicists involve complex patterns of interaction that are self-organizing (Barabasi, 2002; Buchanan, 2002; Capra, 1996). That is, systems or organizations can evolve and create new structures through the processes of development and learning.

The concept of "small world phenomenon" (Milgram, 1967), popularly know as the phenomenon of six degrees of separation, describes how people are connected through randomly linked social networks. Milgram, a sociologist seeking to map social connections, conducted a "lost letter" experiment in which he found that letters misdirected were received by the intended person within six links of people.

A related network theory is found in a branch of mathematics known as graph theory. This theory demonstrates that no matter how many points there are in a distribution, they all can be linked together—even if there are a few randomly scattered points in that distribution. Sociological research conducted by Granovetter (1973) added to this mathematical concept in his discovery of weak links. Applied to communication theory, social connections unrelated to organizational work, which he described as weak links, tend to tie larger networks of people together—and with the fewest numbers of connections. For example, Ms. Apple, a principal at Grandview High School, knows Dr. Mackenzie, a local pediatrician, through their common membership in Rotary Club. At the last Rotary meeting, Ms. Apple discussed with Dr. Mackenzie that many students who were interested in music were not able to take band or orchestra classes, because of the cutback in arts programs and the need for students to take more academic classes. That evening, Dr. Mackenzie mentioned this to her husband, who was an amateur jazz musician. He approached the subject at a meeting of the Jazz Society, and two weeks later, Ms. Apple receives a call from a local group of professional jazz musicians offering to volunteer for after school lessons for some of her students with potential musical talent. As a result of the connections and mentoring between students and professional musicians, two talented seniors received music scholarships to different universities. You get the idea. Social connections, although "weak" links, may provide some of the most powerful connections among various organizations.

Nonverbal Communication

Facial expressions, voice intonation, dress, and body position and gestures play an important part in the communication process. Receivers of messages look for these nonverbal cues to confirm the words being communicated. For instance, the principal who says to a teacher, "I want to hear about your concerns with Mary's progress," while going through papers on her desk and glancing at her watch is sending an inconsistent message to the teacher. Her words say, "I care," but her actions say, "I don't." Mehrabian (1981) concluded that when verbal messages conflict with the vocal (intonation, projection, and resonance) and visual (facial and body expressions) elements accompanying the verbal message, people believe what is being communicated nonverbally. Vocal and visual elements work in tandem with the verbal message and confirm the sender's intent. For instance, the principal who tells a teacher, "I have confidence in your ability to lead the textbook committee" and places a hand on the teacher's shoulder or pats the teacher's back at the same time increases the effect of his message. In fact, Mehrabian (1981) found that only 7 percent of a message's effect comes from the verbal element, whereas 38 percent comes from the vocal and 55 percent from the visual elements.

Communication and Information Technology

As new information technologies (specifically the Internet and World Wide Web) become commonplace, the lines of information access are increasing and becoming more complex. Effective communication in cyberspace is something that educational leaders must take seriously. Computer-based information technologies, like other communication channels, can either promote or impede community building.

Advantages of computer-based information technology include greater access and interconnectivity among a variety of stakeholders, instantaneously and without actually occupying the same space. Through web pages, schools provide information that is more easily updated and less costly than print media and can even offer interactive opportunities through electronic chats, electronic surveys, e-mail, and the like. Conversely, stakeholders most likely to use information-based technologies are those who are computer literate and who have ready access to the technology. Certain segments of a school's community may be left out of electronic communication, thus widening a gap that already exists between various subcultures, particularly related to socioeconomic and age factors. Thus, educational leaders must consider the context of their communities.

Electronic communication channels make it difficult for traditional gatekeepers of information to control or withhold information, but at the same time have given rise to "e-influentials," people who use and know the Internet and influence other Internet users (Fawkes & Gregory, 2000). However, technology allows for customization, a defining characteristic of the information age (Chance & Lee, 2001). Thus, there is potential for information technology to play an increasing role in communication strategies to involve a greater diversity of stakeholders and to respond to individual needs of stakeholders.

Application to School Leadership

Communication is a primary function of leadership and a driving force of the school organization. Anthropologists identify language as an intricate element of culture. Similarly, organizational culture is greatly defined by an organization's communication structures, because such structures enable the transmission of messages, intentions, goals, and work products of the organization. Formal and informal communication structures are also indicative of the power structure of the organization and reflect the norms, values, and beliefs of the organization.

School leaders must remember that communication is bound to the context in which it occurs and that it is not a linear, but rather a transformational process (Kreps, 1990, p. 26–27). Numerous components—including the reactions of people to messages, the meanings people extract from messages, the time and place of communication, the relationship between communicators, past experiences, and purposes people have for communicating—interact simultaneously in the communication process.

Organizations serve to restrict and direct communication. School leaders must be aware of how the organizational structure may affect their receipt and transmission of information, both through the formal and informal systems within the school. From a leadership perspective, the formal and informal systems of communication may act as a check and balance system for ensuring the intent of a message is accurately received. Leaders should use both formal and informal channels of communication to transmit important messages to stakeholders. In addition, educational leaders must be cognizant of the roles individuals play in restricting or enhancing the flow of information. Key players should be identified and used appropriately.

Organizational communication involves not only communication within the school or school system but also information output to and feedback from the external environment. Understanding that schools are open systems, educational leaders should consider all communications in the context of flowing into and out of the system, no matter where the message originates. In addition, leaders must keep in mind that messages received are filtered through channels of other people and through the experiences and perceptions of the receiver. There may be no such thing as a simple, clear message.

To illustrate the inflow and outflow of communication, consider the example of a high school principal who simply asks her secretary to hold all calls and visitors for 10 minutes while she conferences with a teacher. During that 10-minute conference, the secretary receives a call from a parent asking to speak to the principal—to which the secretary replies that the principal is in conference with a teacher and offers to take a message. After leaving his name and number, the caller hangs up and tells his wife, who is leaving for work, that the principal is unavailable. When his wife arrives at her office, a coworker greets her with a "Good morning," to which she replies, "What's good about it?" When the coworker asks what's wrong, she explains that she is worried about some trouble her high school son is having, and that she and her husband have been unable to get in touch with the principal. The coworker then begins to commiserate that she knows what it's like. She tried for a week to get in touch with their daughter's teacher before they made contact. "Schools just don't care about parents," the coworker concludes. As this example illustrates, there is no such thing as a simple message from one person to another. Communication is not static and does not stop with the receiver. Nor does internal organizational communication remain contained within the organization. As a result of the dynamics of an open system, all communications are potential messages for public relations. All messages, no matter how simple and forthright, will be filtered through receivers' belief systems and will be interpreted and decoded by receivers in terms of their experiences.

Summary

This chapter defined four basic elements of communication—source, receiver, message, and channel. The source is the originator of a message, the intent of which is defined by the source. The message is channeled to the receiver through some medium. The receiver then decodes, or interprets, the message. The effect of the message is thus defined by the receiver's perception.

Although this simplified model provides a conceptualization of the basic components of the communication process, organizational communication is much more complex. Organizational structure, in terms of formal hierarchies and channels of communication, serves to restrict and direct communication. Formal communication systems work in tandem with informal communication systems within the organization. In addition, organizational communication involves information output and feedback from the school's external environment. Communication theory applied to organizations provides a perspective from which to view the operations of the total system. Using Rogers and Agarwala-Rogers' analogy of communication as the lifeblood of the organization, educational leaders are urged to see communication as the means by which schools and school systems are sustained. The flow of communication is constant and systemic, and information must circulate to maintain the system.

Educational leaders play a key role in managing the flow of information so that meanings of messages as interpreted by receivers are closely aligned to the intended message of the sender. Communication theory offers educational leaders a framework for analyzing a school system's communication structure and identifying individuals who play key roles in managing information flow. Whereas clear communication is important, too much information can result in overloading individuals and ultimately have a negative impact on the functioning of the system. By taking stock of a school's communication system, educational leaders can deliberately manage those individuals who act as gatekeepers, liaisons, opinion leaders, and cosmopolites.

Educational leaders must remember that communication pervades organizations, especially as information becomes widely disseminated through e-technology. Messages are communicated not only through words but also through nonverbal behaviors. Clear communication means that one's actions are congruent with one's verbal messages. Communication research proves the adage that actions speak louder than words. The fact that we can often better relay our message in person has implications for web-based and e-mail communication forums. Finally, educational leaders must realize that messages are relayed through a network of systems and people. Networks sometimes provide fortuitous opportunities, but they can also result in information becoming distorted in ways that harm the organization.

Theory into Practice

Who's on First? What's on Third?

"Thank goodness it's Friday," thought Betty, as she put away her last file and got ready to leave school. She was glad there were no activities to supervise at Banks Middle School this weekend, because she was tired. She was going to spend this weekend relaxing and decompressing. Betty was troubled and knew that she would need to be mentally prepared Monday morning for her appointment with Dr. Lamb, the principal of Banks Middle School.

This Friday marked the end of the first quarter of school and the 61st day Betty Miller had served as one of three assistant principals at Banks Middle School. (Not that she was counting the days!) Even though Betty was the new kid on the block at Banks, she was not a "green" administrator. She had been an administrative consultant in the Curriculum Department for three years and a Dean of Students at Lincolnshire High School for two years, before being appointed as Assistant Principal at Banks. Beacon City School District was a large, urban district, and Betty had worked for the district as a teacher for 10 years before moving into administration. Betty thought she understood how to work effectively in and through the bureaucracy of a large district until this year.

Dr. Lamb had been principal of Banks ever since it opened six years ago. Betty knew when she signed on that Dr. Lamb was a stickler for rules and regulations and expected people to do their jobs. He was especially particular about reports and paperwork, and he expected perfection on all written communication that left his school. Betty didn't have a problem with that. In fact, she respected and admired Dr. Lamb when she worked in the Curriculum Department. She could always count on his school to do things right, and he had always been very receptive to working with central administration and curriculum consultants.

The administrative team at Banks Middle School consisted of the principal and the three assistant principals, Betty, James Carver, and Marjorie Dixon. James was a seasoned administrator, having been a high school principal for 15 years in another state. He had "retired" from his previous district and had moved to Beacon City to continue in administration while enjoying some additional income and building a second retirement nest egg. He had served as an assistant high school principal in the district before coming to Banks Middle School when it opened. This was his last administrative job, and he had announced that he would retire at the end of next year. Marjorie was in her third year of administration, all of which had been at Banks.

At the first administrative team meeting before school started, Dr. Lamb outlined and delegated the various administrative duties. Dr. Lamb was very traditional in his organization of administrative tasks. He delegated all student discipline matters to the assistants, assigning each a specific grade level. He divided teacher supervision and evaluation equally among the four administrators, giving each of them particular departments to oversee. Other duties were divided by function. Betty had been given responsibilities for supervising the cafeteria, buses, teacher duty schedules, and student recognition programs. James' responsibilities included facilities and maintenance, scheduling, and student activities (including athletics). Marjorie was in charge of special education facilitation and student government. Dr. Lamb retained responsibility over curriculum matters and considered himself the coordinator of total school programming. Dr. Lamb had emphasized in the first administrative team meeting that he expected his assistants to take charge of their responsibilities, and though he expected to be informed of matters that impacted other areas he did not want to manage the details.

Betty had taken Dr. Lamb's words seriously as she began her first days at Banks. She put together duty schedules for teachers and organized cafeteria and bus supervision. During the first two weeks, some conflicts in responsibility appeared, but Betty decided that this was to be expected. One conflict had been whether Betty or James had the authority to direct custodial staff during lunch times when they were assigned to the cafeteria. Another conflict occurred when James did not inform Betty that a bus would be late and she had already pulled staff from duty. When the bus arrived, no one was there to supervise the students. Yet another incident involving bus supervision had occurred when Betty directed a maintenance worker to remove equipment from the sidewalk, because she was concerned that students might get hurt as they loaded on to the buses. The maintenance worker complained to Dr. Lamb that his supervisor, Mr. Carver, had directed him to clean the sidewalks that afternoon. In each of these cases, Dr. Lamb had intervened and given his own directives to the support staff, often contradicting Betty's instructions.

Betty had decided that these were minor conflicts that would resolve themselves as the team got used to working with each other. "How wrong I was," she thought. Such incidents had continued to occur, and each time they did, she felt as if Dr. Lamb overrode her authority. Even worse, the principal often directed cafeteria staff and counselors on duty in the cafeteria to do something without informing her. On several days, she found herself without help during lunch supervision because Dr. Lamb had directed counselors to make emergency scheduling changes during that time.

So far, Betty had been able to discuss issues with Dr. Lamb, and she felt she had been able to gently resolve each issue. The events this week, however, could not be gently pushed aside. Her reputation was on the line, and she decided she must deal with this issue officially and forthrightly.

It had started yesterday when she received a call from Sue Little, a colleague with whom she had worked in the district curriculum department. Sue was seeking help to relocate wood shop tools that had been purchased by federal funds. Banks had been given the equipment six years ago for its vocational program. However, the wood shop class had been disbanded after two years and the equipment stored. There were now three middle schools that were starting programs that desperately needed this equipment. Because Sue knew Betty, she decided to call her to see if she could arrange the equipment transfer. Betty knew that such transfers were standard operating procedure in the district, and because she supervised the vocational and technical department, she saw no problem in doing this. Just to be sure, however, she consulted with Dr. Lamb about the transfer, and he said, "Go ahead and arrange it."

This morning she had asked a custodian to have the room open Monday afternoon when teachers from the other schools would be there to collect the equipment. Not more than an hour later, James Carver was in her office. Angrily, he told her she had no business messing with the equipment stored in that room. "I'm in charge of custodians and facilities. If you need something, you should go through me. I have plans for that equipment!" Betty surprised herself when she retorted, just as angrily, "That equipment isn't your responsibility, and, besides, I cleared it with Dr. Lamb already." James' response was to turn on his heel and walk out. Betty, still angry, marched to Dr. Lamb's office hoping to see him before James did. As it turned out, Dr. Lamb had left campus early for a meeting and would not be back until Monday morning. Betty told his secretary, "Then make an appointment for me to talk to him at 7:30 Monday morning."

Sample Analysis

Dr. Lamb has established a formal structure of communication, which is primarily vertical. His statement that he should be informed of matters of overlapping or conflicting responsibilities discouraged horizontal communication between assistant principals. He further encouraged vertical communication when he described his function as the coordinator of curriculum and total school programming. He obviously expected that all information should be funneled to him so he could arbitrate conflicts rather than having his assistants collaborate with one another. His actions reinforced this process as he intervened with decisions in each instance of conflict.

The organizational structure established serves to effectively restrict the lateral flow of information between assistant principals and direct communication downward. It is evident that the responsibilities as assigned to assistant principals are not mutually exclusive, and the lack of a formal horizontal communication system is interfering with effective and efficient operations. As Katz and Kahn (1966) noted, communication among peers is a necessary mechanism for task coordination and furnishes emotional and social support to the individual. In this case, both task coordination and emotional support are lacking. Betty and James are in regular conflict and both undoubtedly feel disempowered.

Although Dr. Lamb may believe that he must be the information broker and resolve all conflicts to maintain control, he may in fact be setting himself up for information overload. It is even possible that Dr. Lamb's assignment of counselors to pressing issues when they were supposed to supervise students in the cafeteria could have been the result of information overload. Had Dr. Lamb simply forgotten to inform Betty? Omission of some information is one response to information overload.

Dr. Lamb may view this organizational structure as a way for him to stay informed and better coordinate programs; however, he may be overreliant on the formal, vertical communication channels. Communication theory would inform Dr. Lamb that upward communication is less frequent and more likely to be inaccurate and skewed to call attention to positive information rather than negative information.

As for Betty Miller, she had been wise to clear her actions with the principal first. Because Dr. Lamb values the formal chain of command and is a stickler for procedure, she would be well advised to spend this weekend preparing a written report of this incident to give to the principal at their meeting Monday morning.

Reader's Application

I Heard It through the Grapevine

Twin Peaks was a conservative community whose residents valued academic achievement and strong moral guidelines for their children. Parents generally were not opposed to change if they were convinced it would improve student success, but they certainly would not support unproven alterations to a school curriculum they felt was working.

Thus, when Marcia Long, Twin Peaks Elementary principal, decided to introduce the concept of performance-based assessments to Twin Peaks, she had proceeded slowly and carefully. It wasn't just because new state standards and testing required such assessments; Marcia truly felt that performance assessment would benefit students and better prepare them for the future. She had been sure to gain approval and discuss her plans with the superintendent before beginning any discussions with parents or staff. The superintendent had cleared the way with the Board of Education, explaining their rationale for change, including state reform mandates and student benefits.

For the most part, the change process was going well. In fifth grade, teachers had implemented performance assessments that aligned with state tests and curriculum and that became part of their report of student progress to parents. In addition to traditional grades on report cards, a rubric of standards and expectations was also given to parents. The decision to use both forms of reporting had been the result of Marcia's meetings with her Parent Advisory Committee, who felt parents would be more receptive and understanding of change if traditional reporting forms were maintained. In addition to her work with the Parent Advisory Committee, Marcia had consulted with many individual parents who had come to her with questions or concerns. Marcia had arranged for fifth grade teachers to have extra planning time and in-service training to design and incorporate performance assessments into their curriculum.

With the exception of one teacher, Janice French, the fifth-grade faculty was enthusiastic about the project. Unfortunately, the one faculty member who disliked the change was adamantly opposed and very vocal. She voiced her concerns not only in school but also to her friends, many of whom had children in Twin Peaks Elementary School. Janice's naysaying attitude was nothing new, however, and most of the time other teachers just ignored her.

They saw Janice as basically a kindhearted person but only a mediocre teacher. They saw her as unwilling to change her traditional ways of instruction. Parents were of a similar mind. She generally did well with students whose parents preferred the ways of teaching with which they were familiar. That is, whole-group instruction and lots of bookwork and paper and pencil tasks. The other fifth-grade teachers and Marcia believed that Janice would eventually comply with the new process, as was her usual pattern.

Marcia was therefore a little surprised about the phone call she received from Linda Bell, the PTA president. Linda and Marcia had great rapport, and Linda was like Marcia's eyes and ears of the community. Linda had on several occasions given Marcia useful information about the rumor mill in the community. Today's call was in that same vein.

Linda got right to the point. "Your name came up last night at softball practice," she said.

"Okay," replied Marcia. "Tell me more."

Linda relayed the latest gossip. "Seems that Lucy Nellis has a problem with the new fifth-grade assessment program."

"Oh, great," thought Marcia. "I spent two hours with her last week, and she seemed satisfied." Lucy was a member of an extremely conservative, albeit small, church in town. Half of their three dozen members homeschooled their children, and the other half played watchdog over Peak Valley Public School District. Marcia had always tried to openly communicate with parents of this congregation, and Lucy was an active member of her Parent Advisory Council.

Linda continued, "I wasn't too concerned when I heard that Lucy was questioning this new program. After all, she questions everything. What bothered me was the conversation I had with Ellen Slater, the wife of First State Bank's president, and Joann Glade, the School Board president's wife. They were talking about this new, experimental curriculum in the fifth grade. I know they didn't hear it from Lucy, so that means the grapevine is buzzing. I knew you'd want to know."

Student Exercise: Case Analysis

1. Analyze this case in terms of open systems and formal and informal communication channels that Marcia Long used.

2. Identify some of the key players in Peak Valley's communication network.

3. How should Marcia Long react to the information relayed to her by the PTA president?

References

Barabasi, A. L. (2002). *Linked: The new science of networks.* Cambridge, MA: Perseus.

Barnard, C. I. (1938). *The functions of the executive.* Cambridge, MA: Harvard University Press.

Berlo, D. K. (1960). *The process of communication.* New York: Rinehart & Winston.

Buchanan, M. (2002). *Nexus: Small worlds and the groundbreaking networks.* New York: W.W. Norton.

Capra, F. (1996). *The web of life: A new scientific understanding of living systems.* New York: Anchor Books.

Chance, P. L., & Lee, K. (2001). Exploring technology, change, and chaos theory: Moving educational leadership preparation programs into the new millennium. In T. J. Kowalski & G. Perreault (Eds.), *21st Century challenges for school administrators* (pp. 189–202). Lanham, MD: Scarecrow Press.

Fawkes, J., & Gregory, A. (2000). Applying communication theories to the Internet. *Journal of Communication Management, 5*(2) 109–124.

Fayol, H. (1949). *General and industrial management.* London: Pitman.

Granovetter, M. (1973). The strength of weak ties: A network theory revisited. *Sociological Theory, 1,* 203–233.

Hanson, E. M. (1996). Educational administration and organizational behavior. Boston: Allyn and Bacon.

Katz, D., & Kahn, R. L. (1966). The social psychology of organizations. New York: Wiley.

Kreps, G. L. (1990). Organizational communication: Theory and practice (2nd ed.). White Plains, NY: Longman.

Lewis, P. V. (1980). Organizational communication: The essence of effective management. Columbus, OH: Grid Publishing Co.

Mehrabian, A. (1981). Silent messages: Implicit communication of emotions and attitudes (2nd ed.). Belmont, CA: Wadsworth Publishing Co.

Milgram, S. (1967). The small-world problem. Psychology Today, 1, 60–67.

Miller, J. G. (1960). Information input, overload, and psychopathology. American Journal of Psychiatry, 116, 695–704.

Roethlisberger, F. J., & Dickson, W. J. (1939). Management and the worker. Cambridge, MA: Harvard University Press.

Rogers, E. M., & Agarwala-Rogers, R. (1976). Communication in organizations. New York: Free Press.

9

Decision Making: An Essential Function of Leadership

Synopsis of Decision-Making Theories

Decision making is a primary function of leadership. In fact, Griffiths (1959) suggested that school administration was decision making. Decision-making theories can be grouped into two major categories—normative and descriptive. Normative theories offer models, or ideal processes, for decision making. Descriptive theories attempt to explain how decisions actually come about in practice. A major consideration for leaders is the involvement of others in the decision-making process. Both normative and descriptive theories fall along a continuum from the leader as sole decision maker to full participatory decision making.

As in most aspects of organizational theory, decision-making models have changed over time and reflect the historical context from which they evolved. Traditional models of administrative decision making are based on a rational, scientific approach to management. Rooted in the framework of Taylor's scientific management model, these models approach decision making as a rational and deliberate process undertaken by a single authority. As the scientific approach to management has given way to a human resources and systems orientation, decision-making models reflect a more participatory process and more accurately represent the realities of administrative practice.

Decision-making theories inform the practitioner by providing a framework for the procedural processes of decision making and offering guidelines to determine when and to what extent others should be involved in the decision-making process. In addition, descriptive theories point out individual, organizational, and other factors that impact the decision-making process.

Applications for School Leaders

Understanding decision-making theories will help school leaders:

- Outline an appropriate procedure for making decisions
- Determine when and to what extent others should be involved in decision making
- Identify factors within and outside the organization that impact decision making
- Develop strategies to prevent crisis decision making
- Understand the effect of time on the decision-making process

---

The Leader as Decision Maker

Rational Decision-Making Models

Classical theory assumes that decision making is a linear and logical process where the best possible solution is sought after exhaustively examining all possible alternatives (Hoy & Miskel, 1996). Practicing administrators rarely if ever have the time, resources, or knowledge to employ such an idealistic decision-making process. While recognizing the realities of practice, decision-making models that evolved from classical theory continued to put forth systematic strategies with either linear or circular flow patterns. An example of a linear decision-making process is that proposed by **Peter Drucker** (1974). His process consisted of the following five steps:

- Define the problem.
- Analyze the problem.
- Develop alternative solutions.
- Decide on the best solution.
- Convert decisions into effective actions. (pp. 19–20)

Litchfield (1956) described decision making in terms of complex interactions, or as "a series of wheels within wheels" (p 13). **Wayne Hoy** and **Cecil Miskel** (1996) depicted decision making as an **action cycle,** indicating that many stages of decision making may be occurring simultaneously. However, the stages of the action cycle are outlined in sequential steps, as follows:

- ◆ Recognize and define the problem or issue.
- ◆ Analyze the difficulties in the existing situation.
- ◆ Establish criteria for problem resolution.
- ◆ Develop a plan or strategy for action.
- ◆ Initiate the plan of action.

Defining the problem refers to how a problem is conceptualized. At this stage, the perspective that a leader takes on a problem is important and will frame the options and alternatives considered. Leaders must view the problem realistically through a rich and deep understanding of the formal and informal organization and the people and events in the outside environment that impact it. Sometimes a seemingly simple problem or issue may be symptomatic of a larger, more complex issue. The administrator who does not consider an issue within its role in a larger context may err by making superficial decisions that do not resolve, or may make worse, larger and more important problems. For instance, a principal receives what might be considered a routine request from a parent to review the third-grade curriculum guide. A routine response might be simply to provide the requested document to the parent. However, the principal who views this situation in a larger context will consider deeper issues that might have prompted this request. Has the parent previously discussed instructional or curriculum concerns with the third-grade teacher? Have there been recent community conflicts over the school's curriculum? Has the parent had any conflicts with teachers or staff? Does the parent ascribe to particular religious or philosophical views, which may conflict with the official district curriculum? If any of these questions can be answered affirmatively, then this apparently routine request may indicate a larger, more complex issue is at hand. In that case, the administrator may want to explore more alternatives in responding to the request.

In essence, through the process of defining the problem, the leader has initiated the **analysis** stage of decision making. Once the problem has been properly framed and defined, it can be classified as to what type of problem it is. Such classification aids in choosing an appropriate course of action.

Drucker identified two types of decisions—**generic and unique.** Generic decisions are routine or recurring problems that can be solved through established policies and procedures. Unique decisions are those requiring creative solutions where there are no applicable guidelines or policies. Herbert Simon's (1960) model of decision making, discussed more fully later in this chapter, categorized decisions along a continuum from programmed to nonprogrammed. Once a leader determines what type of problem is being faced, analysis continues by evaluating the importance of the problem, ascertaining what further information is needed, and verifying time constraints within which a decision must be made.

The next stage is the identification of the criteria for an acceptable solution. **Criteria** are used to judge or evaluate possible alternatives. Hopefully, the criteria used to judge possible solutions are compatible with the organization's mission and goals. The superintendent who always measures a decision by whether it is in the best interests of students is an exemplary model of this aspect of decision making.

A critical area in decision making is the development of a **plan of action.** This involves brainstorming alternative solutions, identifying consequences of each alternative, and evaluating each solution against the established criteria. Although the ideal decision-making model calls for an exhaustive list of all solutions, in reality, administrators will consider only a limited number of alternatives. This results from both time constraints placed on decision making as well as the limited capacity of an individual to conceive of all possibilities. Because creative and reasonable decisions are time-consuming, administrators often tend to act too quickly. In situations where a leader is pressured to make an immediate decision about a complex problem, it is important to consider temporary solutions.

A **temporary solution** can serve to alleviate immediate, superficial problems while providing time for a more thorough analysis of the problem and the development of more creative alternatives. For example, during a single day, four incidents of vandalism in student restrooms occurred during times when students were in class. Some immediate action is needed until the problem can be further investigated. Thus, the principal may decide to impose a temporary restriction on student access to restrooms; assign teachers or other adults to supervise restrooms during passing times; and, require students to obtain a pass during class time. The principal further imposes a ban on teachers allowing students to leave the classroom except for an emergency. Although this decision may solve the presenting problem, the vandalism incidents may possibly be superficial indicators of a more complex problem. First and foremost, information is needed about who the vandals are so that they can accept the consequences for their actions rather than having all students punished for the actions of a few. Furthermore, these vandalism incidents suggest other questions to consider. Do students generally take pride in their school environment, or do these actions reflect an attitude in which students do not feel a sense of belonging or responsibility to their school community? Are these incidents isolated, childish pranks, or are they symptomatic of an unsafe climate in the school? Until these questions are answered and analyzed, a long-term solution cannot be determined.

This scenario also represents a common mistake made by many administrators, which may be described as "fire fighting." Fire fighting refers to making immediate, short-term decisions that provide temporary solutions to superficial problems. Although temporary solutions are often necessary, as the previous example demonstrates, administrators whose decision making consists of one temporary solution after another, moving from crisis to crisis, are not providing effective leadership. Effective leadership requires thoughtful, deliberate, and visionary decisions, which are made in the best interest of all students and are mindful of the goals and mission of the school.

The final phase of decision making is to **implement the decision.** This requires specifying how a decision will be carried out. A plan of action details what will be done, when it will be done, how and where certain operations will be performed, and who will do them. At this point, communication is vital. Individuals impacted by the decision must be informed of their responsibilities and how their roles relate to others as well as to the overall plan. The leader must oversee and monitor the plan of action to ensure it is carried out appropriately. Further, the decision and plan of action should be evaluated to determine if the decision effectively solved the problem or if unexpected consequences resulted from the implementation of the plan.

Herbert Simon, a professor of computer science and psychology at Carnegie Mellon University, conducted fundamental research on decision making, using computers to simulate human thinking. Simon (1960) conceptualized decision making as a logical, rational process. He identified three stages in the decision-making process: (a) the intelligence activity, (b) the design activity, and (c) the choice activity. The first stage, the intelligence activity, refers to the act of searching for, and finding, occasions that call for a decision. Simon's use of the military term, "intelligence," reflects the historical context of a post-World War II perspective. The second phase, design, involves the invention, development, and analysis of possible alternatives or courses of action. Like the intelligence activity, the design stage is comparable to military practices of scenario development in planning operations for possible future events. The third stage, choice activity, is defined as selecting a particular course of action from those brainstormed in the design stage.

Whereas this model reflects a systematic approach to decision making, Simon recognized that people's thinking and behavior is not always rational. Simon contended that rationality was limited by the organizational environment and that administrators seek a decision that is satisfactory or "good enough" and not necessarily optimal, a process he termed **satisficing.** Thus, decision makers consider only a few relevant factors and are satisfied with oversimplification of the issues.

Simon further described a continuum of decision types from programmed to nonprogrammed. **Programmed decisions** are those that are routine, where a specific procedure is in place. In schools, programmed decisions would include the placement of routine textbook and supply orders, the procedure for teachers taking sick leave and obtaining a substitute, or any normal procedure carried out on a regular basis. **Nonprogrammed decisions** are those that may be new or particularly difficult problems, where there is no established procedure for dealing with them. Examples of nonprogrammed decisions in schools might include responding to a violent action on campus, or dealing with parental complaints about an established curriculum.

Simon contended that information technology and computer simulation have created conditions where more and more decisions can be included in programmed procedures. Although Simon's focus was on decisions made in business and government entities, his conceptualization has proved to be true in the case of educational institutions. A most pertinent example is in situations involving crisis management. Because of recent events of random killings in schools, such as those that occurred in Jonesboro, Arkansas, and Littleton, Colorado, schools throughout the nation have instituted procedures for dealing with heretofore unpredictable crises. Although a specific situation might not be foreseen, general procedures can be established to deal with possible scenarios. The closer decision making comes to the programmed end of the spectrum, the more likely it is that a decision will be rational, at least in terms of the organization's mission and purpose, and the less apt the decision will be based on an irrational or emotional response.

Descriptive Theories of Decision Making

Decision-making models heretofore described focused on a rational approach to decision making. Although some models recognized the difficulties inherent in applying theory to practice, the theories described so far put forth models for how decision making should be approached. Other researchers proposed theories that attempted to describe how decision making actually occurs in organizations.

Charles Lindblom (1959) described an **incremental approach to decision making,** which he characterized as the "science of muddling through." The incremental approach to decision making is a process where setting objectives and generating alternatives occur simultaneously. A limited number of alternatives are considered, and only a few consequences for each alternative are contemplated. Lindblom termed this decision-making strategy "disjointed incrementalism," where changes are made in small increments with apparent disorder. Series of small moves are made away from the problem rather than toward defined goals. Because goals are not considered, ends may be adjusted to the means. That is, objectives can be made to fit with policies. Lindblom describes this feature of decision making as an active reconstructive process. Problems remain more or less permanent and are rarely solved, only alleviated. Disjointed incrementalism is a fragmented process. Problem analysis and evaluation of solutions occur at different times or simultaneously in several places.

Lindblom's model of decision making emerged from his perspective as a political scientist and policy analyst and was specifically applied to decision making in the political sphere and government policy. He argued that it is possible to make changes as quickly by small, incremental steps as it is by making broad, sweeping innovations. He identified the strength of this approach as one of relative safety that ensures at least some movement toward change. To fully analyze hugely complex problems and consider all consequences of an exhaustive list of possible solutions will deter decision makers from taking any action at all.

Schools, as political entities, are often faced with problems that correspond to this disjointed incrementalism approach. In fact, most educational reform efforts can be characterized by fragmented incrementalism, and school leaders at all levels find themselves more or less forced into this mode of decision making. For instance, for the past two decades national attention has been paid to reforming the American public education system. Literature on educational reconstruction often describes these efforts as waves (Murphy, 1990), or periods, of reform. Although educational scholars and political pundits have proposed various idyllic scenarios as the desired vision, to completely restructure an entire educational system through broad-based change would be so complex that to consider the ramifications of the entire process is virtually impossible. However, various federal and state policies have emerged in the last score of years that have attempted to chip away at the perceived ills of the system. Although the "problem" remains largely the same, substantial changes have occurred. The path, nevertheless, continues to meander, and the end continues to be modified in response to current policies. Effective school leaders approach decision making in this arena with a level of flexibility, and visionary leaders do not allow these incremental changes to deter them from their community's valued goals.

Take, for example, the case of recent initiatives to modify academic standards for student achievement. The standards movement may be viewed as an evolution of previous reforms in school accountability, which were characterized by attention to aligning curriculum with standardized testing. New policies have replaced old ones in fragmented ways through federal and state initiatives under various entitlements and legislation; thus, efforts at reforming the desired ends for student achievement have come incrementally. School leaders must respond to the political and legal realities of these policy changes and often find that new mandates conflict with old ones, that new parameters are defined, or that new procedures are required to meet the same objective. Effective school leaders adjust to new policy demands, rather than resist changes, by adhering to new policies without sacrificing long-term objectives. In this sense, school administrators take advantage of incremental decisions made on a larger, political context and use policies in ways that benefit their school site or district.

A second descriptive model of decision making is one proposed by **James March** (1988). March did not view decision making as rational, but rather as bounded rationality. Those boundaries include limits of the mental capacity of decision makers, political limits, and organizational limits. Limited mental capacity refers to the fact that the mind of the decision maker can deal with only a limited amount of information and with a limited number of alternatives. Additionally, decision makers are influenced by their own and others' preferences, and people change their minds about what they want. Political limits pertain to the interaction of various persons and groups within an organization. According to March, organizational goals are not given; they are negotiated and bargained. Each person, department, and unit within the organization has a preference about what the organization should be like and what its goals should be. Organizational limits are set by what March termed **organized anarchies.** Organized anarchies are characterized by three general principles:

- ◆ An organization defines its goals by what it is doing, rather than through aims clearly defined in advance.
- ◆ Organizations work through trial and error rather than by clear processes understood by its members.
- ◆ Organizations are constantly changing.

Decision making is thus affected by these cognitive, political, and organizational attributes. March described the decision-making process in terms of four tendencies: (a) quasi-resolution of conflict, (b) uncertainty avoidance, (c) problematic search, and (d) organization learning.

Quasi-resolution of conflict is inherent in organizations because of their bureaucratic nature. Units or departments within an organization deal with problems from the point of view of their specialized function. When decisions made within a department conflict with decisions made for the benefit of another department, conflict occurs and decisions made may not be in the best interests of the overall organization. For example, when a high school social studies department schedules a major research paper during the school's final basketball tournament, student athletes and other students participating in game-related activities find they cannot successfully complete the research paper and fully participate in the athletic program. One strategy employed to alleviate conflict is termed "acceptable level decision" where each department makes decisions that are acceptable to different interests, but may not be optimal for the overall organization. Such would be the case when the English department enforces strict standards of writing whereas the math department imposes no standards for correct spelling or grammar. Although the two decisions are acceptable to both departments, the overall outcome for students is less than optimal. Another approach is to give sequential attention to goals—first to goals of one department and then to the other.

A second tendency of decision making is uncertainty avoidance. Because future trends and long-term forecasting are uncertain, decision makers respond to current information. Administrators tend to deal with pressing problems and avoid planning for the future. This is related to the third characteristic of decision making—problematic search. That is, administrators seek ways to solve an immediate problem and when one solution is determined, they stop looking for other alternatives. Furthermore, solutions tend to be similar to old approaches; radical change is avoided. This description of decision making is similar to Lindblom's incrementalism strategy (1959). The final characteristic, organizational learning, refers to the phenomenon that decision makers learn through trial and error. They do not begin by knowing all that is necessary to make decisions.

March and his associates (Cohen, March, & Olsen, 1972) put forth the **Garbage Can Model** of decision making, which suggested that certain aspects of the decision-making process are apparently thrown away. For instance, decision makers ask for information but do not use it, people insist on their right to input but do not exercise it, or departments meet for numerous hours to make a decision but do not implement it. Various problems and solutions are dumped into a garbage can. According to this model, decisions are the result of the interaction among problems, solutions, people, and choices; however, all of these are acting independently of one another. Decisions occur when timing is coincidental; that is, problems, solutions, people, and choices end up in the garbage can at the same time. Solutions join with problems and people make choices because they happen to have the time and drive to pursue the solution at the time. Decisions are thus not truly the outcome of some deliberate process.

Participatory and Group Theories
of Decision Making

As organizational theories have evolved, approaches to decision making that emphasized the leader as solely responsible for decision making have been succeeded by decision-making models that highlight employee participation and involvement. Participation in organizational decision making entails interaction between the leader and others in the organization. Modern organizational theory is historically rooted in the human relations period of the 1930s, with the works of such authors as Mary Parker Follett and Elton Mayo. Foundations for many of the concepts expressed during this period came from the studies conducted at the Hawthorne Plant owned by the Western Electric Company (Mayo, 1933). The essential message of the human relations period was that people work harder and are more productive when they are treated well. Later theorists, such as McGregor, Maslow, Herzberg, and Argyris, built on the ideas of participation as a necessary component of effective and productive organizations.

In terms of decision-making theory, participation has not been so much a question of whether or not employees should be involved in decision making but rather to what extent and under what circumstances decision making should be participatory. From studies of people's perceptions of how much influence they and others have in their organizations, Tannenbaum (1968) derived a concept of total control or **area of influence** of workers, supervisors and managers. In essence, Tannenbaum found that through participative decision making, management increased its control by giving up some of its authority.

Robert Tannenbaum and **Warren Schmidt** (1973) presented a continuum that described increasing **freedom of followers to influence decision making.** They outlined the following decision making scenarios, from lowest amount to highest amount of freedom for followers:

- Manager makes decision and announces it.
- Manager "sells" decision.
- Manager presents ideas and invites questions.
- Manager presents tentative decision subject to change.
- Manager presents problem, gets suggestions, makes decision.
- Manager defines limits; asks group to make decision.
- Manager permits subordinates to function within limits defined by superior. (Tannenbaum & Schmidt, 1973, p. 164)

Victor Vroom and **Philip Yetton** (1973) developed a normative model for decision making that prescribed what processes managers should use to solve problems, detailing to what extent and under what circumstances subordinates should be involved in the decision-making process. They identified five processes that a manager might use in dealing with issues affecting a group of subordinates.

- ◆ Leader makes the decision using available information.
- ◆ Leader obtains information from subordinates, then makes the decision. The leader may or may not identify the problem when requesting information from subordinates.
- ◆ Leader shares the problem with relevant subordinates on an individual basis and gets their ideas and suggestions. The leader then makes the decision.
- ◆ Leader shares the problem with subordinates in a group meeting, and then the leader makes the decision.
- ◆ Leader convenes subordinates and facilitates the group toward consensus on a solution to a problem. The leader does not try to influence the group toward a particular solution and is willing to accept the solution that has support of the entire group.

Vroom and Yetton's decision-making model proposed that all of these processes are appropriate depending on the circumstances. They used a decision tree with a series of seven yes or no questions. The leader answers each question and follows a flow chart to determine which decision-making process is appropriate in a particular situation. The questions the leader should address are:

- ◆ Is there a quality requirement such that one solution is likely to be more rational than another?
- ◆ Does the leader have sufficient information to make a quality decision?
- ◆ Is the problem structured?
- ◆ Is acceptance of the decision by subordinates critical to effective implementation?
- ◆ If the leader makes the decision without input, is it reasonably certain that it will be accepted by subordinates?
- ◆ Do subordinates share the organizational goals to be attained by the decision?
- ◆ Is conflict among subordinates likely if this particular decision is made?

Figure 9.1 shows the optimal decision-making process in consideration of these questions. The leader considers information availability, type of problem, and how critical acceptance and commitment of followers will be to the eventual decision. Each decision process indicated in Vroom and Yetton's decision tree represents the optimal process (not the only one available) that involves the least number of man-hours without affecting the quality and implementation of the decision.

Figure 9.1. Vroom and Yetton's Decision-Making Model: To What Extent and Under What Circumstances to Involve Subordinates in Decision-Making Processes

Decision Process	One solution obviously better than another?	Sufficient information?	Structured problem?	Acceptance by subordinates critical?	Accepted by subordinates if leader makes decision?	Do subordinates share goals to be attained?	Is conflict likely?
Leader makes decision using available information	NO			NO			
	NO			YES	YES		
	YES	YES		NO			
	YES	YES		YES	YES		
Leader obtains information from subordinates and then decides	YES	NO	YES	YES	YES		
	YES	NO	YES	NO			
Leader gains ideas from relevant subordinates and then decides					NO		
					YES		
	YES	YES		YES	NO	NO	NO
					NO		
Leader shares with all subordinates and then decides	YES	NO	YES	YES		NO	YES
	YES	NO	NO	YES			
	YES	NO	NO	NO			
	YES	NO	NO	YES		NO	
Leader accepts consensus solution from subordinates	NO			YES	NO		
	YES	YES		YES	NO	YES	
	YES	NO	NO	YES	NO	YES	

A participatory model of decision making specifically applied to schools is a model proposed by **Edwin Bridges** (1967). Bridges' **shared decision-making model** seeks to determine when teachers should be involved in decision making. This model is founded on the following assumptions: (a) participation is less effective when the decision falls within teachers' zone of acceptance, and conversely, (b) participation is more effective when the decision falls outside teachers' zone of acceptance.

The zone of acceptance is determined by two tests: (a) relevance and (b) expertise. **Relevance** is tested by the following question: Do teachers have a high personal stake in the decision? If so, teachers will usually have a high interest in participation. If not, they will most likely be accepting of the leader's decision. **Expertise** is tested by the question: "Do teachers have the expertise to make a meaningful contribution to the solution?" Involving teachers in decisions in which they have no experience or competence likely leads to frustration. If teachers have a personal stake in the decision and the necessary expertise to contribute to the solution, then the decision certainly falls outside the zone of acceptance and teachers should be involved in the decision-making process. Conversely, if teachers do not have a personal stake in the decision and do not have the expertise to contribute to the solution, then the decision definitely falls within the zone of acceptance and shared decision making would not be appropriate.

When the tests of relevance and expertise contradict one another, the level of participation is less obvious. According to this model, if teachers have a personal stake, but little to no expertise, then participative decision making is not recommended. Involving teachers in decisions outside their realm of competence generally leads to hostility and frustration because often the ultimate decision will be made by administrators who do possess the expertise. Under these circumstances, teachers will most likely perceive the process as a pretense of involvement, feeling that their input was not valued and that decisions had already been made.

In the instance where teachers have expertise but do not have a personal stake in the decision, again participative decision making is not recommended. Involving teachers in decisions that do not affect them may lead to resentment and alienation where teachers feel their time is being wasted on matters more appropriately left to the administration.

In both of the above instances where a decision is marginally within teachers' zone of acceptance, teachers may occasionally be involved in decision making, but only in very limited ways. For instance, teachers' involvement may be limited to communicating the rationale for a decision where teachers have a personal stake in the outcome, or teachers' opinions might be solicited when they have expertise but no stake in the outcome. In these cases, it is imperative that administrators clearly define the teachers' role in the decision-making process, making sure that teachers understand that a final decision will be made by the administration and not through consensus.

Group decision making has become widely practiced in schools today, partly because of policies mandating higher levels of stakeholder involvement and partly because of general trends and practices seeking more democratic approaches to educational decision making. Group decision making in schools often is practiced within a framework of learning communities (Dufour & Eaker, 1998; Senge, 1990; Senge et al., 2000).

Richard Dufour and **Robert Eaker** (1998) characterized a professional learning community (PLC) as a school with

- A shared mission, vision, and values
- A process of collective inquiry
- A structure of collaborative teams
- An orientation toward action and experimentation
- A commitment to continuous improvement
- Ongoing assessment of results

Group decision making and PLCs reflect a democratic approach to leadership and a paradigm shift away from an industrial, hierarchical approach to organizational structure.

Advantages of group decision making include the fact that multiple voices increase the likelihood of wider acceptance of decisions; that collective information and knowledge will lead to better decisions; and, that members of the group are motivated by the process and tend to grow professionally (Kowalski, Lasley, & Mahoney, 2008). However, leaders should be aware that there are factors that influence a group's effectiveness in making good decisions. Yukl (2006) identified seven considerations that affect the quality of a group's decision making process.

1. **Size:** The larger the group, the more communication difficulties occur. Groups should represent a balance of perspectives but remain small enough to communicate effectively.

2. **Status:** Ideas and opinions of group members tend to have more influence. Using guidelines for group behavioral expectations can be effective in alleviating this tendency.

3. **Cohesiveness:** A group whose members share similar values and beliefs will tend to be more cohesive. Although a highly cohesive group may reach a decision faster, they may be less creative and not consider all alternatives because of fear of being rejected.

4. **Diversity:** High levels of diversity in a group may lead to a less cohesive group that experience difficulties in communication. However, more diverse groups tend to offer a greater variety of ideas and solutions.

5. **Emotional maturity:** Group members should be selected who are able and willing to collaborate. Those unwilling to do so will disrupt the process.

6. **Physical environment:** Considerations for a comfortable working environment should include a location and seating arrangements that do not represent on member's status or "turf" over another's.

7. **Technology support:** Using information technology to support a group's work can enhance the group's effectiveness. For instance, agendas and documents e-mailed ahead of meetings, electronic message boards, and computer access during meetings are ways to make the group's work more efficient.

Limitations of Group Decision Making: Groupthink

Participative decision making can lead to better quality decisions and enhanced commitment to carrying out decisions by members of the organization. The models previously discussed pointed out that leaders should carefully appraise the appropriateness of involving others in decision making by considering such factors as information availability, group members' expertise, and how the decision will impact group members' jobs in the organization. When a leader does involve others in decision making, he or she should be aware of his or her role as facilitator and be alert to factors involved in group dynamics that may inhibit effective decision making (see Chapter 7). Janis (1972) noted that when a cohesive group's endeavors for unanimity override their motivation to realistically judge alternative solutions, they have fallen victim to a phenomenon he termed groupthink. He defined groupthink as "a deterioration of mental efficiency, reality testing, and moral judgment that results from in-group pressures" (p 9).

Irving Janis and Leon Mann (1977) specified eight **symptoms of groupthink:**

- ◆ Pressure to conform
- ◆ Self-censorship of dissenting ideas
- ◆ Mindguards
- ◆ Apparent unanimity
- ◆ Illusions of invulnerability
- ◆ Illusions of morality

- ◆ Negative stereotypes of persons outside the group
- ◆ Collective rationalization

Forsyth (1983) categorized the first four symptoms as occurring when a group tends toward early consensus resulting from excessive pressures within the group. The first symptom, **pressure to conform** refers to a pronounced, heightened, and overpowering pressure from within the group to seek unanimity. There appears to be no tolerance for any kind of disagreement among the members, even over minor issues. The second symptom, **self-censorship,** is manifested by group members' reluctance to express disagreement; members remain silent rather than raise any questions or concerns. The third indicator of groupthink in this category is **mindguards,** a term used to denote members of the group who act to protect group members from information they think will hurt the groups' confidence and decision-making ability. Mindguards divert controversial information away from the group and may pressure individual members to keep silent about certain information. The final symptom in this category, apparent unanimity, is the result of internal pressures brought to bear on the group. **Apparent unanimity** is characterized by early consensus of a solution and group members' unusual focus on convergence of thinking rather than on an in-depth exploration of alternative solutions.

The remainingfour symptoms of groupthink can be classified as illusions and misperceptions that lead to errors of judgment. The **illusion of invulnerability** refers to a feeling of confidence in group meetings where members feel that a decision made through group consensus could not be wrong. **Illusion of morality** pertains to a phenomenon where group members believe that their decision is morally correct, and they disregard considering apparent ethical questions or consequences. A third symptom in this category is **negative stereotypes** of persons outside the group. Such stereotyping leads to false assumptions and oversimplification of the problem. Finally, **collective rationalization** occurs after the group becomes committed to a decision. The group avoids or minimizes data that may not support the decision and emphasizes facts and information that affirm their decision.

How can leaders avoid the groupthink phenomenon in participative decision making? Janis and Mann (1977) identified four factors that cause groupthink: (a) cohesiveness, (b) isolation of the group, (c) leadership style, and (d) stress placed on the group to make a good decision. Whereas group cohesiveness is normally a positive attribute of group decision making, extreme cohesiveness can be detrimental. Extreme cohesiveness may result when members of the group consider themselves to be good friends, feel a great sense of belonging in the group, and indicate a desire to retain membership in the group. Thus, school leaders should carefully consider their selection of persons involved in a decision-making group and strive to select persons who represent varying viewpoints and associations.

Isolation of the group from outside experts can also hinder a group's decision-making effectiveness and lead to groupthink. The school leader must ensure that group members stay informed and should encourage members to seek outside sources of information and bring in expert consultation when necessary. Group members should be expected to maintain communication with those they represent. For instance, representatives to a school leadership team would be expected to report to and from their department or grade level teachers.

The effect of leadership style refers to the role the leader takes in the group. Leaders encourage more open discussion when they withhold their ideas for solutions until all other members have made recommendations. Limited discussion occurs when leaders describe their solutions first, because group members tend to yield to their supervisor.

The final cause of groupthink is the amount of pressure placed on the group to arrive at a good decision. Interestingly, as the importance of the problem increases, the more concerned group members become with reducing any uncertainty about their solution and become less attentive to processing information rationally. The more important the decision is perceived to be by the group, the more group members feel a need to present a "united front." When leaders place undue emphasis on the consequences of a group's decision, they convey the message that a decision is unchangeable. Rarely is this the case. School leaders would be wise to explain to teacher committees that decision making is a process and that solutions will be evaluated, revised, and altered as needed.

Data-Driven Decision Making

One consequence of recent trends toward accountability and student assessment is the fact that policymakers and publics are demanding that schools "show me the evidence" that students are achieving. For instance, No Child Left Behind legislation demands the reporting of data such as test results, graduation rates, and attendance rates. Schools are using a variety of data to evaluate school programs and student learning. Thus, models of data-driven decision making are beginning to emerge. Theodore Kowalski, Thomas Lasley, and James Mahoney (2008) proposed a four-stage process for data-based decision making: (a) collecting, (b) connecting, (c) creating, and (d) confirming. **Collecting** refers to the compilation of important data. Knowing which data are important requires identifying the questions to be answered and then finding ways to store data so that various data elements can be correlated. **Connecting** involves analyzing data from various perspectives or combining it with other data to answer specific questions. **Creating** is the process of doing something with the data. It is the decision point that answers the question: So what? If data reveal that there is a gap between where students are and where we want them to be, creating means developing strategies to close the gap. The creating process includes articulating hypotheses about the reasons for the gap and formulating plans to address underlying causes. **Confirming** is the process of evaluation, and includes both formative and summative analysis. That is, checking on both the process of implementation and the result of the interventions.

In their research on data-driven decision making (DDDM), Gina Schuyler Ikemoto and Julie Marsh (2007) described models of DDDM as falling into one of four quadrants varying along two continua: (a) the type of data used and (b) the nature of the data analysis. Each of these continua range from simple to complex.

Figure 9.2. Ikemoto and Marsh: Data-Based Decision Making (DDDM) Models

DDDM Model	*Type of Data*	*Analysis and Decision Making*
Basic	Simple	Simple
Analysis focused	Simple	Complex
Data focused	Complex	Simple
Inquiry focused	Complex	Complex

Decision making in the basic model is generally unilateral and relies on one type of data from one point in time from a readily available source. Analysis-focused decision making generally involves a team and employs data taken over time (such as pre- and posttests). However, the analysis focused model does not rely on expert knowledge or empirical evidence. Data-focused decision making is usually done by a group and uses more complex data. However, data is generally taken from only one point in time and does not rely on expert knowledge. Inquiry-focused decision making probes a specific question or problem over a long period of time and integrates professional development as part of the inquiry process.

Differences in the four types of DDDM are attributed to several factors:

◆ Accessibility and timeliness of data

◆ Perceived validity of the data

- Staff capacity and support
- Time provided for the process of data analysis
- Partnerships with external organizations
- Tools to collect and evaluate data
- Organizational culture and leadership
- Focus of state and local policies on accountability

Decision Making Filters

Chris Argyris (1994) pointed out that human behavior involves two types of theories of action. The first is the **espoused theory**, or what people say they believe. The second is their **theory in use,** or what people actually do. Argyris noted that there is often a discrepancy between the two, yet people are unaware of it. Thus, in decision making there is often a tension between what should be and the realities of organizations. Knapp, Copland, and Swinnerton (2007) identified three examples of such tensions, or dilemmas.

- Tension between state or federal mandates and local cultures and contexts
- Tension between short-term "solutions" that show apparent student gains and long-term approaches that could result in larger systematic changes
- Tension between competing belief systems concerning what is desirable and what is politically or culturally possible

Robert J. Starratt's (1991) ethical considerations of care, justice, and critique offers a framework and analytical lens from which to view decision making. The ethic of care focuses on relationships, not from a contractual perspective, but from a human perspective. The ethic of justice refers to ideas of equality and democratic principles. The ethic of critique addresses issues of power that may be rationalized through cultural practices or institutionalized in organizational structure.

These foregoing examples offer us another perspective on decision making. School leaders may want to consider whether or not their decisions mirror their beliefs and values and whether or not their decisions represent thoughtful consideration or expedience. Further, are the processes for decision making appropriate to the situation, and are they congruent with the school's mission and context?

Summary

Decision making is fundamental to the role of any school leadership position. In fact, Griffiths (1959) proposed that school administration was decision making. This chapter has presented decision-making models along a continuum—from decision making as a process undertaken by a leader as the single authority, to participative models that involve others in the decision-making process. This continuum of decision-making models helps school leaders understand under what conditions and the extent to which others' involvement will enhance the decision-making process and lead to better solutions.

This chapter also explored the complexities of decision making. Rational and linear approaches to decision making were contrasted with descriptive models of decision making, which explain that decision making in practice is more complex and less deliberate than rational, linear models would suggest. These theories help school leaders identify the political and organizational contexts within which decisions are made.

Because decision making is a primary responsibility of leadership, it is important for educational leaders to understand the forces that influence the decision-making process and how these forces can impact the efficacy of decisions made. Organizations do not stop while decisions are made. Consequently, a leader's decision-making process is constrained by factors of time, personnel, resources, and information. Thus, not only should the educational leader be concerned with making a decision about a given problem but must also determine the appropriate process for making the best decision in a particular situation. Models such as those outlined by March, Bridges, and Vroom and Yetton can provide guidance to school leaders in developing the most effective decision-making process under a variety of specific circumstances.

Furthermore, it is important for leaders to be aware of their filters when making decisions. Consideration must be given to organizational values and contextual factors. This is especially important given the current political climate of accountability, which may tempt school leaders to opt for the short-term solution rather than systemic change.

Theory into Practice

It's a Dirty Job, and Someone's Got to Do It

Superintendent Johnson wasn't really surprised by the Board of Education's action at last night's meeting, where the Board directed him to bring forth a recommendation for custodial and maintenance operations next month. Dr. Johnson had been dealing with issues and problems related to the district's custodial and maintenance performance almost on a daily basis since he had come on board as Superintendent of Fairville School District four months ago. Fairville was a medium-sized district of approximately 20,000 students with 20 elementary schools, 4 middle schools, and 2 high schools. Recent and continued growth had resulted in the building of 5 elementary schools, 2 middle schools, and a high school within the last 10 years. Buildings in the district ranged in age from those newly constructed to 2 buildings that were 60 years old. Custodial and maintenance services were operated from one department under the supervision of the Assistant Superintendent for Transportation, Facilities, and Operations. Each building was assigned a custodial staff that was directly supervised by building principals. Maintenance operations were centralized and managed by a staff supervisor who received all requisitions for building maintenance and scheduled crews to fulfill job requests, in addition to overseeing regular maintenance duties such as landscaping, building inspections, and routine mechanical maintenance. Custodial and maintenance workers were strongly represented by the support staff union, which had been the source of many of Superintendent Johnson's headaches in recent months. Several grievances from the union had recently reached his desk, ranging from complaints about job duties and hours that violated the negotiated contract to one incident alleging unsafe working conditions. The latter complaint was one that involved a work-related injury. The staff member was now on medical leave, and the case had been referred to legal counsel.

The costs for custodial and maintenance services had been steadily increasing over the last three years. When Dr. Johnson began investigating the finances of this division, he had predicted that increased costs would be related to salary increases over the last three years and would be proportional to the addition of new facilities in the district. What he found, however, was that increased costs associated with custodial and maintenance services could not be accounted for simply as a result of increased salaries and additional staff. Instead, he found that increased costs were almost double what should have been expected with growth. On further investigation, he discovered that staff absences and sick leave had risen sharply in the last two years, requiring the use of more substitutes and temporary workers. In addition, several injuries in the last two years had resulted in substantial workmen's compensation claims leading to increased insurance and legal costs to the district.

Furthermore, principals, teachers, and patrons had been complaining to him about cleanliness and other issues in many of the buildings. Similar complaints had been heard by board members, leading to their directive at last night's meeting. Two board members had strongly urged the superintendent to investigate the possibility of contracting out either or both custodial and maintenance services. They argued this would cut operational costs by saving the district certain insurance and legal-related expenses. Perhaps not coincidentally, one of these board members was a manager at a local manufacturing plant that had recently contracted custodial services. He had been highly complimentary of his plant's contract and in the last few weeks had been lobbying other board members to consider this alternative for Fairville School District. Dr. Johnson knew this course of action would necessitate layoffs and would become a "hot" issue with the support staff union.

As Superintendent Johnson sat at his desk, he thought, "Well, I better get to it. I have only 30 days to bring my recommendations to the board."

Sample Analysis

Dr. Johnson is confronted with making a decision, in the form of a recommendation to the Board, about a significant issue that will impact personnel, facilities and operations, and budget. Several key factors are important considerations for Dr. Johnson. The first factor has to do with the manifestation of the problem itself; that is, custodial and maintenance services are currently not meeting organizational expectations as measured by complaints received from principals, teachers and parents. Second, the superintendent lacks some essential information that may help him define the problem. Questions to which Dr. Johnson should seek answers include: Why have incidents of sick leave and injury been increasing? What factors are contributing to the apparent low morale? Is there inappropriate supervision, lack of adequate training and expertise, or inadequate resources? Third, Dr. Johnson must consider those persons or groups who are affected by the situation and those who have influence on the outcome. A final factor that surrounds Dr. Johnson's dilemma is time. He must present a recommended solution to the board in one month.

Drawing on decision-making models that outline a rational, linear approach, a first step for Dr. Johnson would be to define the problem. Is this simply a budgetary issue or is this presenting problem symptomatic of some underlying conditions that will continue to impact other school operations? To properly frame this problem, the superintendent needs to gather more information. Dr. Johnson should consider the desired outcomes of this decision. Keeping in mind the organizational goals related to this decision will help clarify the criteria by which alternative solutions should be judged. In this case, three primary objectives are: (1) to maintain cleanliness and appearance of school buildings; (2) to provide appropriate maintenance of facilities in terms of safety, comfort, and buildings' structural and operational systems; and (3) to reduce financial costs related to custodial and maintenance operations. By clearly defining goals and criteria, Dr. Johnson will avoid confusing symptoms with goals. For example, the superintendent knows that support staff morale is low, but should not view the improvement of morale as a primary objective, even though some alternative solutions may certainly improve morale. Improved morale may be considered among the criteria by which alternatives are judged, but not at the expense of primary goals.

As Dr. Johnson undertakes his first step in gathering data, he will also be faced with the question of participation in the decision-making process. Who should be involved in the decision and to what extent? Using Vroom's decision process model (see Figure 9.1), Dr. Johnson would likely conclude that he should share the problem with subordinates but ultimately make the decision himself. This is based on the fact that he needs additional information, the problem is not structured or programmed, and it appears that subordinates may not share the organizational goals. Dr. Johnson must also consider the question of the expertise of the staff. Bridges and Vroom and Yetton would suggest that unless the staff has the necessary expertise to solve the problem, the leader should limit the involvement of subordinates and assume responsibility for making the decision.

As Superintendent Johnson proceeds in data gathering and discussions with staff, he may find that an incremental approach may be warranted. This is especially relevant considering the time constraints with which he is faced. An interim decision to involve staff in developing an improvement plan may buy him time to gather more information to make a better long-term decision. Furthermore, if we examine this situation from the perspective of the Garbage Can Decision-Making model, it may result in additional solutions being thrown into the "trash bin." At this point in time, only one apparent solution has been thrown in, and that was the proposal put forth by a board member to contract these services.

Finally, Dr. Johnson should guard against a temporary solution leading away from organizational goals. An interim solution should be used only to "buy time" to gather more information and to deliberate more carefully about alternative solutions that would most likely lead to desired goals.

Reader's Application

Controversy Haunts Spirit Day at Meadows Middle School

Who would have thought that a long-lived tradition would generate so much controversy? Gale Brown, principal of Meadow Middle School, had not given a second thought to scheduling the events of Spirit Day, which had become a customary part of Meadow's homecoming football game. Homecoming usually fell at the end of October near Halloween, and the student council had always sponsored a costume contest. Students were allowed to don Halloween-type masquerade costumes throughout the day. Certain restrictions, of course, were imposed, which prohibited masks, excessive makeup, and inappropriate or revealing costumes. Judging occurred at an after-school event immediately following the pep rally. At that time, students were allowed to complete their costumes with masks or makeup if they wished. This day had always been a great success. Students were generally well behaved but had fun, and it seemed to promote school spirit and pride among the student body.

Meadow Middle School was the only middle school in the Forest Grove School District. The district had a student population of 1,500. Originally a rural farm community, Forest Grove was now a community of large acreages on the outskirts of the city, which had grown up to the district's border over the last 20 years. Forest Grove was not even a municipality. There was no business district, and residents of Forest Grove received services such as police and fire protection through the county government. Even though the farms of Forest Grove were long gone, the district had maintained a rural flavor. Residents of Forest Grove took pride in their community and parents had always been active supporters of the school district. Students at Forest Grove enjoyed high academic success, and recently the school district had attracted many new families with young children. In fact, Meadow Middle School had grown from approximately 350 students 2 years ago to more than 400 students this year.

In the last few days, Ms. Brown had received numerous complaints from parents regarding the wearing of Halloween costumes. The complaints had been received from a group of sixth-grade parents who were new residents in this small school district. They contended that the Spirit Day masquerade costumes were promoting an anti-Christian holiday that celebrated Satanic rituals and myths. Now on her way to school, Ms. Brown was truly taken by surprise at what she had heard on the car radio. The local radio station's morning talk show host, Marvin Powell, was asking callers to phone in their opinion about Meadow Middle School's Halloween celebration. Powell explained he had been talking to Jane Little, a parent of a sixth-grade student at Meadow. Ms. Little felt that the Spirit Day at Meadow Middle School was promoting Satanic cults and was not only immoral but was a violation of the constitution's protection of religious freedom.

The radio talk show host asked: "Should students be allowed to celebrate Halloween in our public schools? Specifically, should Meadow Middle School allow kids to dress up as ghouls and goblins?" Powell took responses from about 15 callers, and at least a dozen of those callers agreed with Ms.

Little. Two or three callers voiced their outrage at this attack on a long-standing tradition to promote school pride. It was obvious that the group of parents opposing the Halloween costume tradition had orchestrated this public protest forum.

As Ms. Brown walked into her office, her secretary informed her that the superintendent had just called and was holding for her on line one. On answering the phone, she listened as Superintendent Michaels asked: "Gale, I suppose you heard Marvin Powell's talk show this morning. What are you going to do about Spirit Day?"

Student Exercise: Case Analysis

1. Analyze this problem from the perspective of decision-making theories.
2. What process should Ms. Brown use in making a decision about Spirit Day?
3. Who should be involved in the decision and to what extent?
4. What would you do if you were Ms. Brown?

References

Argyris, C. (1994). Initiating change that perseveres. *Journal of Public Administration Research and Theory, 4*(3), 343–355.

Bridges, E. M. (1967). A model for shared decision-making in the school principalship. *Educational Administration Quarterly, 3,* 49–61.

Cohen, M. D., March, J. G., & Olsen, J. P. (1972). A garbage can model of organizational choice. *Administrative Science Quarterly, 17,* 1–25.

Drucker, P. F. (1974). *Management: Tasks, responsibilities, and practices.* New York: Harper and Row.

Dufour, R., & Eaker, R. (1998). *Professional learning communities at work: Best practices for enhancing student achievement.* Bloomington, IN: National Education Service.

Forsyth, D. R. (1983). *An introduction to group dynamics.* Monterey, CA: Brooks/Cole.

Griffiths, D. E. (1959). *Administrative theory.* New York: Macmillan.

Hoy, W. K., & Miskel, C. G. (1996). *Educational administration: Theory, research, and practice* (5th ed.). New York: McGraw-Hill.

Ikemoto, G. S., & Marsh, J. A. (2007). Cutting through the "data-driven" mantra: Different conceptions of data-driven decision making. In P.A. Moss

(Ed.), *Evidence and decision making,* (pp. 105–131). Chicago: National Society for the Study of Education.

Janis, I. L. (1972). *Victims of groupthink.* Boston: Houghton-Mifflin.

Janis, I. L., & Mann, L. (1977). *Decision making: A psychological analysis of conflict, choice, and commitment.* New York: Free Press.

Knapp, M. S., Copland, M.A., & Swinnerton, J. A. (2007). Understanding the promise and dynamics of data-informed leadership. In P.A. Moss (Ed.), *Evidence and decision making,* (pp. 74–104). Chicago: National Society for the Study of Education.

Kowalski, T. J., Lasley II, T. J., & Mahoney, J. W. (2008*). Data-driven decisions and school leadership: Best practices for school improvement.* Boston: Pearson.

Lindblom, C. E. (1959). The science of muddling through. *Public Administration Review, 19, 79*–99.

Litchfield, E. H. (1956). Notes on a general theory of administration. *Administrative Science Quarterly, 1,* 3–29.

March, J. G. (1988). *Decisions and organizations.* Oxford: Blackwell.

Mayo, E. (1933). *The human problems of an industrial civilization.* New York: Macmillan.

Murphy, J. (Ed.). (1990). *The educational reform movement of the 1980s: Perspectives and cases.* Berkeley, CA: McCutchan.

Senge, P. M. (1990). *The fifth discipline: The art and practice of the learning organization.* New York: Doubleday.

Senge, P., Cambron-McCabe, N. L., Lucas, T., Smith, B., Dutton, J., & Kleiner, A. (2000). *Schools that learn: A fifth discipline fieldbook for educators, parents, and everyone who cares about education.* New York: Doubleday.

Simon, H. A. (1960). *The new science of management decision.* New York: Harper and Row.

Starratt, R. J. (1991). Building an ethical school: A theory for practice in educational leadership. *Educational Administration Quarterly, 27*(2), 185–202.

Tannenbaum, A. S. (1968). *Control in organizations.* New York: McGraw Hill.

Tannenbaum, R., & Schmidt, W. H. (1973, May/June). How to choose a leadership pattern. *Harvard Business Review, 51,* 162–180. (Reprinted from *Harvard Business Review,* March/April 1958)

Vroom, V. H., & Yetton, P. W. (1973). *Leadership and decision-making.* Pittsburgh, PA: University of Pittsburgh Press.

Yukl, G. (2006). *Leadership in organizations* (6th ed.). Upper Saddle River, NJ: Pearson, Prentice Hall.

10

Organizational Change: Reforming and Restructuring

Synopsis of Organizational Change Theories

The process of change is a primary theme of organizational theory, because the role of leadership is often associated with planning, implementing, and directing change in organizations. In the past two decades, schools have been under constant pressure to change through a barrage of educational reform movements.

Organizational change theories help leaders understand the processes involved in implementing and actualizing innovations and reforms within an organization. Organizational change theories illustrate that reform is the product of internal changes within the organizational system. Although external mandates may provide an impetus for change, reform will not be realized unless people within the organization fully understand the change and believe that it is compatible to the mission and goals of the organization.

Change is a complex process associated with the norms, beliefs, and culture of an organization. Providing leadership for change involves an understanding of motivation and an orientation toward holistic thinking in terms of the dynamics within the organization's social system and the interactions between the organizational system and external forces.

In this chapter, organizational change theories are organized into two principal categories—rational, linear approaches and nonlinear, systemic perspectives. These two classifications reflect an evolution of organizational theory over the last century and provide an historical framework for understanding change. This is important because schools function as institutions within larger political, social, and economic systems. Knowing from whence we come helps us understand where we are going, and we must have a clear vision of our destination if we are to prepare students for the future (Chance, 1992).

Applications for School Leaders

Understanding organizational change theories will help school leaders:

◆ Develop procedures for involving teachers, students, and other stakeholders in the change process

◆ Identify forces within and outside the school that facilitate and inhibit change

◆ Approach change as a process that occurs over time

◆ Think of change in terms of whole systems and interactions among many systems

◆ Use strategies that motivate and teach others the necessary knowledge, skills, and attitudes necessary to implement change

◆ Match change to the philosophical orientation and belief structure of the school's social system

---

Conceptualizing the Change Process

Theories of organizational change have taken various approaches to explain the dynamics and processes involved in change. Organizational change theories have been variously described as distinct categories that usually define the impetus for change, such as planned versus natural; voluntary versus mandatory; internal versus external; and organizational self-renewal versus organizational transformation. Evans (1996) discussed change as first-order change and second-order change. First-order change is defined as having the purpose of improving organizational efficiency and effectiveness whereas second-order change is defined as systemic, meaning that the organizational structure itself is modified and beliefs and perceptions of the members of the organization are changed.

In essence, change theories have mirrored the historical development of organizational theory. Viewing change from a broader historical perspective aids in understanding theories of organizational change. Historians have long referred to large-scale cultural and economic changes as significant events in human development and commonly classify historical eras into (a) the agricultural age, (b) the industrial age, and (c) the information age. Toffler (1990), a futurist scholar, referred to these eras as the first wave, the second wave, and the third wave of human civilization. In discussing these historical eras of transformational change, Toffler contended that human institutions and organizations would naturally evolve as economic, political, and social systems adapted to new technologies that profoundly affected human societies. Over the course of the last century, theories of organizational change apparently evolved from those grounded within the assumptions and perspectives of the second-wave, industrial age to those based on a frame of reference more compatible with the third-wave, information society. Early theories of organizational change tended to define the process of change as something rational and linear. More recent theories discuss change in nonlinear terms and point to the complexity and interaction of a multitude of factors and variables, the effects of which cannot be precisely predicted.

Second-Wave Change Theories: Rational, Linear Approaches to Organizational Change

Two prevailing concepts in second-wave organizational change theories are diffusion and organizational development. Diffusion theories focus on the introduction of an innovation into an organization, whether through external mandate or internal, voluntary change. Organizational development, as defined by Fullan, Miles, and Taylor (1980) is

> a coherent, systematically planned, sustained effort at system self-study and improvement, focusing explicitly on change in formal and informal procedures, processes, norms, or structures, and using behavioral science concepts (p. 135).

The goal of both diffusion models and organizational development is to improve organizational efficiency and performance. Both conceptualizations have direct application to schools and educational leadership.

Change as Innovation

One of the first to study the process of change in public schools was **Paul Mort.** Mort noted that it took approximately 50 years for innovations in education to be generally accepted and practiced in schools throughout the country (Mort & Ross, 1957). Mort found that the best indicator of the speed at which a school adopted change was per pupil funding. During the post–World War II years, Mort postulated that because school funding depended on community support, educational administrators, as change agents, should focus on efforts to educate communities about the need for educational innovations and convince constituents to support these through additional tax levies.

Following the Soviet's successful launching of Sputnik in 1957, educational reform became a national political agenda item, of which one result was the passage of the National Defense Education Act (NDEA) for funding curriculum improvement in science, mathematics, and foreign languages. Funding for curriculum innovation from major foundations soon followed, as did other federal initiatives. During the 1960s and 1970s, federal and foundation support for educational innovations, to a great degree, represented an approach to organizational change that still prevails. This was a **diffusion-based** model of change, sometimes referred to as knowledge production and utilization (Owens, 1995) or research, development, and diffusion (RD&D) (e.g., Clark & Guba, 1967; Havelock, 1973). The authorization and creation of regional educational laboratories, Educational Research and Development Centers, the Educational Resources Information Center (ERIC), and the National Diffusion Network in the 1960s exemplify the concept of bringing about educational change by developing innovations for school adoption. This change model had apparently been successful in the instance of federal legislation establishing land-grant colleges and cooperative agricultural extension agencies. Through applied research and experiment stations, agriculture researchers provided information to farmers concerning new and improved agricultural practices. However, as Chin and Benne (1976) pointed out, this process "worked better in developing and diffusing thing technologies than in developing and diffusing people technologies" (pp. 27–28). They further asserted that the diffusion systems formed for educational innovation lacked adequate linkage between researchers and schools.

Ronald Havelock (1973) specifically addressed the linkage gap by focusing on change from the school perspective, rather than the researcher's. He emphasized tactics for effecting change and directed his remarks to school administrators and teachers, whom he identified as the "change agents of education" (p. 3). Havelock specified four roles of a change agent: (a) catalyst, (b) solution giver, (c) process helper, and (d) resource linker (p. 8–9).

As a **catalyst,** the change agent pressures for change, upsets the status quo, and energizes the problem-solving process. The **solution giver** role involves offering expertise on how to solve a problem and how to help clients adapt innovations to their particular organization. As a **process helper,** the change agent assists in helping the organization implement a problem-solving process. Finally, the change agent acts as a **resource linker** by bringing together various resources to meet the needs of the school.

Havelock further outlined a model for change, focusing on the change agent's role as process helper. This model involves six stages as follow:

- Stage I: Building a relationship
- Stage II: Diagnosing the problem
- Stage III: Acquiring relevant resources
- Stage IV: Choosing the solution
- Stage V: Gaining acceptance
- Stage VI: Stabilizing the innovation and generating self-renewal

Havelock articulated three major strategic orientations along with specific strategies for change. The first orientation is designated as **problem solving.** This orientation stresses that problem solving is a process that is internal to the user and emphasizes that the change agent should be nondirective. Havelock stressed that self-initiated and self-applied innovations yield stronger commitment and have better chances for success.

The second orientation is **social interaction.** The social interaction orientation focuses on the patterns of diffusion through a social system from the perspective of the user of an innovation. Havelock explained (a) that a user's network of social relations greatly influences his or her adoption of an innovation; (b) that the user's place and involvement in the network can predict the rate of acceptance; (c) that informal personal contact is key to influencing the user; (d) that group membership and reference group identification affect an individual's adoption of new ideas; and (e) that the rate of diffusion through a social system follows a predictable pattern where there is a slow beginning followed by a rapid period of diffusion followed by a long, slow-moving period of late adoption.

The third change orientation is **research, development, and diffusion (RD&D).** RD&D models use a rational sequence in the development and application of the innovation. RD&D models assume that the consumer is passive yet rational and will accept an innovation given at the right place, at the right time, and in the right form. Havelock contended that an RD&D orientation was most suitable for mass distribution because of the high initial development costs associated with this approach.

The concerns-based adoption model (CBAM) (Hall & Hord, 2001) addresses the implementation of innovations in school settings. The model focuses on the individuals who implement change, the change facilitators, and the environmental factors that influence the change. The CBAM model delineates 12 principles of change, outlined in Figure 10.1.

**Figure 10.1. Concerns-Based Adoption Model:
Twelve Principles of Change**

Principle 1	Change is a process.
Principle 2	There are significant differences between development and implementation of innovation.
Principle 3	Organizations do not change until individuals within the organization change.
Principle 4	Innovations can be products or processes and vary in scale (simple to complex).
Principle 5	Interventions are the actions and events that are key to success in implementing innovation.
Principle 6	A horizontal perspective, where all levels and all individuals within the organization are involved, works best.
Principle 7	Leadership is essential to long-term success of the innovation.
Principle 8	Mandates can work if accompanied by continuing communication, ongoing training coaching, and time for implementation.
Principle 9	The school is the primary unit for change.
Principle 10	Facilitating change is a team effort.
Principle 11	Appropriate interventions reduce the challenges of change.
Principle 12	The school context influences the process of change.

The CBAM model provides tools to diagnose the innovation itself (what the innovation will look like); the feelings of individuals about change (stages of concern); and the behaviors of people relative to the change (levels of use). In examining individuals' concerns and levels of use, it is important for change facilitators to understand that individuals' reactions and feelings about change will vary. For instance, stages of concern range from self-focused (How will this affect me?) to task (How can I get this done?) to impact (How does this work for the whole system?). In a similar fashion, level of use measures individuals' readiness and use of the innovation from nonuse, orientation, and preparation to mechanical use, routine use, refinement, and renewal.

Further, the CBAM model classifies school principals as falling into one of three distinct change facilitator styles: (a) initiator, (b) manager, or (c) responder. Initiators hold strong visions about their schools' future and push teachers and others toward that vision. Managers, conversely, take more time to study innovations and are less likely to delegate. Responders are focused on the present and allow many teachers with different ideas (which may be disparate) to try things out.

Finally, the CBAM model describes six basic interventions that change facilitators employ. These are

- Develop a shared vision for the change
- Plan and provide resources
- Invest in professional learning
- Check on progress
- Provide continuous assistance
- Create a context supportive of change

Organizational Development

Kurt Lewin's (1947, 1952) force field analysis has been recognized as a building block and analytical tool for organizational development. Force field analysis describes an organization as being effected by two opposing sets of forces: (a) driving forces and (b) restraining forces. **Driving forces** are those factors that push for change, and **restraining forces** are those that push against change. Organizations, viewed as social systems, seek equilibrium where balance between driving and restraining forces results in an organizational status quo. Lewin proposed that to bring about organizational change, the equilibrium of the opposing force fields must be broken, which he referred to as "unfreezing the organization." This is done by weakening or strengthening one or more of the forces. At that point, change can be introduced to the organization. After the change has been accepted, the organization must be refrozen. Thus, a new equilibrium in the organization is reached in which opposing forces are once again in balance. This represents a new status quo where change has become institutionalized (Figure 10.2).

The force field analysis model is most useful to educational leaders as a diagnostic and analytical tool for planning change. For instance, the high school principal who is considering introducing block scheduling might use the force field analysis model to identify driving forces and restraining forces.

Figure 10.2. Force Fields in Balance Maintain Status Quo

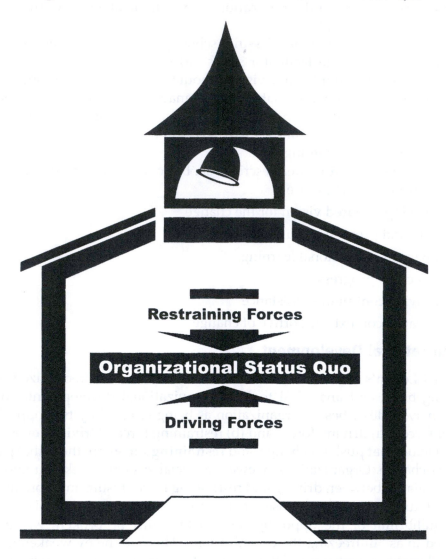

In this case, chances are that both restraining forces and driving forces will include individuals and subgroups from all elements of the school's social system. In other words, driving forces may include some teachers, some parents, some administrators, some students, and some other community members. Restraining forces are likely to include other members of these same groups. Thus, the principal must specifically identify which teachers, which administrators, which parents, and so on, represent driving forces for change and which represent restraining forces for change. By doing so, the principal can better plan and design appropriate strategies for change.

However, the force field analysis model does not inform the leader about strategies to weaken or strengthen forces, other than to suggest that increasing force in one direction may likely bring strong reaction from the opposing force to maintain organizational equilibrium.

Organizational development as a change process paralleled the human relations movement in organizational theory and was based on premises inherent to social systems theory. **Richard Schmuck and Philip Runkel** (1985) characterized organizational development in schools as (a) a sustained effort, (b) focusing on the dynamics of the social system, (c) using self-study for planned change, (d) centering on improvement in organizational functioning through formal and informal procedures, processes, and norms, and (e) directly impacting educational issues. In relation to school improvement, Schmuck and Runkel delineated six assumptions underlying organization development processes.

- *Groups differ from a sum of the individuals.* Whereas individuals possess various abilities and attitudes, the ability of the group to function effectively stems from the interaction among individuals.

- *Change occurs through subsystems.* An organization can better implement change through intact, existing work groups.

- *Members' goals and motives have relevance.* Because individuals' actions are influenced by their goals, knowledge of personal goals and motives is important.

- *Members' feelings have relevance.* Individuals' actions are influenced by emotions. Thus, knowledge of individuals' feelings can aid in the coordination of work.

- *Untapped resources have relevance.* Abilities, information, and skills possessed by individuals within the organization should be sought and used.

- *Change comes from within.* People within the organization often possess the knowledge and skill to effect change, reorganize school structure, and alter ways in which staff members work together. Although initial help may need to come from outside, internal-driven change results in adaptability and self-renewal.

Organizational development as a general approach to change specifically addresses processes and strategies for effecting change, taking the perspective that change is sustained and institutionalized as a result of an organization's internal (rather than external) forces. Organizational development focuses on interpersonal and group interactions within the school's social system and particularly centers on the norms of the organization. Norms, whether formal or informal, are the accepted ways of behaving and involve the roles, structures, and procedures within the organization. Organizational development as a model of change is oriented toward modifying organizational norms. Schmuck and Runkel (1985) noted that "when innovations are undertaken in schools, norms must be changed, because they hold the current structures and procedures in place" (p. 19–20). Schmuck and Runkel identified three areas with which organizational development must be concerned: (a) organizational adaptability, (b) individual motive satisfaction, and (c) effective subsystems.

Organizational adaptability means that the school constructively manages change itself rather than simply responding to external mandates. To manage change, schools must diagnose whether or not they are actually doing what they want to be doing and whether their actions match their words. In addition, schools must seek information and resources needed to solve problems. Most importantly, change must be implemented collaboratively. This involves open communication throughout the school so that individuals gain a level of comfort and develop expertise over time in a new way of doing things. Even if change is agreed on, it cannot be magically implemented by some artificially determined start-up time or administrative mandate where everyone is expected to transform at once. Finally, schools must continuously monitor their abilities to diagnose, gather information, and mobilize.

Because norms are influenced by individual beliefs and values (see Chapter 4), **individuals' satisfaction motives** must be considered. Organizational development concerns itself with developing an organizational culture where individuals' needs for achievement, friendship, and influences are satisfied through their work (see Chapter 7).

Finally, Schmuck and Runkel contended that organizational development depends on building **effective subsystems** through increasing the skill levels of seven, key, interdependent capabilities:

◆ Clarifying communication

◆ Improving group procedures in meetings

◆ Establishing goals

◆ Uncovering and working with conflict

◆ Solving problems

◆ Making decisions

◆ Assessing changes

Organizational development (OD) emphasizes the involvement of individuals in these processes and identifies intact groups (subsystems) as the most appropriate focus for developing these capacities. Organizational development often uses an outside consultant to facilitate school renewal.

The organizational development facilitator, however, does not focus on the content of change but rather on helping the school develop internal processes for implementing change.

New approaches to organizational development are incorporating more nonlinear thinking in terms of organizational change including such practices and theories as appreciate inquiry; large group interventions; organizational transformation through changing mindsets; attention to diversity and multicultural realities; and, complexity theories (Marshak, 2006). "New OD" promotes the concepts that change is continuous and results from creating new social agreements involving multiple, networked systems. This more complex approach to change is discussed more fully later in this chapter.

Total Quality Management

In the 1980s, large American corporations, most notably Ford Motor Company, began to turn their attention to the work of **W. Edwards Deming** and the concepts of total quality management (TQM). Deming, an American and one-time statistician for Bell laboratories, had been teaching the ideas of total quality to Japanese firms since 1950. In 1950, the words "Made in Japan" denoted a product that was cheap, poorly made, and easily breakable. By 1980, Japanese products were in high demand and represented highly regarded standards of quality. The imbalance of trade between the United States and Japan by 1980 was evidence of this 30-year turnaround, with the United States importing 30 percent more in manufactured goods from Japan than the United States exported to Japan in raw materials. American automobile manufacturers were especially concerned as they saw their sales decline as consumers increasingly preferred to purchase more reliable, fuel-efficient Japanese cars.

The transformation of Japanese manufacturing industries was in large part attributable to their commitment to the concepts and philosophy of **total quality management.** The concept of total quality centers on the goal of making every manufactured part as right as possible, doing it right the first time, and constantly striving for perfection. Deming contended that this was possible only if management changed their behavior toward workers, focusing on empowerment, mutual respect, and participative decision making. Deming further asserted that inspecting for quality after parts had been manufactured was inefficient; rather he suggested that designing a process to produce better quality in the first place would yield better products and eliminate the need for testing and inspection.

Central to the philosophy of TQM is the principle of kaizen, or continuous improvement, a concept manifestly more compatible with Japanese culture than American culture. Americans tend to seek innovations with whole new approaches or new technologies to provide quick fixes to problems. The Japanese, conversely, prefer patient, day-to-day improvements, making something better in small increments, which is the fundamental principle of kaizen. Whereas kaizen involves everyone in the organization and is collaborative in nature, American innovation is typically led by one person or a small group of creative champions.

Deming (1982) summarized the basic principles of TQM in what he termed the "fourteen points for management," as follows:

- Create constancy of purpose toward improvement of product and service.
- Adopt the new philosophy.
- Cease dependence on inspection to achieve quality.
- End the practice of awarding business on the basis of price tag.
- Improve constantly and forever the system of production and service.
- Institute training on the job.
- Institute leadership. The aim of supervision should be to help people and machines and gadgets to do a better job.
- Drive out fear, so that everyone may work effectively for the company.
- Break down barriers between departments.
- Eliminate slogans, exhortations, and targets for the work force asking for zero defects and new levels of productivity.
- Eliminate work standards, quotas, and management by objectives.
- Remove barriers that rob workers and managers of their pride of workmanship.
- Institute a vigorous program of education and self-improvement.
- Put everybody in the company to work to accomplish the transformation (p. 23–24).

As American industry turned to Deming's teachings and the ideas of total quality, so did school systems attempting to effect educational reform. Deming suggested that educational leaders create school environments where mutual respect and trust prevail, thus driving out fear, suspicion, and division. He called for the empowerment of students and teachers to continuously work toward improvement and opposed using grades (e.g., A, B, C, etc.) to measure student performance. Deming contended that educational leadership must take responsibility for removing barriers that prevent teachers and students from successful accomplishments and advocated that less emphasis should be placed on supervision as an act of inspection. Rather, assessment of learning and teaching should be an ongoing, participatory process (Bonstingl, 1992; Deming, 1982; National Educational Service, 1993).

John Jay Bonstingl (1992), in applying TQM to schools, identified four pillars of quality schools:

- ◆ A customer-supplier focus
- ◆ Dedication to continuous improvement (kaizen)
- ◆ A process and/or systems approach
- ◆ Management's constant dedication to total quality

A customer-supplier focus applied to schools is not as clear cut as it is in business. Bonstingl asserted that school stakeholders act variously as consumers and suppliers. Dedication to continuous improvement by schools refers to a commitment to lifelong learning and continual professional development. A process and/or systems approach relates to the quality of experiences, where learning is relevant to real-life situations. Management's constant dedication to total quality concerns the principle of maintaining focus on an organizational culture that supports continual improvement over the span of years rather than seeking the quick fix.

Total quality management represents an initial shift in ways of thinking about change, leadership, and organizational structures, and, not coincidentally, appears during a time of large-scale shifts and evolution in human civilization, from a second-wave industrial society to a third-wave information age.

Third-Wave Organizational Change: Transforming Organizational Structure

The information age is not necessarily changing the inherent nature of social systems and organizations, but it is changing the way we see things. As Peter Vaill (1996) observed, "Our own growth, education, increasing sophistication, and knowledge of other cultures and value systems may also be contributing to our feelings of uncertainty and confusion" (p. 16). Vaill used the metaphor of **permanent white water** to describe a different perspective on organizational systems theory and asserted that "the model of a smooth-running macrosystem and component parts is intrinsically invalid" (p. 8). Senge (1990) discussed this similar notion as **mental models,** citing Einstein's observation that theories determine what we measure (p. 175). Senge contended that innovations fail to be implemented because "they conflict with deeply held internal images of how the world works, images that limit us to familiar ways of thinking and acting" (p. 174).

Both Vaill's and Senge's observations about change are conceptually derived from recent scientific theory emerging from quantum physics known as chaos theory. Chaos theory (also referred to as complexity theory) and evolutionary theory emanating from the biological sciences, are providing new metaphors and new ways of thinking about organizational systems and change.

In physics, **chaos theory** is actually a search for patterns at the subatomic, or quantum, level and explains the notion of relationships between seemingly disparate and random events. In discussing studies of meteorology patterns, Lorenz (1979) introduced the often-cited aspect of chaos theory referred to as the butterfly effect, in which he proposed that the flap of a butterfly's wings today in Brazil could set off a tornado in Texas next month. The butterfly effect serves to illustrate the notion that a tiny change to a system can result in far-reaching, unpredictable consequences. Chaos theory describes systems in terms of nonlinear dynamics. Thus, change is not simply the function of adjusting one (or more) variables. An altered state in one system affects the state of another system, which in turn alters the original system, which in turn...and so on. Furthermore, quantum physics teaches us that apparently random variations, when plotted through various mathematical models, form a pattern; however, how changes will be manifested at a specific point in time is not predictable.

Griffiths, Hart, and Blair (1991) applied seven concepts from chaos theory to the practice and study of educational administration. Concepts explored included:

- The butterfly effect
- Onsets of turbulence
- Dissipative structures and attention to ostensibly minor details in everyday events
- Random shocks
- Strange attractors
- Recursive symmetries
- Feedback mechanisms (p. 439)

As discussed above, the butterfly effect refers to the idea that systems are sensitive to slight changes in initial conditions. The **onset of turbulence** is often not apparent because the catalyst may be so far removed from the consequence that it is difficult, if not impossible, to trace it. Applied to schools, educational leaders should note that major problems often grow out of seemingly minor events. Take, for instance, the middle school principal investigating what he described as a "racial incident coming near riot conditions." The problem manifested itself as a gang fight involving approximately 40 African American and white boys, which erupted in the school's hallway during passing time between early morning classes. Teachers and administrators were able to quiet the disorder and launch an immediate investigation into the disturbance. Administrators did not allow any of the students involved in the fighting to return to classes and proceeded to systematically interview all students involved, sometimes in small groups and sometimes individually. By the end of the day, administrators had determined the initial catalyst of the racial confrontation. The fight had started as a single incident between a white youth and an African American student. The white boy admitted taking the first swing at the other child. Administrators asked if there had been any name-calling of a racial nature preceding physical contact. The white youth replied, "No, that other boy was behind me going up the stairs, and he breathed on me." What appeared to adults (and perhaps to other students who entered into the brawl) as a racially divisive foray was not caused by racial tension but rather was a consequence of preadolescent hormonal reactions. This example points to the nonlinear relationships that exist between systems. In this case, the biological and emotional systems of preadolescence interacted with a middle school social system, causing unpredictable and disproportional consequences.

The concept of **dissipative structures** refers to a concept from chemistry involving a loss of energy. Dissipation is not the demise of a system, but rather a process by which a system lets go of its present form and reemerges in a new form (Wheatley, 1992). If school systems are viewed as dissipative structures, this would mean that as an educational system becomes less functional it will eventually reconfigure itself to better cope with the new environment. Dissipation can be the result of a random shock to the system. Wheatley proposed that new and different information can act as a **random shock** to an organizational system, creating so much internal disturbance, and resulting in such disequilibrium, that the system falls apart. Viewed from a broad perspective, dissipation and random shock may be analogous to Toffler's prediction that industrial-based systems will give way to organizations better suited to civilization's needs in the information age.

Strange attractors, recursive symmetries, and feedback mechanisms are concepts related to what physicists and mathematicians know as fractals. Wheatley (1992) defined a **strange attractor** as "a basin of attraction, an area displayed in computer-generated phase space that the system is magnetically drawn into, pulling the system into a visible shape" (p. 122–123). **Recursive symmetry** refers to these shapes, which often appear as familiar natural shapes of clouds, galaxies, or spirals. Additionally, shapes of whole systems are often repeated in the system's parts, as where individual florets of broccoli mirror the dominant shape of the whole vegetable. Mathematically, these shapes are generated through equations that feed back on the previous iteration and formulate fractals of the whole. In terms of organizational systems, output is fed back into the system as input. Griffiths, Hart, and Blair (1991) cited student achievement as an example of the **feedback mechanism,** where measurements of student achievement (output) are fed back to the school (input). This tends to reinforce the way in which parents and community perceive the school and the way in which teachers and students perceive themselves and the system.

Fractals have been referred to as qualitative, rather than quantitative, measures because there is no precise measurement of a fractal. Measurement depends on the perspective one takes to measure. In topography, perspective equates to whether one zooms in to measure more closely or zooms out to measure more generally. In physics, fractal patterns appear when measuring the movement of subatomic matter. Furthermore, patterns differ depending on what is being measured, because quantum entities such as electrons exist simultaneously in two forms, waves and particles. Consequently, as Einstein observed, theories determine what we measure and influence what we see.

Looking at organizational systems, these concepts teach us about the importance of the whole. Thus, effective leadership involves systems thinking—being able to envision the "big picture." As Senge (1990) commented, "The real leverage in most management situations lies in understanding dynamic complexity, not detail complexity" (p. 72). The leadership concept of modeling is analogous to the concept of fractals and recursive symmetry, where students and teachers replicate a leader's behavior. As learning theory has proved, the most powerful teaching mechanism is modeling, and students (or followers) will act in accordance with a teacher's (or leader's) behavior.

The concept of measurement offered by chaos theory is referred to by physicists as **contextualism** (Wheatley, 1992, p. 63) and is an especially pertinent conceptual lens for analyzing organizational change. Senge referred to contextualism when he discussed localness, where decision making is moved down the organizational hierarchy, as far from the top as possible. He contended that "localness is especially vital in times of rapid change" (p. 288) because local members of the organization have more current information and are in a better position to adapt to continuous change. Vaill also spoke of local innovation as individuals' way of coping with the stress of change representing creative maneuvering through, and adaptation to, a complex system. He further cautioned, as did Wheatley, that attempts to control innovation at the system's macro level increase the complexity and fragility of the system and work against operationalizing the innovation at the local level.

Chaos theory offers an alternative frame of reference from which to consider change, portraying change as a complex, nonlinear, and often uncertain process. And although chaos theory may provide an academically challenging perspective, practitioners ask what insights it provides for educational leaders concerned with implementing change in schools. **Michael Fullan** (1999) combined concepts from the biological sciences with principles of chaos theory in discussing strategies for educational change. He suggested that evolutionary theory may provide some insights into strategies for encouraging and adjusting to change. Fullan proposed that collaboration is an essential element for effecting organizational change, which he illustrated through an example from zoology, contrasting the adaptation of two species of birds to new environmental conditions. Scientists concluded that birds that are social learn faster and thus increase their chances for survival and evolve more quickly. Others have also identified collaboration and attention to human relationships as essential leadership qualities for effecting organizational change. **Seymour Sarason** (1990) asserted that current power relationships in schools prevent educational reform, suggesting that collaborative efforts are needed to effectively implement change in schools. Sarason commented that "educational reformers have trouble understanding that change by legislative fiat or policy pronouncements from on high" (p. 101) does not result in change, and that reformers often "confuse a change in policy with a change in practice" (p. 101). **Margaret Wheatley** (1992) wrote that "nothing exists independent of its relationship with something else" (p. 34) and what is critical is the relationship between the person and the setting. These observations about collaboration, relationships, and adaptation also fit within the concept of contextuality discussed earlier.

Robert Evans (1996) proposed that successful implementation of change depends on the meaning attached to the change by those who must implement it. For an organization and those in it to accept change, the change must fit within their beliefs and understanding of the world. Evans considered cultural change as requisite to organizational change. Cultural considerations again point to the concepts of contextuality and wholeness inherent in chaos theory. Evans suggested that coherent, personal, and continuous retraining must take place before and during implementation of change. Moreover, leaders must recognize that change involves loss; an innovation is not simply a substitute for the traditional way of doing something. The innovation must be seen as fulfilling traditional values, and the old way must be mourned. Thus, change is analogous to the grieving process and requires time. This is also why the personal involvement of the leader with individuals implementing the innovation is vitally important.

And what about the impact of the digital revolution on organizations? **Rosabeth Moss Kanter** (2001) has explored the impact of the Internet in her studies on e-culture. Kanter (2006) noted that "working in e-culture mode requires organizations to be communities of purpose" (p. 860). Successful e-culture organizations were found to have the following characteristics:

- Departments collaborate.
- Conflict is seen as creative, rather than disruptive.
- People can do anything not explicitly prohibited, instead of doing only what is explicitly permitted.
- Decisions are made by the people with the most knowledge, rather than those with the highest rank.

Kanter described community as somewhere midpoint on a continuum from bureaucracy to democracy. Thus, e-culture communities that work well have a balanced governance structure that connects informal and formal systems—newstream with mainstream. In addition, communities have shared disciplines and routines, facilitated by common vocabulary and tools, and they employ multichannel and multidirectional communication. Further, e-culture communities require that networks are managed and integrated. Unlike committees, networks of people working together are fluid and open-ended but not necessarily spontaneous. Finally, personal relationships remain important, even in e-cultures. Ways are found to get people together, to develop a shared identity, and carry people across "silos."

The concepts of e-culture and communities may have significant implications for educational leadership, as educational organizations change in accordance with the digital age. Principles of curriculum, instruction, and parent–community relations, for example, are changing as schools incorporate web-based technology into everyday activities. Parents often have immediate access to information about their children's grades and homework assignments. As well, parents and other community stakeholders have access to master calendars and accountability reports. Conversely, web sites such as My Space are available to educators and other agencies, sometimes informing police or school principals about potential threats to student safety. On a larger scale, the proliferation of K–12 virtual schools represents a new paradigm for schools' organizational structure, which will undoubtedly require new ways of thinking about leadership, community development, and perhaps most importantly the culture of schooling. Schools in the information age may look different and may cause us to examine basic, underlying values about the purposes of education and the role of schools in the larger cultural context.

Chaos theory and complexity science add to the knowledge base of systems theory underpinning organizational development models of change, providing a fuller understanding of why organizational development processes work and offers insights into how to enhance these processes. Chaos theory and complexity science consider the interactions among various systems, whereas organizational development models emphasize only the internal mechanisms within the school's social system.

Application to School Leadership

Educational leaders today are increasingly being placed in the role of change agent, as stakeholders question the effectiveness of current school practices and demand that schools be accountable for meeting new standards for student achievement. In light of this emphasis on school reform, it is essential that educational leaders have an understanding of organizational change theory and its applications to school systems.

First and foremost, organizational change theory illustrates that change is more about process than innovation. Reform is mere rhetoric without implementation and, as Sarason pointed out, legislation does not directly result in change in practice. While external forces may push for school reform, change will occur only if teachers and other stakeholders accept ownership of the change process. For the school leader, this means involving teachers, parents, students, and others who will be impacted by the change. Involvement includes building relationships among staff, administrators, parents, and students that are based on trust and mutual respect. To effectively implement change, new programs or innovative approaches to curriculum and instruction must be fully understood by educators and leaders. In addition, those implementing change must see value in innovative practices that achieve desired organizational outcomes, in which by people in the school community believe.

From a leadership perspective, organizational change theories recommend the establishment of procedures that involve teachers and others in problem identification, problem analysis, and problem solving. Even though diffusion models of change continue to dominate educational reform thinking, school leaders should note that this approach has not worked well in educational settings. Organizational development models and chaos theory suggest that this may result from the contextual nature of schooling.

To contextualize change, that is, to adapt innovations to a particular school setting, educational leaders should involve stakeholders in conversations about organizational beliefs, values, and norms. All those involved in the change process must have a clear vision for their school and see how the innovation fits within their belief system and how it will help them attain the desired outcomes. This requires a high level of participation from teachers, parents, students, and community and is a time-consuming process.

Moreover, change is a complex process because schools are open systems that interact with various external systems and internal subsystems. Chaos theory, in particular, suggests that the effects of change cannot be precisely predicted because of the large number of variables involved, and further demonstrates that change is not necessarily a linear process. Knowing this, leaders should be comfortable in making adjustments as changes are implemented. This is essentially the concept that TQM refers to as kaizen, or continuous improvement.

Flexibility to make adjustments does not mean losing sight of the ultimate goal, however. Total quality management also puts forth the principle of management's constant dedication to total quality. Thus, organizational change theory teaches school leaders the importance of preparation and initial time investment for effecting change. Educational leaders who understand organizational change theory will invest their time and preparation to develop a school's human resources and to put in place procedures and structures that enable a high level of collaboration.

Summary

This chapter presented an historical perspective on the development of organizational change theories. Theories of organizational change explain how organizations adopt and implement innovations, and these theories describe processes for effective problem solving and improvement efforts. This chapter characterized organizational change theories as explaining change through either rational, linear models, or nonlinear, systemic approaches. Rational, linear theories, termed "second-wave theories," are grounded in the assumptions of an industrial era, whereas nonlinear, systemic approaches, designated as "third-wave theories," consider change as a process involving interactions among numerous variables and systems.

Rational, linear approaches to organizational change include diffusion and organizational development models. Diffusion approaches have dominated change efforts in schools, and many legislative and other external change forces prescribe or use a diffusion approach. Diffusion models approach change as a rational act based on implementing programs or innovations that have been proved effective in pilot projects and research. Organizational development approaches change contextuality and emphasizes the establishment of systematic procedures for problem solving within the organizational system.

Total quality management also stresses process but further prescribes specific organizational systems and belief systems that drive change. A primary concept of TQM is the idea of kaizen, or continuous improvement, which sets TQM apart from organizational development and diffusion models. Continuous improvement defines change as something different than a single innovation or a distinct solution to a particular problem. Total quality management is predicated on the belief that quality is the result of small, incremental improvements over time.

Finally, change was discussed using recent theories emanating from physical and biological sciences, such as chaos theory and evolutionary theory. Applied to organizations, these theories perceive change as the product of interactions among various systems. Such theories encourage educational leaders to view change in a broad perspective and to orchestrate change through "systems thinking."

A common theme among all theories of organizational change is that change is a process that must involve the people who will be affected by the change. Change cannot be imposed. For innovations to be implemented within a system, people in the organization must be actively engaged in problem solving, self-study, and communication. Organizational change is inextricably tied to the beliefs, values, and norms that define the organizational culture. Thus, to be institutionalized, school leaders must ensure that changes fit within the belief structure and philosophical orientation of the school.

Theory into Practice

Curriculum Change Not Flying at Eagle Elementary School

After reviewing her student scores on the state standardized tests, Terry Greenfield, principal of Eagle Elementary School, was not pleased. She was meeting next week with the Assistant Superintendent for Curriculum and would have to explain to her why students' reading scores showed no improvement and were still averaging below the 40th percentile nationally. Greenfield had been assigned to Eagle Elementary School two years ago when it was deemed an "at-risk" school based on its low reading scores. The fact that students at Eagle Elementary School scored low on standardized test scores was not a recent occurrence. The faculty at Eagle Elementary School remained largely the same as they had been two years ago when Greenfield took over, and teachers' average length of service at Eagle was eight years. Many of the teachers seemed complacent about student achievement and blamed low student performance on families' lack of interest in education and students' issues with poverty and difficult home lives. Teachers, however, were very caring toward the children and felt they were doing their best to help students succeed.

Two years ago, a committee of teachers had volunteered to attend a training workshop for a reading program, endorsed by the state and school district, that had been credited with raising students' reading levels in schools similar to Eagle Elementary. Teachers who attended the workshop conducted in-service training for the staff, and the reading program was implemented in all classrooms. Greenfield had reinforced the curriculum's implementation by observing teachers' reading lessons and conferencing individually with teachers about their instruction. Greenfield had noted that although teachers appeared compliant in implementing the new reading program, many appeared less than enthusiastic about it. It was as if they mechanically "went through the motions" in their reading lessons. When reading scores did not improve after the first year, Greenfield was not really concerned, because the reading program was new, and she knew any curriculum change needed more time to show any effects. However, now, after two years Greenfield was sure she needed a new plan for improving reading achievement, and she wanted to be prepared with that plan when she met with the Assistant Superintendent next week.

Sample Analysis

This case represents a diffusion approach to change. By using the diffusion model, Terry Greenfield fell victim to the underlying assumption of this change model—that teachers, as rational people, would accept the change because it had proved successful elsewhere. Greenfield, as a change agent, had assumed some, but not all, of the roles Havelock described. She had served as a catalyst, solution giver, and resource linker but had failed to fully address her role as a process helper. The role of process helper is one that helps the organization develop a problem-solving process. It is evident in this case that the teachers at Eagle Elementary School had not been fully involved in the decision to adopt the reading curriculum. Critical steps of relationship building, teacher involvement in diagnosing and analyzing problems associated with low reading achievement, and participation in a solution were not implemented. Only teachers who attended the original training workshop were fully involved in the change process.

Involving others in the change process is time consuming, which is probably why it is so often ignored or overlooked. It is tempting, and may even seem logical, for Greenfield to mandate an obvious solution to students' low reading achievement. And although such an approach is expedient and straightforward, it by no means assures that the change will be implemented. In this case, teachers did not overtly rebel against the new reading program, but they did engage in subtle sabotage as evidenced by Greenfield's observation that teachers just seemed to go "through the motions" of their reading lessons. Furthermore, focusing on the process of change puts the innovation within the context of the social system. Both organizational development and TQM focus exclusively on the process of change and the interactions of people within the organizational social system. Chaos theory, too, addresses the issue of contextualism. Wheatley pointed out that attempting to control innovation from the top works against operationalizing the innovation.

Greenfield must first be resolved to the fact that change will take time, and she should be prepared to discuss a reasonable time line for change with the Assistant Superintendent. Her time line should include a reasonable period (perhaps up to a year) for involving the entire staff in discussion and research about the reading achievement problem and possible approaches to solving it. Her initial task might be to develop a procedure for the faculty to become involved in dialogue about their beliefs and values related to teaching, learning, and student achievement. If a particular reading program contradicts teachers' beliefs, then teachers will not implement it. Failure to implement may not even be deliberate, but may result because teachers don't fully understand the program because it conflicts with firmly held mental models.

Undoubtedly, Greenfield and the faculty at Eagle Elementary School will face the pressure of improving test scores; however, they will be no worse off by taking the time to focus on the organization and process of change. During this relationship-building stage, they may want to explore other ways of measuring student progress in reading, and may want to examine factors other than reading curriculum and instruction that impact student achievement. Greenfield and her faculty may then discover less obvious solutions that may lead to systemic change which will substantially influence student learning.

Reader's Application

No Raise in Taxes
If the Old School Is Razed

It was Lee Thompson's fourth year of his superintendency in Midville, a school district of approximately 2,000 students located in a small mid-western town. Like many other schools throughout the United States, Midville's facilities were old and in desperate need of repair or replacement. Two years ago, the Midville Board of Education had proposed a bond issue to build a new high school and renovate three elementary schools. However, the bond issue was soundly defeated by a 2 to 1 margin. The primary forces against the bond issue were lifelong residents of Midville, many of whom were retired or near retirement. Their opposition to the tax levy had centered around the proposed destruction of the district's oldest building, which had served as the town's first high school. Built in 1915, the building had housed Midville Junior High School students until three years ago. At that time, a state inspection of the building revealed unsafe conditions related to asbestos exposure and outdated electrical wiring and heating systems. The junior high students were moved "temporarily" to one of the elementary schools, and the elementary students in that school were split between the other two elementary schools. The proposed facilities plan, after construction of a new high school, had been to relocate the junior high to the present high school building and recover the elementary building to ease overcrowding in the other K–6 schools.

Dr. Thompson had investigated the feasibility of renovating the 1915 high school, but the costs of asbestos removal, electrical and heating and air-conditioning updates, along with other necessary improvements would have been more costly than building a new school. Thus, he had recommended to the board that the old school be torn down and the land be used as the site for a new high school building.

Now, two years after the defeat of the last bond issue, the board was prepared to put the issue before the people again. Dr. Thompson had been confident that this time there would be little opposition, because two months ago much of the old building's roof had been destroyed in a storm. Dr. Thompson thought this might convince voters of the futility of trying to save the structure. But after tonight's board meeting, Dr. Thompson knew that approval of this bond issue would not be any easier than the last. A group of community members had spoken tonight at the board meeting to renew their opposition to the bond issue if it involved tearing down their high school. They assured the board they would actively work to defeat the tax levy.

Dr. Thompson knew that change was hard, but he considered this reaction irrational. Somehow he must provide the leadership to gain the support of this group and convince them that razing the old high school and building a new one would benefit Midville's children and future.

Student Exercise: Case Analysis

1. Use organizational change theories to explain voters' opposition to the proposed bond issue.

2. What concepts from organizational change theories could Dr. Thompson apply to help him gain the support of the community?

3. Should Dr. Thompson be concerned about the butterfly effect? Explain.

4. What would you do if you were the superintendent of Midville?

References

Bonstingl, J. J. (1992). *Schools of quality: An introduction to total quality management in education*. Alexandria, VA: Association for Supervision and Curriculum Development.

Chance, E. W. (1992). *Visionary leadership in schools: Successful strategies for developing and implementing an educational vision*. Springfield, IL: Charles Thomas.

Chin, R., & Benne, K. D. (1976). General strategies for effecting changes in human systems. In Bennis, W. G., Benne, K. D., Chin, R., & Corey, K. E. (Eds.), *The planning of change* (3rd ed., pp. 22–45) New York: Holt, Rinehart and Winston.

Clark, D. L., & Guba, E. G. (1967). An examination of potential change roles in education. In Sand, O. (Ed.), *Rational planning in curriculum and instruction*. Washington, DC: National Education Association.

Deming, W. E. (1982). *Out of the crisis*. Cambridge, MA: Massachusetts Institute of Technology Center for Advanced Engineering Study.

Evans, R. (1996). *The human side of school change: Reform, resistance, and the real-life problems of innovation*. San Francisco: Jossey-Bass.

Fullan, M. (1999). *Change forces: The sequel*. Philadelphia: Falmer Press.

Fullan, M., Miles, M. B., & Taylor, G. (1980) Organizational development in schools: The state of the art. *Review of Educational Research, 50*(1) 121–183.

Griffiths, D. E., Hart, A. W., & Blair, B. G. (1991). Still another approach to administration: Chaos theory. *Educational Administration Quarterly, 27*(3), 430–451.

Hall, G. E., & Hord, S. M. (2001). *Implementing change: Patterns, principles, and potholes*. Boston: Allyn and Bacon.

Havelock, R. G. (1973). *The change agent's guide to innovation in education*. Englewood Cliffs, NJ: Educational Technology Publications.

Kanter, R. M. (2001). *Evolve! Succeeding in the digital culture of tomorrow*. Boston: Harvard Business School Press.

Kanter, R. M. (2006). From cells to communities: Deconstructing and reconstructing the organization. In J. V. Gallos (Ed.), *Organization development*, (pp. 858–887). San Francisco: Jossey-Bass.

Lewin, K. (1947). Frontiers in group dynamics. *Human Relations, 1*, 5–41.

Lewin, K. (1952). Group decision and social change. In Swanson, G. E. (Ed.), *Readings in social psychology*. New York: Henry Holt.

Lorenz, E. N. (1979). Predictability: Does the flap of a butterfly's wings in Brazil set off a tornado in Texas? Paper presented at the annual meeting of the American Association for the Advancement of Science, Washington, DC.

Marshak, R. J. (2006). Emerging directions: Is there a new OD? In J. V. Gallos (Ed.), *Organization development* (pp. 833–841). San Francisco: Jossey-Bass.

Mort, P. R., & Ross, D. H. (1957). *Principles of school administration.* New York: McGraw Hill.

Owens, R. G. (1995). *Organizational behavior in education.* Boston: Allyn and Bacon.

Sarason, S. B. (1990). *The predictable failure of educational reform.* San Francisco: Jossey-Bass.

Schmuck, R. A., & Runkel, P. J. (1985). *The handbook of organizational development in schools* (3rd ed.). Prospect Heights, IL: Waveland Press.

Senge, P. M. (1990). *The fifth discipline: The art and practice of the learning organization.* New York: Doubleday/Currency.

Toffler, A. (1990). *Powershift: Knowledge, wealth, and violence at the edge of the 21st century.* New York: Bantam Books.

Vaill, P. B. (1996). *Learning as a way of being: Strategies for survival in a world of permanent white water.* San Francisco: Jossey-Bass.

Wheatley, M. J. (1992). *Leadership and the new science: Learning about organization from an orderly universe.* San Francisco: Berrett-Koehler Publishers.

11

Applying Theory to School Leadership: Concluding Comments

Teaching theory without application to practice is merely an intellectual exercise. It adds little value and produces no change or improvement in schools. By the same token, teaching about practice disconnected from theory is simply a retelling of "old war stories" and serves only to maintain the status quo. This primer on organizational theory for educational leadership has attempted to bridge the gap between theory and practice. I have endeavored to provide the reader with basic concepts of organizational and leadership theories that have direct relevance to the practice of leadership in schools today. In addition, I have attempted to structure this book in such a way that readers will be able to see both the big picture regarding the complexities of school organizations, and at the same time glean useful information about specific functions and activities of leadership.

As a way of reviewing the major concepts explored throughout this book, consider the familiar Indian fable about the six blind men and the elephant. Each man, blind since birth, approached the elephant to investigate its shape. The first man approached the elephant's side and described the elephant as a wall. The second took hold of the elephant's tusk and concluded that the elephant was shaped like a spear. The third man came upon the trunk of the elephant and decided that the elephant was similar to a snake. The fourth happened to touch the elephant's knee and leg, thus deducing that the elephant was much like a tree. The fifth man felt the elephant's ear and determined that it must be like a fan. The sixth blind man grabbed the elephant's tail and figured it was akin to a rope.

In each of the preceding chapters, readers were exposed to one specific perspective of organizational theory and its application to leadership, much as each blind man perceived the elephant. At this point, it is important for the reader to step away from the elephant so that the entire animal can be seen. By viewing the elephant with a broader lens, one can see that its tail, its trunk, its ear, its knee are all components of the whole animal. The elephant needs and uses all of these parts, and they operate together for the elephant to exist. Thus, if the elephant is the organization, leadership is the elephant's brain. The brain simultaneously exists as a component of the elephant and as the director of the elephant's activities, just as the leader is a member of the organization who interacts with other individuals and systems within the organization.

An educational leader must function as the director of the school or district to orchestrate its effective operation, to facilitate harmony among the various players, and to maintain synchronization with the culture of the audience. Knowledge of organizational theories helps the leader understand the dynamics of schools and how people are likely to be affected by certain behaviors and events. Organizational theories do not provide certainties or absolute predictability, but they do offer the leader a framework from which to work. They remind the leader that his or her behaviors, such as communication and decision making, are not isolated events but rather actions that may have long-reaching consequences for others within and outside the organization.

Framed within an historical context, organizational theory offers a perspective on the relationship of schools to the larger culture. People and social institutions such as schools are both products and creators of culture. Educational leaders who are aware of the roots and traditions on which schools have been built understand how and why they operate as they do. This knowledge places leaders in a better position to plan for the future and to influence change for school improvement. However, leaders must also know where they want to lead their organizations and what they want to accomplish. Although organizational theories, in and of themselves, do not inform us about what will be, they can suggest trends of the future and how institutions and organizations are bound to change in light of a postindustrial society. Futurists propose that institutions designed for an industrial society, marked by highly bureaucratic structures, top-down management, and close supervision and inspection, are not compatible with modern society's information-based culture. New technology allowing instant, easy access to information is changing the way we live and work.

Future trends have implications for educational leaders and the ultimate structure of schools. The deeply held cultural image of learning taking place in a classroom bound by four walls is beginning to erode. People of all ages are now turning on their computers and seeking information they need, when they need it. More and more adult workers are maintaining "virtual" offices via electronic networking. The boundaries of organizations are less visible and more fluid. Will educational institutions follow this pattern? It seems likely that they will, given the part schools play in the overall culture. Systems theory is particularly applicable to understanding the possible nature and form of evolving school organizational structures.

And whereas the structure of school organizations may change, the human factor will not. We must remember that organizations are not things, but a collection of human beings working together for some common purpose. Principles of communication and decision-making and motivations for human behavior will remain constant factors, and, in fact, should influence how we structure our organizations. If we don't attend to cultural forces and human needs in shaping the form of our organizations, they will cease to be effective, viable institutions. Educational leaders have a choice. They can continue to manage schools from an industrial-age, factory-model perspective, or they can proactively lead schools through institutional changes necessary to function within a post-industrial society. Those who choose the former path choose to let the forces around them control their destiny; those who choose to lead choose to take risks to influence the reshaping and transformation of schools.

The following comment from Will and Ariel Durant's (1968) classic work, *The Lessons of History*, is a noteworthy reminder for educational leaders.

> Consider education not as the painful accumulation of facts
> and dates and reigns, nor merely the necessary preparation of
> the individual to earn his keep in the world, but as the trans-
> mission of our mental, moral, technical, and aesthetic heritage
> as fully as possible to as many as possible, for the enlargement
> of man's understanding, control, embellishment, and
> enjoyment of life (p. 101).

History can teach us about the future if we seek to find the patterns and traditions that define our culture. Organizational theory can inform the practice of leadership if we choose to use it. The connection of theory to practice brings a greater hope for school leaders to shape the future of educational organizations and a greater promise for making a true difference in the lives of our children.

References

Durant, W., & Durant, A. (1968). *The lessons of history.* New York: Simon and Schuster.

Name Index

Abbott, Max, 50–53
Adler, Paul, 24
Agarwala-Rogers, Rehka, 154–155, 159–161
Argyris, Chris, 71, 191
Avolio, Bruce, 94
Banks, James, 74–75
Barnard, Chester, 6
Bass, Bernard, 94
Blake, Robert, 93
Blair, Billie Goode, 212
Blanchard, Ken, 118
Blau, Peter , 13, 23, 68
Bolman, Lee, 29
Bonstingl, John Jay, 211
Borys, Bryan, 24
Bridges, Edwin, 185
Burns, James MacGregor, 93
Burns, Tom, 25, 111
Coons, Alvin, 91
Croft, Don, 67
Crowson, Robert, 29
Cubberly, Elwood, 5
Deal, Terrence, 29, 73, 97
Deming, W. Edwards, 209
Drucker, Peter, 174, 175
Dufour, Richard, 186
Eaker, Robert, 186
Etzioni, Amitai, 14–16
Evans, Robert, 215
Fayol, Henri, 4
Fiedler, Fred, 113–116
Firestone, William, 70
Foster, William, 97
French, John R. P., 87–88

Fullan, Michael, 215
Getzels, Jacob, 43–50
Glasser, William, 132–134
Goldring, Ellen, 29
Griffiths, Daniel, 173, 212
Gronn, Peter, 99
Guba, Egon, 43–50
Gulick, Luther, 4
Hall, Gene, 203
Halpin, Andrew, 67, 91
Hanson, E. Mark, 71
Hart, Ann Weaver, 212
Havelock, Ronald, 202–203
Hemphill, John K., 91
Hersey, Paul, 118
Herzberg, Frederick, 134–136
Hord, Shirley, 203
House, Robert, 116
Hoy, Wayne, 24, 174
Ikemoto, Gina Schuyler, 190
Janis, Irving, 187
Jensen, Mary Ann, 140
Kahn, Robert, 111, 157, 159
Kanter, Rosabeth Moss, 315–216
Katz, Daniel, 111, 157, 159
Kowalski, Theodore, 189
Lasley, Thomas, 189
Lawler, Edward, 137–138
Leithwood, Kenneth, 95
Lewin, Kurt, 205
Lindblom, Charles, 178–179
Locke, Edwin, 138
Mahoney, James, 189
Mann, Leon, 187
March, James, 71, 180–181

Marsh, Julie, 189
Maslow, Abraham, 130
Mayo, Elton, 5
McGregor, Douglas, 88–90, 134
Mintzberg, Henry, 25–28, 90–91
Miskel, Cecil, 174
Mitchell, Terence, 116
Mort, Paul, 201–202
Mouton, Jane, 93
Ogawa, Rodney, 29
Parsons, Talcott, 12
Pavlov, Ivan, 129
Peterson, Kent, 97
Raven, Bertram, 87–88
Rogers, Everett, 154–155, 159–161
Runkel, Philip, 207
Sarason, Seymour, 215
Schein, Edgar, 65
Schmidt, Warren, 182
Schmuck, Richard, 207
Scott, W. Richard, 13, 23, 54, 68
Senge, Peter, 42, 71–72, 211, 214

Sergiovanni, Thomas, 72–73, 95–96
Simon, Herbert, 6, 177–178
Skinner, B. F., 129
Spillane, James P., 99
Stalker, George M., 25, 111
Starratt, Robert J., 191
Sweetland, Scott, 24
Tannenbaum, Robert, 182
Taylor, Frederick, 3–4
Tuckman, Bruce, 140
Vaill, Peter, 211, 214
Von Bertalanffy, Ludwig, 41
Vroom, Victor, 136–137, 182–184
Weber, Max, 17–23
Weick, Karl, 112
Wheatley, Margaret, 213–215
Wilson, Bruce, 70
Winer, B. J., 91
Yetton, Peter, 182–184
Yukl, Gary, 85–87, 98–99, 186–187

Subject Index

alienation, 14–16
authority, 17
behavioral science, 5–7
bureaucracy, 4, 17–25, 27–28
change, 199–219
    agent, 202
    and information technology, 215–217
    as diffusion process, 201–205
    as organizational development, 205–209
    transformational, 211–217
Chaos Theory, 212–214
Choice Theory, 132–134
classical organizational theory, 3–5
climate, 64, 67–68
communication, 153–166
    and information technology, 163
    networks, 159–162
    nonverbal, 162–163
Compliance Theory, 14–17
Concerns Based Adoption Model, 203–205
contingency planning, 112
contingency theories, 109–122
critical theory, 97–98
culture, 63–76
decision making, 173–191
    action cycle, 174
    data driven, 189–191
    filters, 191
    Garbage Can model of, 181
    incremental, 178
    linear model of, 174–178
    participatory, 182–187

    programmed vs. nonprogrammed, 178
    shared, 185
diversity, 73–75, 187
equilibrium, 44
Expectancy Theory, 136–137
Force Field Analysis, 205–207
formal organization, 48–52, 69–70
goal theory, 138–140
group dynamics, 140–144
groupthink, 187–189
Hawthorne studies, 5
hierarchy, 22
idiographic systems, 47–53
industrial model, 4
informal organization, 23–24, 48–52, 69–70
information overload, 159–162
information technology, 163, 187
Institutional Theory, 54–55
Leader Behavior Description Questionnaire (LBDQ), 91
leaders, 15, 85–96, 113–116, 118–120
    behavior of, 88–92
    formal, 15
    informal, 15
    leader-member relations, 114
    officers, 15
    traits of, 85–87
leadership, 83–102
    authority of, 95
    achievement-oriented, 117
    behavior, 88–92, 118–120
    directive, 117
    distributed, 99
    flexible, 98

matrix, 92
participative, 117
roles, 90–91
situational, 114–116, 118–120
skills, 86–87
style, 49–50, 53–54
supportive, 117
traits of, 85–87
transactional, 93
transformational, 94–95
learning communities, 71–72, 186–187
Least Preferred Coworker (LPC), 113–115
loose coupling, 112–113
Managerial Grid, 92
mechanistic organizations, 111
motivation, 127–144
Motivation-Hygiene Theory, 134–135
network theory, 159–162
nomethetic systems, 47–53
norms, 43, 44, 65, 69
Ohio State Studies, 91
organic organizations, 111
Organizational Climate Description Questionnaire (OCDQ), 67
Organizational Development, 205–209
organizations

as communities, 71–73
as living organisms, 7
dilemmas of, 29–31
mechanistic, 25
organic, 25
roles in, 45, 49, 143
structure of, 25–28, 66–68
types of, 12–16
path-goal theory, 116–118
postmodernism, 73–75
power, 14–18,, 87–88
problem solving, 174–177, 203
regulations, 19–20
Research, Development, and Diffusion (RD&D), 203
rules, 19–20
scientific management, 3–4, 173
Situational Leadership, 118–120
S-M-C-R model, 154
social justice, 73–75, 97–98
social relations, 68
social systems (See System Theory)
system theory, 7–8, 41–57, 110
systems thinking, 72
task structure, 114
Theory X-Theory Y, 88–90, 134
Total Quality Management, 209–211
University of Michigan leadership studies, 92